THE HISTORICAL GEOGRAPHY AND TOPOGRAPHY OF BIHAR

BY

MITHILA SHARAN PANDEY

Department of Ancient Indian History and Archaeology,

PATNA UNIVERSITY, PATNA

MOTILAL BANARSIDASS

DELHI :: PATNA :: VARANASI

FIRST EDITION, 1963

ISBN: 978-81-2082-657-1

Also available at:

MOTILAL BANARSIDASS
41 U.A. Bungalow Road, Jawahar Nagar, Delhi 110 007
8 Mahalaxmi Chamber, Warden Road, Mumbai 400 026
120 Royapettah High Road, Mylapore, Chennai 600 004
Sanas Plaza, Subhash Nagar, Pune 411 002
16 St. Mark's Road, Bangalore 560 001
8 Camac Street, Calcutta 700 017
Ashok Rajpath, Patna 800 004
Chowk, Varanasi 221 0011

PRINTED IN INDIA
BY JAINENDRA PRAKASH JAIN AT SHRI JAINENDRA PRESS,
A-45 NARAINA, PHASE I, NEW DELHI 110 028
AND PUBLISHED BY NARENDRA PRAKASH JAIN FOR
MOTILAL BANARSIDASS PUBLISHERS PRIVATE LIMITED,
BUNGALOW ROAD, DELHI 110 007

DEDICATED TO THE MEMORY OF
MY FATHER
PANDIT BALDEO PANDEY

ABBREVIATION

A.	Aṅguttara Nikāya
A.A.	Aṅguttara Nikāya Aṭṭhakathā
A.I.G.	Ancient Geography of India
Ait. Bra.	Aitareya Brāhmaṇa
A. S. I.	Archaeological Survey of India.
A.S.I.A.R.	Archaeological Survey of India, Annual Report
Atharva	Atharva Veda
Bāl.	Bāla Kāṇḍa
Bu.	Buddha Vaṁsa
D.	Dīgha Nikāya
D.A.	Dīgha Nikāya Aṭṭhakathā
Divy.	Divyāvadāna
D.P.P.N	Dictionary of Pali Proper Names
E.I.	Epigraphia Indica
E.R.E.	Encyclopaedia of Religions and Ethics
G.D.A.M.I.	Geographical Dictionary of Ancient & Medieval India.
I.A.	Indian Antiquary
I.C.	Indian Culture
I.H.Q.	Indian Historical Quarterly
J.	Jātaka
J.A.O.S.	Journal of American Oriental Society
J.A.S.B.	Journal of Asiatic Society of Bengal
J.B.B.A.S.	Journal of Bombay Branch of Asiatic Society
J.B.O.I.	Journal of Bhandarkar Oriental Institute
J.B.O.R.S.	Journal of Bihar and Orissa Research Society
J.B.R.S.	Journal of Bihar Research Society
J.I.H.	Journal of Indian History
J.O.C.	Journal of Oriental Conferences
J.R.A.S.	Journal of Royal Asiatic Society
M.	Majjhim Nikāya
M.A.	Majjhima Nikāya Aṭṭhakathā

M.A.S.B.	Memoir of Archaeological Survey of Bengal
M.A.S.I.	Memoir of Archaeological Survey of India
M.M.K.	Manjuśrīmūlakalpa
Mbh.	Mahābhārata
Mtu.	Mahāvastu
P.H.A.I.	Political History of Ancient India
Rig.	Ṛig Veda
S.	Saṁyutta Nikāya
S.A.	Saṁyutta Nikāya Aṭṭhakathā
S.B.M.	Śramaṇa Bhagavān Mahāvīra
S.N.	Sutta Nipāta
S.N.A.	Sutta Nipāta Aṭṭhakathā
Sat. B.	Śatapatha Brāhmaṇa
Thag.	Thera Gāthā
Thig.	Therī Gāthā
Thig. A.	Theri Gāthā Aṭṭhakathā
V.	Vinaya Piṭaka

ACKNOWLEDGMENT

I am deeply obliged to Dr. B. C. Sen, the Reader in the department of A.I.H. & C., Calcutta University for suggesting to me the topic of this thesis and for pointing out the immense possibility of work in this field of historical geography hitherto so little explored, particularly, in respect of the geography of ancient Bihar. I had started to work upon this subject in India, but later circumstances made it possible for me to go to England. Prof. A. L. Basham kindly accepted me as his student. His able supervision and unfailing encouragement enabled me to complete this work so soon. I am grateful to him for all his valuable help, he gave and what is more I have learnt a lot by coming in contact with his rich personality.

I must also thank Shri B. L. Sethia and Mrs. Jaysree Sethia, without whose financial aid I could not have completed this work. I cannot express in words what I owe to this couple. I must express my deep gratitude to Prof. Ramsharan Sharma, M. A., Ph. D., the Head of the Deptt. of History, Patna University, who took great interest in getting this book published.

Thanks are also due to my friends Dr. Upendra Thakur and Shri Basudeva Narayan, M. A. who took special care to go through the proof of this book.

Moreover I am indebted to my predecessors in this field who made the path clear for me and for others to follow. Last but not least I am obliged to the authorities of the S. O. A. S. and of its Library for providing me with all the necessary facilities for research.

FOREWORD

The region which is now known as the state of Bihar is one of the great foci of Indian history. From before the days of the Buddha it was a major centre of Indian political life, and from South Bihar there came the primary impetus which led to the foundation of the first all-Indian empire, that of the Mauryas. Not only has Bihar played a very important part in political life, but also the region has been one of the most significant cultural centres of the subcontinent, especially in respect of Buddhism. It was in Bihar that the Buddha achieved enlightenment; many of his most important sermons were preached in Bihar; and from Bihar the doctrines of later Buddhism spread to South-East Asia and the Far-East. In the middle ages great Buddhist monasteries such as Nālandā and Vikramaśīla were centres of pilgrimage for Buddhists coming from all over Asia, and the vigorous intellectual life of these monastic universities made an impact upon the whole history of Asia.

Hitherto the student of Ancient India has been rather badly provided with geographical and topographical studies. The pioneer work of Sir Alexander Cunningham in many respects remains to this day the most significant text book of its kind and various later efforts at compiling geographical and topographical dictionaries of early India have been in general completely inadequate and in many cases thoroughly unscholarly. For a few regions of India a little work of a more detailed type has been done, notably for Gujrat, but the detailed study of the ancient geography and topography of India is still largely in its infancy.

My friend and former student Dr. M. S. Pandey has made a very significant contribution to the subject in his work on the historical geography of Bihar. He has ransacked a very large range of sources for information and has produced a survey of the subject which may in many respects serve as a model to students working on other regions of India. A detailed analysis along these lines of all the geographical evidence relating to the earlier past for each region of India is much to be desired, and should result in the production of a number of monographs on the basis of which it might be possible to compile a gazetteer of ancient India such as has long existed for classical Europe. I understand that some such project is already afoot, and this work will do much to help it forward. I commend Dr. Pandey's study to all students of ancient India. It is written with scholarly acumen and clarity, and is very evidently the work of a man with a deep affection for his native land.

A. L. Basham

CONTENTS

CHAPTER I

INTRODUCTION

The term 'Historical Geography' has been applied to a variety of subjects—to the story of geographical exploration and of geographical science to the history of changing political frontiers and to the study of the influences of geographical factors upon historical events. All these are most illuminating themes and this is not a place to embark upon a discussion of terminology. Yet the fact remains that historical geography has been increasingly identified with another line of thought whose data are, of necessity, historical, but whose outlook is geographical. This study—to use Professor E.G.R. Taylor's words 'strictly speaking merely carries the geographer's studies into the past, his subject matter remains the same.'[1] Scholars are apt to disagree among themselves, and so we are more concerned with the subject matter than with the definitions of the term. We have concentrated ourselves on the geographical materials which we could find in the different works—foreign and indigenous, which help us in reconstructing the history of the past.

The importance of geography for the study of history cannot be overestimated. It plays a dominant role in shaping the events of human life. It has been accepted on all hands that the study of history without the perspective knowledge of geography is not complete. This maxim can be applied to the history of any quarter of the sphere, but it is particularly essential for the history of India, which covers a span of almost four thousand years and has seen the rise and fall of many dynasties—indigenous and foreign. The rise of early urban civilization in the Indus valley and its disappearance, the composition of the Vedic hymns, still reverberating on the banks of the everflowing Sindhu and Gaṅgā, the emergence of Magadha on the political stage of Northern India, and the series of invasions from the north-west devastating the green

1. Preface to *Historical Geography of England Before 1800*.

lands of the Āryāvarta, each in itself tells a tale of the influence which geography has displayed from time to time in the making and unmaking of a nation. Although at present scientific researches have lessened the degree of natural calamities, we cannot yet feel ourselves to be wholly safe from the unleashed forces of nature, finding that "in Central Africa 'the desert is on the move', the wide spread soil erosion in parts of Africa and in the Middle-West of United States, and finally the continual threat of drought which hangs over the great grain lands of the world-alike in the United States, Canada and South Russia."[1]

If this is the condition of the world, when man is progressing on the path of scientific knowledge with terrific speed and is challenging the superiority of the gods at every step, we can imagine how weak and poor our ancestors were in the hands of cruel Nature. Thus it is explicitly clear that the human chronicles which have been handed down to us contain some subtle chapters which can be fully studied only with the help of geography.

The history of Europe has been studied according to this pattern by numerous scholars, but in Indian history good geographical studies are conspicuous by their absence. There have been scholars who have tried to pursue this sort of study. But their number is very limited. Major General Sir A. Cunningham tops the list among such scholars, although the work was started long ago by Wilford. Cunningham attained considerable success in his efforts, but his work suffers from certain defects, for which he alone cannot be held responsible. His *Geography of Ancient India* (1871 A.D.) contains a lot of information about India's past, but the greatest defect in his work is that his study followed the route of Hsüan-Tsang only. Naturally, therefore, he has left all those places which lay outside the route of the pilgrim. As archaeological exploration was in its infancy in his time, certain conclusions arrived at by him have been proved wholly baseless. He depends solely upon the information supplied by the pilgrim, which may not be correct in the light thrown on it by sober modern students of history. He literally believes

1. *The Geography Behind History*, p. 11.

in Hsüan-Tsang's account and has tried to prove it correct by his own inferences and sometimes twists the texts to support his own explanation. In the indigenous sources which Cunningham utilized for his study, he entirely relied upon the Buddhist works. He scarcely refers to the facts dealt with in the Jain and Brāhmaṇical sources. Despite these defects, the work of Cunningham is of superb quality and deserves every praise.

Cunningham was followed by several scholars. But the majority of them did nothing substantial besides writing a few stray articles. Dr. B.C. Law, however, has contributed immensely in this field. His *Historical Geography of Ancient India* deals with many topics concerning India's past history. But he has not gone into the depth of the subject. His work covers names of rivers, mountains and places which were never heard in ancient India. So far as the sources are concerned, he hardly refers to any save Buddhist texts.

This sort of historio-geographical work on different regions of India has been pursued to some extent by other scholars such as H.C. Ray-Chaudhury, B. C. Sen, H. D. Sankalia and the like, but none has so far attempted to write about the historical geography of Bihar, whose past has been so glorious. We have concentrated our efforts on the study of the mountains, rivers, regions, districts, places and routes of that region, which have been so often referred to in our ancient literature.

As in the case of history, so in geography, ancient Indian scholars never wrote any thing deliberately with the intention of recording geographical information. Not until a late period was any text book dealing with their country composed. It is true that there is some information in early Indian literature upon which the historical geography of India can be reconstructed, but a novice has always to be alert about the materials he is going to utilize. The very nature of the works where these materials lie buried is not above suspicion. They are generally epics, Purāṇas, Kāvyas, fictional prose-works, scriptures, astrological and astronomical works etc. As the aim of these works was not to supply any historical or geographical data, they seem to care very little about the precision of the facts they allude to. The materials which we use for our purpose are mostly casual references by authors interested in other topics and it is our duty to scrutinize them thoroughly before we arrive at any conclusion. The Buddhist sources are more definitely precise and trustworthy so far as Bihar is concerned. It was on the soil of Bihar that Buddhism was born, grew and flourished, and so it is but natural for the Buddhists to have recorded many details about Bihar in their works.

The Jain works also give some information. But much information in the Jain sources has not yet been utilized, for many important texts are still unpublished. However, there are several defects in the Jain works. Most of them were composed in later centuries in the western part of India; therefore their authors did not know much about Bihar. The rivers, hills, territories and places referred to in the Jain scriptures are not precisely located and they are rarely corroborated by other sources. Sometimes one comes to the conclusion that certain places or regions are mythical ones.

Among the poets none save Kālidāsa seems to possess wide knowledge of the country.

The materials gathered from the indigenous sources are sometimes supplemented and corroborated by foreign accounts. Most of the foreign writers had never visited India and they based their accounts upon the writings of a few travellers who visited the country and left first hand impressions of what they experienced in a strange land. Therefore, their accounts are sometimes exaggerated or show imperfect knowledge of the facts. The Chinese pilgrims recorded the accounts of their travels after their return to China. It is therefore natural that they may have forgotten many details of what they had seen or heard in India. A foreigner is apt to make mistakes about directions. Even a well-informed and widely learned pilgrim such as Hsüan-Tsang was not above these common errors. Another difficulty which we have to tackle in the itineraries of Fa-hsien and Hsüan-Tsang is the measurement of the distances. Fa-hsien uses the term *Yojana* while Hsüan-Tsang employs the Chinese *li*.

The *Yojana* in India differed from region to region and the *Yojana* of Magadha was definitely slightly different from those employed in other parts of the country. As Fa-hsien has used the term *Yojana* for his whole journey in India, we are not in a position to determine which *Yojana* he had in his mind while travelling in Bihar.

The *li*[1] of Hsüan-Tsang is a term which is used for measurement of distances in China. It has varied from time to time and region to region. There was never a standardized *li* in China itself. The *li* differed in measurement also according to the nature of the land. We cannot say exactly in what sense it was used by Hsüan-Tsang in India. Cunningham, on the basis of his rough measurements, standardized it as six *lis* equal to one English mile. In some cases his estimate is almost correct. But his calculation is little more than a matter of guess work. In recent centuries, it was generally taken that three *lis* make an English mile. Thus we see that there may be much difference of opinion in interpreting the measurements recorded by Hsüan-Tsang. So the pilgrim's calculations cannot be accepted at their face value and require new interpretation in the light of further research. And these measurements suffer from one general shortcoming which is true for all ages and all people. Whenever a man feels *fatigued*, even short distances seem very long. This must have been the case with the Chinese pilgrims who travelled on foot from place to place. A student must be careful of such inaccuracies, which become apparent if observed minutely. Even on Cunningham's estimate of 6 *lis* to a mile, many of Hsüan-Tsang's distances seem to be exaggerated.

Besides the itineraries of the Chinese pilgrims, we have other source-materials which are definitely more authentic; they are inscriptions and seals. The inscriptions dealing with the grants of land or villages mention the boundary of the land granted or the administrative unit in which a particular village was situated. The inscriptions of the Pāla kings are of great help in this respect. Sometimes we find spurious Copper Plates forged in the name of past kings. In such cases, the date, palaeography, and names may be challenged, but this does not invalidate the geographical importance contained in these inscriptions. The places mentioned in inscriptions cannot be incorrect, because the very purpose

1. We are grateful to Mr. M. Loewe for supplying much of the information contained in this paragraph.

of forging the plate would not be served if the place was not in existence.

A large number of village names have been found on the seals discovered at Nālandā. The seals are inscribed with the name of the village which possessed a Buddhist monastery or a corporate body which contributed some amount to meet the expenses of the big monastery at Nālandā. These villages were generally situated in the vicinity of Nālandā. Some seals have been found also at Vaiśālī. But they do not help much in geographical studies.

These are the raw materials which we have utilized to build the edifice of our *Historical Geography* . Here we must make a few points clear, without whose proper understanding we shall fail to appreciate the difficulty of the researcher, particularly in this type of work.

In spite of immense research work on the history of ancient India, there are still certain lacunae which a student has to fill in with his own imagination and inference. This can be done more correctly and authoritatively by those students who have a correct idea of the locality, language and culture of the regions concerned. In the absence of precise knowledge of these things, it will be very difficult for a student to distinguish between two different regions. For instance, we can take the Tirhut division of modern Bihar. It is the ancient Tīrabhukti, which roughly corresponds to Mithilā of even earlier days. But the district of Saran is also included in the modern Tirhut, although it does not bear any resemblance culturally, ethinically and linguistically to Mithilā.

The identification of ancient place names is a major problem which is difficult to tackle all over the world, let alone in India, where much remains to be achieved in this field. No authoritative village survey has yet been made in India, and archaeological explorations conducted at certain places are quite insignificant in comparison to the length and breadth of the country and its vast number of ruins. The places have both Sanskrit and Prakrit names which were pronounced differently and thus confusion arose. Last but not the least, some of the place-names were affected by the Persian names which were later imposed upon them. Some of these names are found transliterated in foreign accounts in such a corrupt and degenerate form that it is very difficult to identify and locate the places referred to. In face of all these problems it is often very difficult even to establish the real original name of a place. The means which we can apply to solve this problem, is philology. On the basis of philological studies, we can hope to discover the original names of places. We often find names having symbolical or explanatory meanings, which can be easily interpreted with the help of philology. However the philological solution of the problem cannot be accepted as final. There may be certain places bearing the same name in a certain locality. We have found such cases in dealing with the modern place-names in the region round Rājagṛha and this can be true for any part of India. Some of the places bearing old names may have sprung up quite late, and hence there is always some uncertainty in the location and identification of a place in the absence of an authoritative village survey.

The problem of major routes is not less complicated. The pilgrims, no doubt, generally travelled on high roads, but from their descriptions it seems that they may also have used tracks in travelling from one village to another. The Sanskrit and Jain literature is almost silent in this respect. It does mention places sometimes, but it does not give a correct idea of communications. The Buddhist litrerature excels the others in this field, for it describes in some detail the destination of the roads and the places lying on them. But these sources are not of very great help in preparing a chart of the ancient routes. No doubt, we can show different places on high roads, but we do not know in detail how they ran from place to place. Nobody could have had exact knowledge of these routes in the absence of maps and as yet we have no evidence that there were any maps in ancient India. Thus in reconstructing ancient routes we have to depend on our own historical imagination and our knowledge of the regions through which a particular road might pass. Our attempt to trace these routes on a map will be largely hypothetical, and many of our tentative reconstructions cannot be supported with very strong arguments, if challenged. But to suggest any other alternative routes is also full of the same or greater risks, and we believe that our reconstruction of the main routes in ancient Bihar is the most probable in the light of the knowledge available. Despite all these difficulties we have attempted to draw a sketch map of the ancient routes in Bihar. Although hypothetical, it shows how these routes probably connected the ancient cities of Bihar.

Mankind from the beginning of his journey on the earth has normally followed the easiest and most comfortable routes in travelling from place to place. This principle holds good in general and even at present the main lines of communications in India are, no doubt, those which existed in ancient days, with changes here and there owing to shifting populations and improved means of transport and road making.

In tracing the ancient routes we have therefore always kept in mind those lines of communications which are used for traffic at the present time.

Before dealing with the actual historical geography in our thesis, we deemed it necessary to give an outline of the ancient history of Bihar. The chapter helps us in understanding the geographical forces behind historical events of the state. As it was not our aim to carry on research in the political history of Bihar, it is futile to expect any thing new in this chapter. We would like to say that this is simply a synthesis of researches carried on by numerous scholars in this field. This is followed by a chapter on the ancient rivers of Bihar. A large number of small rivers flowing in the modern Bihar has not been mentioned at all. We have included only those rivers in our list which have been mentioned at least once in early literature. This does not of course imply that the rest of the rivers were not in existence in ancient Bihar. We can only say that they probably did not play any important role in the history of the time and hence they have not been referred to.

Most of these rivers rise from mountains and hills which have been fully discussed in a separate chapter. The land of north Bihar is level and there is no hill worth mentioning except a few unimportant ranges in the Champaran district. We do not find any of these hills mentioned in our sources. It will be mere repetitions to emphasize more than once that Magadha, being the cradle land of Buddhism, has received great attention from the Buddhists and almost every hill or cave has been an abode of some known or unknown mendicants. The Purāṇas explicitly deal with the Mandāra, the well-known hill of the Bhagalpur district. The Hindus and the Buddhists had probably not penetrated into the heart of the modern Chhotanagpur, which is full of hills. The Jain literature, however, throws some light in this direction but it is limited to a few places only. Their attention was directed more to the Pārśvanātha hill and so we are quite in the dark about the rest of the hills.

The land of Bihar, physically divided into three broad divisions, had more political fragmentations. The districts of Shahabad and Saran seem to have been originally a portion of those territories which now form a part of the eastern Uttar Pradesh. The rest of the country was fairly well-known except the Jhārakhaṇḍa. The Jains mention a few kingdoms in this area, but we should use these sources with some reserve. A few inscriptions of early medieval India have revealed the names of some administrative units of different categories. But we learn little about the nature of these administrative units.

CHAPTER II

HISTORICAL OUTLINE

The history of the territory now comprising the state of Bihar, though it has some degree of unity, is in large measure the history of two distinct regions, separated by the Gaṅgā. To the North of the great river lay Mithilā, and to the South Magadha. The former was first Aryanized, but it early lost its prominence to Magadha, which became the centre of great empires. The former was usually a stronghold of Brāhmaṇic orthodoxy, while the latter was one of the earliest homes of Buddhism, and remained a centre of that faith until the Muslim conquest. Thus the character and fortunes of the two parts of Bihar have been very different.

Archaeological discoveries of prehistoric or protohistoric material have not been plentiful in Bihar, and we have little indication of the earliest inhabitants of this region. Finds of copper implements at Ranchi and elsewhere have not been satisfactorily dated, and may belong to pre-Aryan times, but may equally well be later. The great wall of Rājgir gives positive evidence of an organized state system in the time of the Buddha, but for the period before this time we have only traditions, not written down until a much later date, and in many respects evidently unreliable. There are, however, a few references in Vedic literature which throw a little light on the earliest history of the region.

As far as the northern part of the state is concerned, our first reliable reference is to be found in the story of Māthava Videha, to be found in the *Śatapatha Brāhmaṇa*.[1] We are told that this chief, accompanied by his family priest Gotama Rāhugaṇa, travelled from the banks of the Sarasvatī to those of the Sadānīrā; here he stopped, for the land on the further bank of the river had not been purified by Agni. Agni, at the behest of Māthava, agreed to cross, and from that time forward the land was purified, and fit to be lived in by Aryans.[2] Māthava is said to have dried up the marshes,

1. I. 4; I. 10.
2. Ibid.

cleared the jungle, and established a kingdom. It seems fairly certain that this story, told as it is in a very ancient source, contains a recollection of the first Aryan settlers in the region, if we accept the usual identification of the Sadānīrā as the Gandak,[1] and the fire-god's part in the story seems to be a recollection not only of the introduction of the Vedic fire-cult into the region, but also of the clearing of forests by fire, a practice well attested in early Indian literature.

Though the Purāṇic and Epic traditions give us the names of numerous kings of Videha, the name the land acquired from the clan-name of its first Aryan colonist, only one of these kings seems to have been remembered in the earlier traditions as contained in the Vedic literature. This is Janaka, who is recalled in the Upanishads and in Buddhist and Jain literature also as a powerful king, and a keen patron of the ascetic teachers of the new wisdom of the *Upanishad*. Much is told of him in later tradition, but there is little that can be relied on as sober history, except this fact. As he appears to have been the contemporary of the great sage Yājñavalkya, and thus to have lived towards the end of the Vedic period, we can date him somewhere in the 7th century B.C.[2]

The Jain and Buddhist scriptures, though they remember Janaka and other kings of the region north of the Gaṅgā, tell of the existence of a confederacy of republican tribes there at the time of the Buddha, referred to usually as the Vṛjjis or Lichchhavis. It appears that the former name was applied to the whole confederacy, while the latter was its leading tribe.[3] The origin of these tribal peoples, and the means whereby they took over the region from the older kings, have been the subject of much speculation and controversy,[4] which can perhaps only be solved if archaeologists are successful in discovering sites which can be definitely dated to these times.

Both Buddhist and Jain sources preserve many traditions of these republican peoples, governed apparently by a large assembly of heads of families, and a smaller inner council

1. Weber - Indische Studien, pp. 112, 181.
2. For details see Thakur, History of Mithilā, chap. II.
3. D. A. II. p. 159; *Kalpa Sūtra,* section 128.
4. I. A. Vol. XXXVII, pp. 58-90 ; Mishra, *Early History of Vaiśālī,* Thakur, *op. cit.* chap. III.

of tribal chiefs.[1] They appear to have been for a while powerful, but they were suppressed by the kingdom of Magadha soon after the Buddha's death, and did not rise again to prominence for many centuries, and then only to be merged in the Gupta empire.

The region to the south of the Ganges, though according to later tradition it was a flourishing kingdom at the time of the Mahābhārata War, is referred to even less frequently in the early literature than the territory to the north of the river. Magadha is not mentioned in the *Ṛg-Veda*, and though some authorities believe that the tribe of Kīkaṭas referred to therein resided in Magadha, the evidence is very faint, and contrary evidence is stronger.[2] Magadha occurs first in the *Atharva Veda*, as a land wherein the *vrātyas* dwell.[3] The term *Magadha* also occurs in later Vedic literature, whether in the sense of a Māgadhan, a bard, or a member of the caste of that name.[4] But it is evident that throughout the period when the Vedic literature was being written that part of Bihar south of the river was looked on as an impure non-Aryan region. Buddhist and Jain sources show that even in the time of the Buddha it was by no means thoroughly Aryanized. Aṅga, the eastern neighbour of Magadha, receives equally scant mention in this literature. In the *Atharva Veda* the Aṅgas, like the Magadhas, are mentioned as an impure people.[5] The *Aitareya Brāhmaṇa*, however, mentions them as conquering the world,[6] which would suggest that for a while Aṅga made some impression on the politics of the time. But the evidence is shadowy in the extreme, and only at the time of the Buddha do we find some real light on the subject.

When about 530 B. C. the Buddha began to preach his new doctrines Magadha had become a well organized kingdom, and its king Bimbisāra had annexed Aṅga.[7] This was the first Magadhan conquest, beginning a series of annexations,

1. S. B. E. Vol. XI. p. 3.
2. *Ṛg Veda*, III. 53. 14.
3. Atharva V. 22. 14.
4. Vedic Index II. 117.
5. V. 22. 14.
6. VIII. 22.
7. S. B. E. XVII. p. 1.

which, extending over a period of some 200 years, were to lead to the first great Indian empire. There is no clear evidence on the origin of Bimbisāra. Hindu and Buddhist sources are at variance on this matter, and no earlier king of Magadha, except Jarāsandha of Epic tradition, plays an important part in any legend. It would seem probable that Bimbisāra's reign saw a very rapid growth of Magadhan power, not only through the conquest of Aṅga but also through his marriage alliance with Pasenadī of Kosala, which appears, reading between the lines of a rather garbled Buddhist tradition, to have brought him control of further territory to the west, in the direction of Banaras.[1] He appears to have been on the whole a man of peace and to have kept on good terms with his neighbours, consolidating his kingdom and improving his system of government in preparation for further expansion at a later date.

Bimbisāra was put to death by his son Ajātaśatru some seven years before the Buddha's death, probably in 493 B.C.[2] The new king seems almost at once to have commenced a policy of expansion. According to Buddhist tradition he was immediately involved with his uncle Pasenadī, king of Kosala, to the West, and appears to have acquired further territory in the region of Banaras as a result of this war.[3] He then invaded Vajjian territory across the Gaṅgā, and, after what appears to have been a long war, annexed the region to his empire.[4] Thus Magadha became master of the whole of modern Bihar, with full control of both sides of the Gaṅgā from the neighbourhood of Banaras to Bhagalpur or beyond. We hear little more of the great rival kingdom of Kosala, and it seems likely that it fell to Magadha soon after. There is indeed one reference to an attack on Ajātaśatru's capital on the part of Pajjota, the king of far-off Avanti (Malwa),[5] but this is only mentioned in passing, and very obscurely, and if such an attack took place at all it was unsuccessful.

1. Jātaka No. 239, 283, 492.
2. Mahāvaṁśa Ch. II.
3. The Book of the Kindred Sayings, I. pp. 109-110, J. Nos. 239, 282, 439.
4. S. B. E. XI. pp. 1-5; XVII 101.
5. D. P. P. N., 1.34.

With the reign of Ajātaśatru it was evident that Magadha was the predominant Indian kingdom.

Many factors, some of them geographical, contributed to the success of Magadha. The mighty Gaṅgā on the North, and the Soṇa on the West gave the region a natural defence, and a useful means of communication. Control of the Gaṅgā, and of the river port of Champā, the chief city of Aṅga, must have considerably enriched the Magadhan kings, for even at this time trade had become vigorous, if we are to believe our sources, and though we have no positive archaeological evidence of sea-trade with south India at this period, there is every likelihood that coastal shipping was already bringing up the Gaṅgā the gold of Mysore, the jewels of Hyderabad and Ceylon, and the spices of the Tamil country. This trade with the south was to increase in later centuries, and must always have been a valuable source of wealth to the ruler who controlled the lower Gaṅgā. Perhaps even more important was the fact that the Magadhan kings controlled access to one of the main sources of metals in India. From their capital of Rājagṛha Bimbisāra and Ajātaśatru could levy tribute on the iron and copper brought from the region of Ranchi to the Gangetic plain, and could always be sure of an abundant and cheap supply of these metals for themselves. Ethnic factors also may have played their part in the success of Magadha. The land, even in the days of Bimbisāra, was still only on the fringes of Brāhmaṇism. While the lands of earlier Aryan occupation, such as the Kuru-Pāñchāla territory, seem by this time to have become priest-ridden, squandering much of the national wealth in expensive sacrifices, this was not the case with Magadha, where the Brāhmaṇa was by no means so influential. It was an early home of Buddhism and Jainism, which encouraged a somewhat more positive and realistic approach to life than did the sterile sacrificial brāhmaṇism of the regions further West. And a final factor in the success of Magadha may well have been the genius of her kings. It is evident that Bimbisāra was a brilliant organizer.[1] He is recorded as being in contact with the king of distant Gāndhāra,[2] and he may even have learnt something of the mighty imperial

1. *Vinayapiṭaka*, VII. 3.5.
2. J. I. 399, II. 218.

system of the Achaemenids. Ajātaśatru, though remembered chiefly as a fierce conqueror, must have maintained the tradition of good administration established by his father, which was to culminate in the highly centralized state of the Mauryas, which is reflected in the great *Arthaśāstra*.

Though no doubt most of them contributed something to the progress of Magadha, the successors of Ajātaśatru are shadowy figures. One of them, Udāyin, is said to have moved his capital from Rājagṛha to Kusumapura, or Pāṭaliputra,[1] a clear indication of the growing strength and confidence of Magadha, and of the growing importance of the Gaṅgā both for trade and politics. Śiśunāga, apparently a usurper,[2] is said to have destroyed the Pradyotas, the rulers of Avanti;[3] this evidently indicates a further westward expansion of Magadha. Around the middle of the 4th century B.C. a new Magadhan dynasty, founded by the base-born Mahāpadma Nanda, appears to have gained a foothold in Orissa[4] and perhaps in part of the Deccan.[5] When Alexander of Macedon reached the Beas he was told that the whole of India beyond that river was in the hands of Xandrammes,[6] presumably a Nanda king. It is evident that, even before the rise of Chandragupta Maurya, Magadha controlled most of northern India.

The last Nanda was overthrown by Chandragupta Maurya, who appears to have been a young man at the time, and, according to some classical sources, had been in touch with Alexander,[7] whose satraps he expelled from the Panjab.[8] The century following his accession, in *c.* 321, was one in which nearly the whole of India was governed by a Mauryan emperor from Pāṭaliputra. Under Chandragupta or his successor Bindusāra, great accessions of territory were gained in the Deccan.[9] By his war with Seleucus Nicator Chandragupta gained much of what is now Afghanistan, and paved the way

1. *Pariśiṣṭaparva*, VI. 34; 175-180.
2. *Mahavamśa*, Ch. IV. 6.
3. *Vāyu Purāṇa*, pp. 314
4. *Select Inscriptions* p. 208.
5. *Pariśiṣṭaparva*, VII. 81.
6. *Invasion of Alexander*, pp. 221, 281.
7. Justin. p. 142.
8. *Alexander* (Plutarch) LXII.
9. *Beginning of the South Indian History*, Ch. II.

for close contact with the Hellenic powers of the West.[1] As we can gather from the account of Megasthenes and from the *Arthaśāstra* ascribed to Chandragupta's mentor Kauṭilya, which, whatever its true origin, must surely reflect Mauryan conditions. The Mauryans, no doubt largely inspired by the earlier system of government, but contributing much of their own, built up a highly organized administration, which for a century succeeded in controlling an area as large as British India before partition, despite primitive means of communication. Their success must be counted as the highest achievement of Indian statecraft, despite its temporary nature.

The third Maurya, Aśoka, is so famous that he hardly requires any mention. He followed the traditional policy of conquest in the early part of his career, and eight years after his coronation, annexed the powerful territory of Kaliṅga to his empire. He thus ruled over a large empire extending from Bengal to southern Afghanistan and from Kashmir to Mysore in the Deccan from his capital at Pāṭaliputra. But the Kaliṅga war gave him a great psychological shock. He changed the policy of *digvijaya* for *dharmavijaya* and devoted his whole energy and the resources of his vast empire to the preaching of dharma and the welfare of the mankind. During his reign cordial relations were established with the Hellenic countries[2] of the west. He died about 232 B. C.

The successors of Aśoka may have inherited the large empire of their predecessors, but certainly not their capacity and energy. Soon they lost every part of their empire one after another and a day came when the last Maurya king Bṛhadratha was assasssinated by his general Puṣyamitra in the presence of the army in 187 B.C.

Puṣyamitra founded a new dynasty, that of the Śuṅgas. The first king ruled over most of the provinces of northern India, but the centre of power seems to have shifted from Magadha to Vidiśā in Central India. This can be inferred from the *Mālavikāgnimitraṁ* and the Śuṅga sculpture in Central India. The *Mahābhāṣya*[3] and the *Mālavikāgnimitraṁ*[4]

1. Justin. p. 143.
2. *Select Inscriptions* p. 37.
3. II. 32.8
4. *Mālavikāgnimitraṁ*, p. 353.

inform us that during the reign of Puṣyamitra, a certain Yavana attacked India and was defeated. According to the *Gargīsaṁhitā*[1] the Greeks at one time penetrated into Magadha and beseiged Pātaliputra, but were forced to retreat owing to internal dissensions. The king who led this invasion was probably Menander[2] or Demetrius.

The Hāthīgumphā inscription[3] of the aggressive Jain king of Kaliṅga tells us that Khāravela invaded Magadha during the reign of Bahasatimitra. Dr. Raychaudhuri[4] thinks that invasion took place in the 1st century B.C., but earlier scholars generally believed that it occurred in the 2nd century B. C. Puṣyamitra's successors had no capacity and energy to control the empire and the kingdom soon passed over to the Kāṇva dynasty. Vāsudeva Kāṇva was the first king of the line. We have no detailed information of the Kāṇva rulers. Their line came to an end about 30 B.C.

After the extinction of the Kāṇva dynasty, we have no authentic knowledge of the dynasties which ruled over Bihar. The Purāṇas say that the Āndhras ruled over Magadha after the Kāṇvas but this is not proved by any other source. Dr. K. P. Jayaswal[5] on a very obscure basis had tried to show that the Nāgas, Vakāṭakas and Bhāraśivas were ruling in northern India before the Guptas. But his view is not taken very seriously by the historians. As far as the Kuṣāṇas are concerned some coins have been discovered in Bihar, but, that is not the sure sign of their rule there. The available sources show, however, that the Kuṣāna power reached for a while as far as Banaras.[6]

The post-Kāṇva and pre-Gupta period is still a dark one in the history of Bihar and we cannot say any thing about it with certainty unless fresh materials are available.

Chandra Gupta I of the Gupta line came to power some time about 320 A.D. The Gupta inscriptions name two predecessors of Chandra Gupta I but we know hardly anything

1. J.B.O.R.S. Vol. XIV, Part III, p. 402.
2. *Ancient India* (Majumdar) p. 125.
3. *Select Inscriptions*, p. 208.
4. P.H.A.I., p. 378
5. *History of India.* (Jayaswal), pp. 2—61.
6. *Select Inscriptions* pp. 132-133.

about them. His title '*Mahārājādhirāja*' shows that he had strengthened his power. He married the Lichchhavi princess Kumāradevī and probably inherited the Lichchhavi territory in north Bihar on account of this marriage. Chandra Gupta I started an era from A.D. 320, which is known as the 'Gupta-kāla'.

Samudra Gupta was the product of the union with the Lichchhavi princess. During his reign, Magadha regained the vitality and energy which she had lost after the death of Aśoka. Samudra Gupta came to the throne about A.D. 335 and ruled till 375-76 A.D. He made at least three compaigns, to conquer the rājās of the Āryāvarta and the eastern part of Deccan. At the completion of his conquests, he performed the *Aśvamedha* sacrifice to celebrate his *digvijaya* and commemorated the ceremony by issuing special coins.[1] He had diplomatic relation with several foreign kings.[2] The Allahabad pillar inscription[3] throws a flood of light upon the personal and political career of the great Gupta monarch.

Samudra Gupta was succeeded by his son Chandra Gupta II, also known as Vikramāditya, who under the latter title has become a famous figure of tradition. He was the worthy son of his worthy father. He extended the conquests of his father by annexing the Satrapal territory of Gujarat and Saurāshṭra. The ports on the western coast were now under the Guptas. Through these ports, there was a brisk trade between the east and the west, which brought immense riches into the country. Chandra Gupta II made a matrimonial alliance with the Vākāṭakas and thus further extended the sphere of his influence.

In the latter part of his career, the capital was probably shifted to Ujjayinī from Pāṭaliputra if we are to believe tradition, but Vikramāditya of Ujjayinī may be a legendary king about whom we have no authentic evidence. If he was Chandra Gupta II, soon after his death Pāṭaliputra regained its former position, since it seems to have remained near the centre of the Gupta empire until its end. The reign of Chandra Gupta II is very famou sfor literary and cultural activities.

1. *Select Inscriptions*, p. 258.
2. Ibid.
3. Ibid.

Chandra Gupta II was succeeded by his son Kumāra Gupta in A.D. 415. He reigned till 455 A.D. He maintained intact the empire he had inherited from his father. But it seems that the empire had begun to weaken even during the reign of Kumāra Gupta. We find mention of rebellion and invasions[1] which shook the Gupta empire. The Crown prince Skanda Gupta rose equal to the occasion and maintained the falling fortune of the family.[2] The chief invaders appear to have been the fierce Hūṇas of Central Asia, who now for the first time appeared on the Indian scene.

Skanda Gupta reigned till A.D. 467. His inscriptions speak of the bravery which he showed in quelling the rebellion and repelling the Hūṇas. We have no detailed account of his reign.

After Skanda Gupta, there are many geneological and chronological complications. The historians are not unanimous about the succession of kings and their dates. However no king had the capacity to check the Hūṇas who were coming in, horde after horde. It is not improbable that the Hūṇas had attacked Magadha, the heart of the empire. Yaśodharman of Mālawā probably wiped out the remaining power of the Gupta kings. However they survived at least in north Bengal till circa 540 A.D. as we learn from the Damodarpur Copper Plates.[3] After the fall of the Guptas, small principalities came to power in different parts of the empire.

Two poweful dynasties also appeared on the stage. They were the Maukharis of Kanauj and the later Guptas of Magadha and Mālawā. The ambitious kings of both these dynasties strove to extend their territories and war between them continued for several generations with many vicissitudes. The later Guptas had initial success and extended their territories at the expense of their rivals, but Iśāṇavarman, the third king of the Maukhari dynasty, defeated Mahāsena Gupta and captured Magadha. This is indicated by the Deo-Barnark inscription.[4] The later Guptas retired to the distant province of Mālawā. We do not know for certain how long

1. *Select Inscriptions*, p. 314.
2. Ibid.
3. *Select Inscriptions*, p. 337.
4. C. I. I. Vol. III, p. 213.

the Maukharis ruled over Magadha. There seems to have been dissension[1] among the Maukharis as a result of which they lost control of it. It is possible that this internal trouble gave an opportunity to Śaśāṅka, the king of Bengal, to assert his independence. He probably conquered the land upto the Sona.

Dr. R. C. Majumdar[2] thinks that Śaśāṅka in his early career was a feudatory, who ruled from Rohtasgadh. In any case he became a powerful king. That his dominion was vast is attested by Bāṇa, Hsüan-Tsang and *Mañjuśrīmūlakalpa.* His coins have been found at Gayā and Nālandā. With his capital at Karṇasuvarṇa in north Bengal, he ruled over the whole of Bihar, Orissa and the eastern part of Uttar Pradesh.

When Śaśāṅka killed Rājyavardhana, the elder brother of Harshavardhana of Thāneśvar,the latter resolved to destroy him as soon as possible. It is not improbable that Harsha drove him out of Bihar in his early career, because we find no record of Śaśāṇka in this part of India after Harsha's coronation.

Mādhava Gupta ruled in Magadha as a deputy of Harsha. He probably became independent in A. D. 647 after the death of Harsha. By that time Mithilā seems to have passed under the control of Arjuna or Aruṇāśva, the provincial governor of Harsha. He attacked a Chinese embassy headed by Wang-Hiuen-Tse. The latter escaped to Nepal and Tibet and with the help of the kings of these lands, he conquered a large part of northern Bihar. The Chinese account of Wang-Hiuen-Tse's conquests seem to be rather exaggerated.

Mādhava Gupta was succeeded in circa 672 A.D. by Ādityasena, who assumed the imperial title.[3] He brought Mithilā too under his suzerainty. If Śrī Ādi Siṁha of the Dudhapani inscription is to be identified with him, we can assume that he held sway upto Hazaribagh in south Bihar.[4]

The last king of the dynasty was Jīvita Gupta II. He was probably killed fighting with Yaśovarman of Kanauj about A.D. 725. An inscription has been recently found in the Muzaffarpur district (which has not been edited) which shows that the line continued till the end of the eighth century A.D.

1. *The Catalogue of Coins of the Guptas, Maukharis etc. in the Provincial Museum of Lucknow*, p. 39.
2. *History of Bengal,* Vol. I, p. 59.
3. C. I. I. Vol. III, p. 204.
4. E. I. Vol. II. pp. 343-47.

The meteoric rise and fall of Yaśovarman of Kanauj, in the first half of the eighth century A.D. brought about anarchy in the country. The fish logic[1] (*Matsyanyāya*) had become the order of the day. The life and property of none was safe. At this critical juncture, Gopāla came as the saviour of the country and laid the foundation of the Pāla dynasty which ruled over Bihar and Bengal for more than 300 years.

We have no information about any permanent capital of the Pālas. Their inscriptions were generally issued from their *Jayaskandhāvāras* (Victorious camps). It is not improbable that the Pālas had their capital somewhere in Eastern Bihar, as their more important inscriptions were generally issued from places located in the Bhagalpur or Monghyr district.

Gopāla came to power some time in the later part of the eighth century A. D. According to Tāranātha[2] "Gopāla began to reign in Bengal and afterwards reduced Magadha also under his power." He might have reigned from about A.D. 756 to 783. It was Gopāla who brought Mithilā also under his subjugation, because we do not find the names of Mithilā and Magadha in the list of the countries conquered by Dharmapāla.

Gopāla was succeeded about A.D. 783 by his son Dharmapāla, who ruled till A.D. 815 or 819. At this time, the Pratihāras and the Rāshṭrakūtas had also risen to power. All the three states were bent upon to capture the fertile Gangetic plains. This was the main reason of the tripartite struggle which lasted for more than one hundred years. Dharmapāla achieved initial success, but he was driven back by Nāgabhaṭa II, the Pratihāra king. The latter attacked Dharmapāla's territory and a severe battle was fought at Mudgagiri, as attested by the Gwalior inscription of Bhoja[3] and the Jodhpur inscription of Bāhuka.[4] This invasion seems to have been no more than a raid and the Pratihāras probably could not annex any part of the Pāla dominion. The

1. E. I. Vol. IV. p. 249.
2. I.A. Vol. IV. p. 366.
3. E.I. Vol. XVIII, pp. 108-112.
4. Ibid. pp. 96-98.

Rāshṭrakūṭas soon attacked Nāgabhaṭa II and gave him a crushing defeat. This gave ample opportunity to Dharmapāla to retrieve his position.

He was succeeded by his son Devapāla, who reigned for 48 years. His inscriptions speak in eulogistic terms of his conquests with evident exaggeration, but he definitely had control over the whole of Bihar, as is proved by the find spots of his inscriptions. During his reign, Mihira Bhoja of Kanauj tried to snatch the western portion of the Pāla dominion, but he met with little success. After Devapāla, a confusion creeps into the line of succession of the Pāla dynasty. Dr. B. P. Sinha thinks[1] that the empire was divided between Vigrahapāla and Surapāla. But it is generally believed that Vigrahapāla and Surapāla were one and the same person.

Nārāyaṇapāla came to the throne after Vigrahapāla. We have found no inscription of his in Bengal. Even in Bihar, after his 17th year,[2] there is no record till 54th year of his reign.[3] The thirty seven years' interval evidently saw a great decline in the fortune of the family. At this time, we find four inscriptions[4] of the Gurjara king Mahendrapāla in south Bihar and one inscription in Paharpur in the Rajshahi district of north Bengal. These inscriptions prove that Mahendrapāla captured Magadha and north Bengal from the Pālas. This is supported by the Deoli Plate[5] of Kṛshṇa II which distinguishes between Gauḍa and Magadha at the time of his invasion of Magadha. But the Udandapur image inscription of Nārāyaṇapāla shows that he managed to restore the rule of his family in the eastern part of Bihar.[6] During his reign a Rāshṭrakūta family ruled in Bodh Gayā and its adjoining region, as can be inferred from the inscription of Tunga Dharmāvaloka.[7] They captured the fort of Manipur which is identified with the Manivāṭaka of Devapāla's Nālandā grant.

1. *The Decline of the Kingdom of Magadha*, p. 381.
2. J.A.S.B. XLII. p. 354 etc.
3. I. A. (1918) p. 110.
4. Dighba Dubauli Plate, The Ramagaya inscription, Itkhori inscription, the Guneriya inscription.
5. E. I. Vol. V, p. 193.
6. I. A. (1918) p. 110.
7. *Buddha Gayā* p. 193.ff.

Nārāyaṇapāla was succeeded by Rājyapāla. He brought Nālandā[1] under his control. Allan[2] and H. C. Ray[3] are of the opinion that the Gurjaras crossed the Sona and overran the whole of Tirthut about this time.

Rājyapāla was succeeded by Gopāla II. The Chandel king Yaśovarman easily defeated the Pālas. At this time north Bihar probably formed a separate province outside the Pāla jurisdiction. It is mentioned separately in the list of territories conquered by Yaśovarman.

Vigrahapāla II came after Gopala II. The Chandras and the Kāmbojas established themselves in Bengal during his regime. These Chandras hailed from Rohitagiri. Some scholars identify it with the Lalmai[4] hill of the Tippera district, but it is generally identified with the Rohatasagadh of Bihar.[5] It is possible that they were driven from Bihar during the invasion of the Gurjara king Mahendrapāla. At this time, there ruled in Arakan another Chandra family which came from Basarh of north Bihar. We do not know if the two Chandra families were related in any way. Tāranātha informs us that a king named Balachandra ruled over Tirhut and Kāmarūpa.

Mahīpāla, the son of Vigrahapāla tried to retrieve the position of his family. When he came to the throne only Rāḍha and a portion of Bihar were left of the whole Pāla empire. He tried to extend his dominion and met with some success. Several inscriptions found at Bodh Gayā[6] and Nālandā,[7] and the Bangarh[8] grant issued from Vilāspur in the Patna district prove his rule over south Bihar in the early part of his career. The Chandel king Dhaṅga[9] seems to have attacked Rāḍha and Aṅga either during the reign of Mahīpāla or of the Kāmbojas. But he soon withdrew and the Chedis took his place as the chief invaders of Bihar.

1. I. A. (1917) p. 111.
2. *Cambridge Shorter History*, p. 144.
3. D. H. N. I. Vol. I, p. 305.
4. I. H. Q. (1926) pp. 325-27; (1927) p. 418.
5. *History of Bengal* Vol. I, p. 194.
6. A. S. R. III, p. 122.
7. Ibid. pp. 122-23.
8. J. A. S. B. (1892), Part I, p. 77 ff.
9. E. I. Vol. I, pp. 138, 145.

A manuscript of the *Rāmāyāṇa* by a Nepalese Kāyastha completed in the year 1019 A.D. speaks of a certain Gāṅgeyadeva as the ruler of Tīrabhukti. Bendall[1] identifies him with the famous Chedi king of the same name. But Lèvy[2] thinks that he might be an unknown king belonging to the Kalachurī family of Gorakhpur. Scholars generally take him to be the Chedī king. He may have defeated Mahīpāla and captured Mithilā. But we have neither epigraphic nor numismatic evidence to prove the rule of this king over this part of the Pāla empire. The Imadpur[3] image inscription proves that Mahīpāla soon took back Mithilā from the Chedis. He died about A.D. 1032.

After the death of Mahīpāla, the empire fell on evil days. Mahīpāla was succeeded by Nayapāla. He and his son Vigrahapāla III have been credited with no military exploits. The Chedī king Karṇa invaded Magadha several times during the reign of Nayapāla. However a treaty was concluded between them through the mediation of Dipāṅkara Atīśa, the famous Buddhist teacher.[4] The Kṛshṇa Dvārikā temple inscription[5] and the Narasimha temple inscription[6] at Gayā show that Nayapāla had paramount control over the western part of Bihar. According to the *Rāmacharita*[7] Vigrahapāla III defeated Karṇa. From Nawalagadh inscription too, on paleographic grounds, the rule of Vigrahapāla III seems to have extended to Tirhut.[8] But it is possible that the image may have been taken to Nawalgadh from some place in south Bihar. A certain king Nānyadeva, a Karṇāṭa warrior, had established a principality in Mithilā by A.D. 1097.[9] Vijayasena, the Sena king, probably made an invasion against this king, who is referred to in Deopara inscription.[10]

After Vigrahapāla III, Rāmapāla came to the throne. During the rule of his ancestors, the conditon of the Pāla

1. J. A. S. B. (1903) Part I, p. 18.
2. *Le Nepal* Vol. II, p. 202 note I.
3. I. A. Vol. XIV, p. 165, n. 17
4. *History of Bengal* Vol. I, pp. 144-45.
5. J. A. S. B. (1900) Part I, pp. 193-95.
6. Ibid. p. 191 n. I,
7. Ch. I. 9 (Commentary).
8. G. D. College Bulletin No. I.
9. Thakur, History of Mithilā, chap. V.
10. E. I. Vol. I, pp. 305-315.

territory had sunk to the lowest level. Gauḍa had passed into the hands of the Kaivartas and the Varmans seem to have established their power in Aṅga. Rāmpāla consolidated his power. His maternal uncle Mathana or his family drove away the Varmans from Aṅga. He defeated the Kaivartas and Magadha[1] was fully under his control. He died about A.D. 1109.

Rāmapāla was succeeded by a few minor kings such as Rājyapāla, Kumārapāla, Gopāla III and Madanapāla. There were merely phantoms ruling only a small part of the once powerful empire reared by the genius and strength of Dharmapāla and Devapāla. They were titular kings bereft of power. During Rāmapāla's reign, a Sūra dynasty had established itself in western Mandara. Choḍagaṅga, the Utkal king attacked it and rooted out the family.

In Bengal, Karnāṭa Kshatriyas had established their rule. Madanapāla was the master of a few districts in the eastern part of Bihar, as we infer from an inscription[2] found at Jayanagar near Lakhiserai in Bihar. The Pāla dynasty came to a close with the end of Madanapāla.

During the week successors of Rāmapāla, the Gahaḍavalas had occupied a portion of Magadha, as can be inferred from the Rahan Plate[3] of Govindachandra. He issued a grant[4] of the village Paḍalī from Maner in the Patna district in A. D. 1126. He issued another grant[5] from Mudgagiri in A.D. 1146. This goes to prove that the major part of Bihar was under his control. His son Vijayachandra had also control over parts of Magadha, as is shown by the Tārāchaṇḍi[6] Plate found near Sahasram. The territory of Jayachandra definitely extended upto Gayā in the east. This is proved by an inscription[7] found at Gayā itself.

After the collapse of the central authority, local chiefs raised their heads and founded small principalities in different parts of the state. The inscriptions furnish us with a few

1. J.A. S. B. (1900) Part I, p. 100.
2. C. A. S. R. III, p. 125, No. 17.
3. I. A. XVIII, pp. 14-19.
4. J.B.O.R.S. (1916) pp. 441-47.
5. E.I. Vol. VII, pp. 98-99.
6. J. A. O. S. VI pp. 547-59.
7. A. S. I. (1903-4) p. 55.

names ending in Pāla, but they probably had no connection with the imperial Pālas. They are Yakshapāla, Palapāla and Govindpāla. The name of Palapāla is mentioned in the Jayanagar[1] inscription which was issued in the 35th year of his reign. Dr. B.C. Sen thinks that he may be connected with Madanapāla, whose inscription comes from that very place.

The name of Yakshapāla is mentioned in an inscription at Gayā.[2]

From the Govindpur[3] inscription, we know about a new family named Māna. Two princes referred to are Varamāna and Rudramāna. We find a reference to the Māna family in the 8th century Dudhpani inscription also. But it is difficult to say if they were related with each other.

The Māna family probably came into collison with Yakshapāla's family in their northward advance.

While these families were quarrelling over the carcase of the Pāla empire, the Gahaḍavālas came and wiped them from the stage.

Such was the condition of Bihar in the latter decades of the 12th century A.D., when the ferocious Muslim horde was rapidly marching towards the east. The powerful dynasties of Delhi and Kanauj had tried their strength separately and were swept away by the terrible storm. This time, no Mahāpadmananda or Chandragupta rose equal to the occasion to repel the foreign hordes. The consequence was evident. There was no king to offer even feeble resistance and the whole of Bihar was conquered without any difficulty. Bakhtiyar Khilji overran the whole of the state from one end to another and the last vestiges of the Buddhist learning and culture disappeared from Bihar in the storm.

1. C. A. S. R. III No. 33.
2. A. S. I. (1901-2) p. 2.
3. E. I. Vol. II pp. 33-42.

CHAPTER III

THE MOUNTAIN SYSTEM OF ANCIENT BIHAR

The modern state of Bihar is divided into two parts by the river Gaṅgā. These two divisions have developed on rather different political and social patterns from remote antiquity. Their physical distinctions played a significant part in their progress. North Bihar has plain lands with fertile soil. There is no trace of mountain range or hill throughout the region, except in the extreme north of the Champaran district, which actually forms a part of the Nepalese Terai. These hills, locally known as the Dun and Someswar, extend over an area of 364 miles.

South Bihar is quite different from north Bihar in physical features. The land is quite fertile in the plain along the south bank of the Gaṅgā but the farther south one goes the more hills and mountain ranges one finds. There is hardly any district in south Bihar which has no hills. Those of Gayā, Patna, Shahabad and Bhagalpur districts are the most famous and we often find remains of flourishing culture on the summit or in the vicinity of these mountains. Of the hills of the Chhotanagapur area, there is hardly any worth mentioning from the historical point of view other than the Pārasnātha hill of the Hazaribagh district. The ranges of the Chhotanagpur area are no doubt lofty and important from the geological and mineral points of view, but they were probably hardly inhabited, except perhaps by a few savage tribes, in ancient days, and thus they have been rarely referred to in our literature.

It would be tedious and unnecessary to enumerate all these hills but we discuss the chief among them districtwise. The names of these hills have been given after important villages in their vicinity or events which may have happened there. But we often see that the same range assumes another name after some distance, when it is associated with another important village.

In the Patna district there are hills at Rājagṛha only. In the district of Gayā, there are the Bhundas, Jethian range, Hadia, Durvāsāṛshi, Mahabar hills, Bramhayonī, Kowadol, Barabar, Hasra Pahar, Chirki hills, Lohabar hills, Powai, Śṛṅgīṛkhī and the like. The Shahabad district has the Rohtas and the Kaimur ranges. The Mandāra hill, Pathar-ghata, Barai and Cologong rocks lie in the jurisdiction of the Bhagalpur district, while the Monghyr district has the Kharag-pur hills extending from Jamalpur to Jamui, a peak called Śṛngīṛkhi, Marak, Giddhaur hills, Satapahari etc.

The most important hills of Chhotanagpur are the Pārasnātha and the Rajamahal hills. Besides these, there is a large number of lesser ranges—Dalma, Sawai, Karanti, Panchet, Latehar Peaks, Brijka hills, Khaira hills, Netarhat hills, Kotam Turgenik, Tatakora, Butbul, Burhi, Mahagarbhi etc.

The hills named above are actually spurs of one mountain range, the Vindhyās. But the term Vindhyā as used in Sanskrit literature, needs clarification; it is said to be one of the "family mountains" (*Kulasparvata*)[1] and in this sense it has not been finally identified.

The Purāṇas supply a list of seven mountains besides the Himavat which they term *Kulaparvatas* or *Kulāchalas*. We do not know what the term actually denotes. It may be interpreted as "family mountains" or a group of mountains linked together around one central peak. If we minutely observe these mountains identified with modern ones, we shall not fail to mark that these mountain ranges are actually connected in one form or other. The Kulaparvatas[2] Mahendra, Malaya, Sahya Śuktimān, Ṛksha, Vindhyā, Pāriyātra or Pāripātra are seven in number. Besides them, we are told, there are thousands of mountains[3] near them.

Some of these mountains lie in the southern part of the state of Bihar. Most of the Kulaparvatas have been successfully identified by the scholars, but a doubt is still entertained by them about the location of the Śuktimat

1. *Mārkaṇḍeya Purāṇa* Ch. 57.
2. Ibid. Mahendro Malayaḥ Sahyaḥ, Śuktimanṛiksha parvatah Vindyāścha Pāripātraścha saptaivātra Kulāchalāḥ. (10-11).
3. Ibid. Teshāṃ sahasrashonye bhudharā ye samipagāḥ.

range. Cunningham[1] thinks that this range "must correspond with the high range of mountains to the south of Sehoa and Kanker, which gives rise to the Mahānadī, Pairi and the Seonath rivers and which forms the boundary between the Chhatisgarha and the feudatory state of Bastar."

C. V. Vaidya[2] identifies the Śuktimat range with the mountains of Kathiawar, but these are famous in literature as the Raivata mountains.

Pargiter[3] was first inclined to identify this range either with the Arāvalī or with the southern portion of the Eastern-ghats, but later on he preferred to identify it with the Gora khasi[4] hills of Assam beyond the Brahmaputra.

Dr. R. C. Majumdar[5] and Harit Krishnadeva[6] propose to identify the Śuktimat range with the Sulaiman mountains on the basis of similarity of names.

According to Prof. H.C. Raychaudhuri[7] the name should be "applied to the chain of hills that extends from Sakari in Raigarha, C. P. to the Dalma hills in the Santhal Parganas washed by the influents of the Babla."

Cunningham confuses the Śuktimat range with the south eastern Vindhyā and the Mahendra ranges which are Kula-parvatas in themselves. The *Mahābhārata*[8] gives a clue to the location of this mountain by associating the Bhallāṭa people with the Śuktimat range. Pargiter, no doubt on this basis, followed the route of Bhima's conquest in the eastern region but he forgot that Bhīma did not cross the Lauhitya or the Brahmaputra beyond which are the Garo and Khasi hills.

So far as its identification with the Sulaiman range is concerned, it can be said that the Sulaiman range forms a part of the Himālayas.[9] It had no separate identity in ancient India, as far as our knowledge goes.

1. A. S. I. Vol. XVII p. 69.
2. *Epic India* p. 276.
3. *Mārkaṇḍeya Purāṇa* p. 285.
4. Ibid p. 306.
5. Proceedings of Second Oriental Conference 1923 pp.
6. Ibid. Z. D. M. G. 1922. p. 281.
7. *Studies in Indian Antiquities*. p. 120.
8. II. 30. 5.
9. *Kumārasaṁbhava* I. 1. Kālidāsa mentions the Himalayas sloping on the eastern and western sides as if embracing the oceans.

Dr. Ray-Chaudhuri gives a wider range to the Śuktimat Kulaparvata, which has been identified by Beglar[1] with the hills in the north of the Hazaribagh district. We think Beglar is probably right in his supposition from the fact that it is associated with the Bhallāṭa people[2] who, it appears lived in this district. From the evidence of the *Mahābhārata*[3] it is obvious that the Śuktimat range must be somewhere in the eastern region.

The Bhallāṭas seem to be a forest people. The *Mahābhārata*[4] mentions them after Kosala and Malla, hence we should seek for their abode somewhere in the forest tract of Chhotanagpur. The more important tribes such as the Videhas, Aṅgas and the Magadhas had occupied certain parts of the Bihar state, the location of which is quite certain. Chhotanagpur is the only area about which we are still in dark. It is, therefore, possible that the Bhallāṭas may have occupied the Hazaribagh region. We, therefore understand that the hills in the north of Hazaribagh district are the ancient Śuktimat mountains.

Modern geologists look upon the hills in the Chhotanagpur division and other parts of south Bihar as offshoots of the Vindhyan range. The Purāṇic chroniclers have divided this range into three parts—the Ṛksha, the Vindhyā and the Pāriyātra or Pāripātra. The Pāripātra is generally identified with the ranges to the west of Bhopal together with the Arāvalī mountains. A great confusion prevails regarding the identification of the Ṛksha and the Vindhyā mountains. The rivers rising from one have been described as issuing from another and vice-versa in different Purāṇas. However it is supposed that the mountains to the north of the Narmadā in the Central Vindhyan region are the Ṛksha, while those to the south of the Narmadā are the Vindhyās of the Purāṇas. It appears that the name Vindhyā was some times loosely applied to the whole range extending from the Rajamahal hills to Gujarat as at the present time. Thus the Barabar

1. A.S. I. Vol. VIII. p. 125.
2. MBH. II. 30. 5.
3. Ibid.
4. II. 30. 5.

cave Inscription[1] of Maukhari Anantavarman mentions that an image was placed in the caves of the Vindhyā mountains.

This proves that even about the Gupta period, the mountains of south Bihar were taken as the offshoots of the Vindhyā range.

Thus we have shown that probably the whole of the Kulaparvata Śuktimat, and part of the Vindhyā Kulaparavata lie in the state of Bihar. Hence each of the hills in this region is either a branch of the Śuktimat mountain or of the Vindhyā. We shall deal with the more important of them separately.

Ptolemy[2] has given a few names of these mountains. His Ouindion is identified with the Vindhyā range by all authorities. E. H. Johnston[3] identifies Sardonyx with the Śuktimat range, but he locates the mountain in the Bundelkhand area. He seems to be wrong in the location of the range, but his identification should be acceptable to all.

THE RĀJAGṚHA HILLS

Rājagṛha occupies a unique place in ancient Indian literature. We find poetic descriptions of its mountains in Pāli, Prākrit and Sanskrit literature. The *Vimāna-vatthu commentary*[4] explicitly mentions the five hills at Rājagṛha. The other Buddhist texts too, enumerate five hills only. Their statements are corroborated by the *Rāmāyaṇa*[5] and the *Mahābhārata*.[6]

The hills were given different names in different periods. The *Isigilli Sutta*[7] states that all the hills at Rājagṛha except the Isigilli had different names in different ages. The *Mahābhārata* supplies two lists of the hills at Rājagṛha. The Buddhist texts use invariably the same names, but they differ in their evidence for the position of the hills.

Cunningham[8] and Marshall[9] have shown that the hills

1. C. I. I. Vol. III. p. 227.
2. *Ancient India* (Ptolemy) VII, 19-25 Maccrindle pp. 75-81.
3. J. R. A.S. (1941) pp. 208-22.
4. p. 82; Pañchānaṁ Parvatānamatare vemajjhe.
5. Bal. 32. 8. Eshā Vasumatī Rāma Vasostasyamahātmanaḥ. Ete śailavarāh pañcha prakāsante samantataḥ.
6. II. 30. 3. Ete pañchamahāśṛingāḥ parvatāh śitaladrumāḥ. Rakshantīvābhisaṁhatya sañhātañgā Girivrajam.
7. M. III. p. 68.
8. A. S. I. Vol. I. pp. 21-27.
9. A. S. I. A. R. (1905-6) pp. 86-106.

at present are named the Baibhāragiri, the Sonagiri, the Udayagiri, the Chhatagiri, the Ratnagiri and the Vipulagiri, altogether six hills. The highest peaks of the whole range of hills have been named according to a later tradition by the local people and thus their number comes to six. In fact there are four ranges[1] which can be distinguished separately, from which the six peaks rise : (i) the Baibhāragiri, (ii) the Sonagiri, (iii) the Udayagiri, (iv) the Chhatagiri, (v) the Ratnagiri and (vi) the Vipulagiri are the peaks of the Chhotagiri range.

The Pāli *Isigilli Sutta* refers to the five hills as the Isigilli the Vebhāra, the Pāṇḍava, the Gijjhakūṭa, and the Vepulla or as the Vebhāra, the Pāṇḍava, the Gijjhakūṭa, the Isigilli and the Vepulla. The order is changed in the commentaries. The *Suttanipāta commentary*[2] enumerates them as the Pāṇḍava the Gijjhakūṭa, the Vebhāra, the Isigilli and the Vepulla, while the *Vimānavatthu commentary*[3] gives them as the Isigilli, the Vepulla, the Vebhāra, the Pāṇḍava, and the Gijjhakūṭa.

The *Rāmāyaṇa* does not mention their names, but the *Māhābhārata*[4] speaks of the five hills at Rājagṛha as

"Vaiharo Vipulaḥ śailo Vārāho Vṛisabhastathā
Tathārṣhigiristāta Śubhachaityaka panchamaḥ."

The verse speaks of the number of the hills as five only but if we take the word 'Vipula' not as an epithet of the Vaihāra or Vārāha, but as a separate mountain, we see that there are six hills. At another place in the same work, only five have been enumerated but bearing different names. They are Pāṇḍura, the Vipula, the Vārāha, the Chaityaka and the Mātaṅga.

The Buddhist texts agree among themselves in the names of the hills, but they differ from the *Mahābhārata*, while the latter itself differs in its two lists. Some scholars[5] take the Vipula of the first list to be an adjective of the Vārāha. But we do not see any reason why the Vipula should be taken as an adjective when all the lists—Buddhist and Hindu agree in taking it as a separate hill. If we accept Vipula as a separate hill then we have the Vipula, the Vārāha and the Chaityaka

1. Ibid.
2. Vol. II. p. 382.
3. p. 82.
4. II. 21. 2.
5. M. A. S. I. No. 58 (B. C. Law).

common to both lists of the *Mahābhārata*. The Ṛshigiri of the first list is probably the Mātaṅga of the second list. There have been seers of this name in ancient India in different periods and it is not improbable that the Ṛshigiri may have had some association with a seer named Mataṅga whose abode might have been there at some early time.

The Vṛshabha of the first list has not been included in the second list of the *Mahābhārata* or in the Pāli literature. We think, this hill should be taken as an epithet of Vārāha, since this hill gives an impression of breadth and strength suggesting a bull.[1] Another explanation, might be suggested however. There are actually six peaks in the whole range of hills, at present known as the Baibhāra, the Sonagiri, the Udayagiri, the Chhatagiri, the Ratnagiri and the Vipulagiri. It is possible that the compiler of the *Mahābhārata* enumerates these six hills, but speaks of their total number as five only, following an old tradition.

If, however, we accept our first suggestion, the *Mahābhārata* will give the Vaibhāra, the Vipula, the Vārāha, the Ṛshigiri and the Cahaityaka. The Pāṇḍura of the *Mahābhārata* seems to be the Pāṇḍava of the Pāli literature because there is much similarity in the names. But the difficulty arises that the Pāṇḍava is included in the Pāli list with the Vaibhāra and the Pāṇḍura of the second list of the *Mahābhārata* is present with the Vārāha. It appears that either the compiler of the *Mahābhārata* or the Pāli texts has made a slight mistake in arrangement of the names. If the Pāṇḍura is the Pāṇḍava, as we definitely suppose, there should be either Vaibhāra or Vārāha. If we accept this proposition, we shall have to identify the Pāṇḍava or Pāṇḍura either with the modern Vaibhāra or with the modern Ratnagiri as D. N. Sen[2] has done.

B. C.[3] Law is inclined to identify the Isigilli with the Sonagiri. The Isigilli seems to be the Prakrit form of the Ṛishigiri, which is probably the Mātaṅga of the second list of the *Mahābhārata*.

1. I have personally visited all the hills at Rājagṛha The top of the Vārāha hill is flat and high while other parts are low. From some distance, the top looks like the hump of a bull.

2. J. B. O. R. S. Vol. IV. pp. 113-35.

3. M. A. S. I. No. 58 (B. C. Law) p. 29.

The Śubhachaityaka of the first list of the *Mahābhārata* can be no other than the Chaityaka of the second list. We may suggest that this hill abounded in the Chaityas which were highly revered at Rājagṛha during the pre-Buddhist and early Buddhist period. The people later on forgot the importance of the Chaityas and corrupted the name of the hill Chhaṭagiri, by which it is known even now.

The Śubhachaityaka seems to be the Gijjhakūṭa of the Pāli literature. The Buddhist literature is full of praise for the Gijjhakūṭa. It seems to have been a favourite resort of the religious people even in time gone by.[1] Many events in the life of the Master happened on this hill. The Buddhist and Brāhmaṇical religions have flourished side by side in India and the sacred sites of the Buddhists have been taken over as places of pilgrimage by the Hindus also, and it is, therefore, not beyond possibility that the Gijjhakūṭa, which is so associated with the life of the Buddha and where stūpas and chaityas must have been raised by his disciples, was taken by the Hindus also as very sacred. Therefore, the *Mahābhārata* calls it the Śubhachaityaka, the Chhaṭagiri of our days.

On the basis of a statement in the *Saṁyutta Nikāya*[2] B.C. Law[3] has identified this hill with the Udayagiri. No doubt, at present the river is nearer to this hill, but rivers are apt to change their course, so we cannot rely much upon them. Secondly the directions indicated by Fa-hsien[4] and Hsüan-Tsang[5] point to the Chhaṭagiri as being the ancient Gijjhakūṭa. Their description agrees more closely with the Chhaṭagiri than any other hill, as Broadley[6] and Marshall[7] have pointed out. Moreover, the name Udayagiri bears no resemblance to the name Gijjhakūṭa. We, therefore, think there should be no doubt in identifying the Gijjhakūṭa with the Chhaṭagiri.

Since Udayagiri cannot be identified with any other ancient name, it may be identified with the ancient Pāndava or Pāṇḍura by a process of elimination.

1. J. II. 55.
2. S. I. p. 109.
3. M. A. S. I. No. 58. p. 6.
4. *Record of the Buddhistic Kingdoms*. Ch. XXIX. p. 69.
5. On Yuan-chwang Vol. II. pp. 151-52.
6. I. A. Vol. I. pp. 18-21, 69-74. 106-110.
7. A. S. I. (1905-06) pp. 86-107.

Thus we can give an approximate identification of the five hills at Rājagṛha.

1	2	3	4
Pāli Script.	*Mbh. 1st list.*	*Mbh. 2nd list*	*Mod. Names.*
Vebhāra	Vaibhāra	—	Baibhāra
Pāṇḍava	—	Pāṇḍura	(Udayagiri)
Vepulla	Vipula	Vipula	Vipulagiri
Gijjhakūṭa	Śubhachaityaka	Chaityaka	Chhaṭagiri
Isigilli	Ṛshigiri	Mātaṅga	Sonagiri
—	Vārāha	Vārāha (Vṛshabha)	Ratnagiri

VAIBHĀRA

The Vebhāra hill is probably referred to in the *Mārkaṇḍeya Purāṇa.*[1] The *Vāyu Purāṇa*[2] reads Vaihāra which is a synonym for Vaibhāra at Rājagṛha. There are many places of interest in this hill. The Pīpal cave and the Sattapaṇi cave of Buddhist literature have been located on the north eastern slope of the Vaibhāra. Near the hot spring, on this hill, is a massive stone building called 'Jarāsandha Kī Baithaka'. Behind this, is the cave called the Pīpal Cave (Pin-po-lo) by the pilgrims. It was discovered for the first time by Cunningham.[3] This was the cave where Buddha took his meals. We are not sure how this cave took the name associated with the Pīpal tree. It is possible either that there was a Pīpal tree in front of the cave or that, as the Buddha sat in that cave in meditation, the cave was associated with the Pīpal tree under which he had attained enlightenment. Hsüan-Tsang says that "To the west of the hot springs stands the stone house of Pi-po-lo, in which Buddha formerly lived. The deep cave which opens behind its wall was the palace of the Asuras."[4] The identification of the cave is supported by the statement of Hsüan-Tsang, but it seems to us from the statement that the stone building itself was called the Pīpal Cave and the Asura Cave was the actual cave behind the stone structure. Cunningham[4] is of the opinion that the stone

1. Ch. 57.
2. Ch. 45. 90.
3. A. S. I. Vol. III. p. 141.
4. Hwen-Thsang (Julien) III. p. 117.
5. A. S. I. Vol. III. p. 142.

building was constructed probably during the life of Buddha. We do not find any detailed information as to the necessity of erecting the house on a hill. Did it serve as a watch house or was it meant for the abode of Buddha himself? We suppose that the building was actually meant for the Buddha to live in, and it was made of rough blocks taken from its vicinity which resulted in an artificial cave where the Bhikshus may have lived later on. As time rolled on, people seeing its dimensions and roughness called it the cave of the Asura. We cannot agree with Cunningham[1] in his supposition that that the cave was named after Jarāsandha who was an Asura. The people of Rajagṛha are still proud of Jarāsandha as their powerful king in the past.

Cunningham[2] identified the Sattapanni Cave of the *Mahāvaṁśa*[3] with the Sonabhadara of modern times. He points out that Sattapanni is equivalent to Śrotaparṇī[4] in Sanskrit. In the Tibetan works, this cave is called the Nyagrodha cave. The Nyagrodha is a Banyan tree and we do not find any relation between Nyagrodha and Śrotaparṇī. We prefer to look on Sattapanni as the Prakrit form of Saptaparṇī, which is a kind of creeper. This creeper might have been planted outside the cave for its decoration when it was prepared by Ajātaśatru for the first Buddhist synod. Fa-hsian[5] calls this cave Chuti but he does not explain the word. It may have some connection with Chaityas.

VIPULA

The hill stands on the north-eastern side of the hot springs and to the north of the Gijjhakūṭa hill. This hill is actually the biggest and the highest of the whole range. It is possible that it was named Vipula on account of its dimensions. At one place in the *Saṁyutta Nikāya*,[6] the Vipulagiri is declared to be the best of the Rājagṛha hills. At another place,[7] in the same work it is described as a massive hill. No doubt,

1. Ibid.
2. Ibid.
3. 3. 19.
4. A. S. I. Vol. III. p. 144.
5. *Record of the Buddhistic Kingdoms* Ch. XXX, p. 72.
6. Vol. I. p. 67. Vipulo Rajagahiyanam giri setho pavuchchati.
7. Vol, II, p. 185. Akkhato Vepullo pabbato mahā

the names of all the hills at Rājagṛha have changed from time to time, and we find clear evidence of this changing of names in reference to the Vipula in the *Saṁyutta Nikāya*, which claims to give a history of the hill. The hill was once known as the Pāchinvaṁsa and the people of the neighbourhood were known as the Tivaras. Then it was called as the Vankaka and the people were called the Rohitasas. In the third stage the hill was known as the Supassa and the people of the locality were known as the Supassīya. The fourth and the last stage was when it was called the Vepulla and the people the Magadhakas.

The whole passage merely mentions the antiquity of the hill and is not to be taken too seriously. The hill may have been known by some of these different names at the same time. Such cases are not rare even at the present day.

PĀṆḌAVA

We are not sure of the identification of this hill. Neither the Pāli nor the Sanskrit literature throws any light upon the subject. We have shown, however, that it was probably the modern Udayagiri. Is it that the hill might have been known by this name owing to some creeper or trees of yellowish colour ?

GIJJHAKŪṬA

The Sanskrit name is Gṛidhrakūṭa. This hill seems to have derived its name from the vultures[1] which lived upon its peak. On this hill, we are told, the Master patted the head of Ānanda, when he was attacked by Māra in the disguise of a vulture.[2] It seems possible that the story may be a later fabrication in view of the abundance of vultures on its peak. There are still some remains on the hill which deserve our notice. Hsüan-Tsang[3] recorded about this hill, "In the middle of the road, there are two small stūpas, one called Hia-shing (dismounting from the chariot), because the King when he got there went forward on foot. The other is called Tui-fan (sending back the crowd), because the King,

1. S. A. II, p. 417; AA I. p. 412; MA I. p. 291 etc.
2. *The Record of the Buddhistic Kingdoms* XXIX pp. 69-70.
3. *On Yuan Chwang*, p. 151 (Vol. II).

separating the common folk would not allow them to proceed with him. There is a brick Vihāra on the borders of a steep precipice at the western end of the mountain. It is high and wide and beautifully constructed. The door opens to the east."

The remains recorded by Hsüan-Tsang have been successfully identified by Marshall.[1] A path-like road leads to the Gṛdhrakūṭa. We meet the two stūpas on this very path. The Vihāra on the western end has fallen. There are more remains on this hill which have not been successfully identified.

ISIGILLI

This hill stands on the south-western side of the Rājagṛha hills. Neither the Pāli literature nor the pilgrims tell us anything in particular about this hill. On this hill the wall of rough stones which encircles the hills of Rājagṛha is higher than at any other place.

VAIDYAKA

The *Dīgha Nikāya*[2] mentions a hill under the name of Vaidiyaka. But this hill is seldom mentioned in other works More famous than this hill is the Indraśāla cave which it contains. It is said that Indra[3] himself asked forty-two questions to the Buddha in this cave and therefore the cave was named after Indra. The cave became so famous that sometimes the whole hill is designated by this name. The Ghoshrawa[4] Inscription calls it the Indraśaila.

The identification of this hill has been a matter of interesting controversy among a scholars. Cunningham[5] identified this hill with the Giriyek, which is to the south-east of Rājagṛha. He based his arguments on the records of Hsüan Tsang and, after ascertaining distances, direction and description of the peak, he arrived at the conclusion that the hill at Giriyek represents the Buddhist Indraśīlaguha. Broadley[6]

1. A. S. I. (1905) pp. 86-106.
2. Vol. II. pp. 263-64.
3. D. II pp. 263-64.
4. J. A. S. B. (1848) pp. 492-501.
5. A.S.I. Vol. III pp. 145-59.
6. I. A. Vol. I. pp. 18-21, 69 74.

preferred Fahsien as the source of his identification and came to the conclusion that the hill at Bihar Sharif, first proposed by Kittoe, was the probable site of the Indraśīlaguha. Both scholars have relied much upon the direction and distances given by the pilgrims. But we should bear in mind that the Chinese pilgrims were definitely not furnished with modern apparatus to measure the distances accurately; moreover they wrote the accounts of their travels when they returned to their own country. It was therefore but natural to forget accurate distances and directions. We should thus depend rather upon the general description of the place given by the pilgrims than on their distances. Hsüan-Tsang[1] mentions that the hill consists of two peaks, the one containing the cave itself and the other Hansasanghārāma. The Ghoshrawa Inscription[2] also speaks of the "two gems of Chaityas." which were erected by Vīradeva "as beautiful as the peak of mount Indraśaila". Both pilgrims speak of the cave in the southern side of the hill. At a distance of two miles to the south-west of Giriyek, there is a big cave which is at the present time called Giddha-dvāra. This resembles the description given by the pilgrims. There are still remains of the Buddhist monasteries in the vicinity of the village.

Broadley[3] argues that Fa-hsien speaks of a solitary peak wherein the Indraśailaguha was situated. But we do not find any cave in the hill at Bihar Sharif, besides which its top is flat, and cannot be compared to a monastery, as described in the Ghoshrawa inscription. The hill at Bihar Sharif is not connected with any anecdote in the life of Buddha or his disciples, while the Giriyek hill is a part of the Rājagṛha hills—the cradle of early Buddhism. All the hills at Rājagṛha are connected in one way or another with the Buddha, so it is not improbable that the Giriyek hill was the site of Indraśīlaguhā.

The *Dīgha Nikāya* states that to the east of Rājagṛha was the village of Ambasanda and, to the north of the latter was the Indraśīlaguhā. Accordingly the Indrasilaguha should be to the north—east of Rājagṛha. But, if we accept the

1. *On Yuan Chwang* II. p. 173.
2. J.A.S.B. (1848) pp. 492-501.
3. I. A. Vol. I, pp. 18-21, 69-74.

statement of the *Dīgha Nikāya* as trustworthy, we shall be put to further trouble, because there is no hill either small or big to the north-east of Rājagṛha. There is no possibility of any change in the position of the hill. The author of the *Dīgha Nikāya* appears to have made a slight mistake in putting north in place of south. We therefore endorse the identification of the Indraśilaguha with the Giriyek hill as proposed by Cunningham.

Cunningham may be right in explaining the name as Giri-ek (=solitary peak), although it is an offshoot of the Rājagṛha hills. At present the hill is known as the Khirakiya. We do not think the modern name has any association with Giri-ek. It is possible that the door of the cave itself looked like a window (Khirki), so the people named the whole mountain by this epithet. M.A. Stein[1] also agrees with the identification of Cunningham.

HILLS IN THE NEIGHBOURHOOD OF GAYĀ

In the city of Gayā and its neighbourhood, there are several hills which are famous in the Purāṇas and the Buddhist literature alike. The city itself stands on a low range of hills whose spurs have been named in the *Gayāmahātmya* variously, either in association with the name of Viṣṇu or Asura Gaya Such spurs are not actually hills but are high levels of rocky ground. The Gayā Brāhmaṇas attach much importance to these rocks or *Śilās*, since they are important centre of pilgrimage and the main source of their livelihood. However there are a few big hills among them, namely—Brahmayoṇī, Pretaśilā, Ramśilā etc.

THE BRAHMAYOṆĪ

The Brahmayoṇī is the principal hill of Gayā and stands to the south west of the city in its vicinity. The *Vinaya Piṭaka*[2] calls it the Gayāsīsa. The *Mahābhārata*[3] knows it by the name of Gayāsīra. The Purāṇas[4] too call it the Gayāśira. It is also known as the variant Gajaśīśa.[5]

1. I. A. (1901) pp. 54-63, 81-97.
2. I. 34 ff, II. 199.
3. III. 95. 9.
4. *Vāyu Purāṇa* Ch. 106. 65.
5. *Gayā and Buddhgayā* p. 278.

Buddhist scholars explain the name of this hill by its resemblance to a sitting elephant. The *Vāyu Purāṇa*[1] states that Viṣṇu pressed the head of Gayā under this hill with his foot. The modern temple of Viṣṇu at Gayā is located as the site of Viṣṇu's foot print, so the hill should be identified with the rocky site of the temple. But this place is not a hill and in the light of the Buddhist literature, the Purāṇic legend carries little weight. The Buddha is said to have started for Uruvelā from this hill.[2]

Hsüan-Tsang[3] clearly refers to this hill as the Gayā mountain, standing to the south-west of the city. At present this hill is famous under the name of the Bramhayoṇī, which seems to be a name given at later times.

PRETAŚILĀ

The Pretaśilā is to the north-west of the town at a distance of a few miles. This hill is referred to in the *Vāyu Purāṇa*.[4] There is a block of stone lying on the top of the hill whence it is known by this name.[5] This hill is a great centre for the performance of Śrāddha rituals and is referred to as such in the *Vāyu Purāṇa*. It plays no role in the Buddhist literature.

RĀMAŚILĀ

The Vāyu Purāṇa[6] mentions the Rāmatīrtha in the Phalgu where Rāma is said to have bathed with his spouse Sītā, This Tīrtha is a small pond located at the foot of this hill. But it is not clear how this hillock was associated with the name of Rāma. It is not referred to in any other literature.

MORĀ MOUNTAIN

Fa-hsien and Hsüan-Tsang have referred to this hill in their itenararies. Their accounts are similar. They say that Buddha[7] performed austerities on this hill and it was here that he had resolved to attain perfect enlightenment. After prediction by gods he left the hill and went to Bodh Gayā.

1. Ch. 106. 48.
2. *A Study of the Mahāvastu* p. 81.
3. *On Yuan Chwang* Vol. II p. 111.
4. Ch. 108. 15 "Sītāñgushṭhaikadeśo yaḥ sa cha Pretaśilā Smṛtaḥ.
5. *Gayā and Buddha Gayā* p. 86.
6. Ch. 108. 16.
7. *On Yuan Chwang* Vol. II. p. 112.

Fa-hsien[1] explicitly says that the hill is half a *yojana* north-east of Bodh Gayā. Hsüan-Tsang[2] shortens the distance to 14 or 15 *li*. Cunningham[3] almost agrees with their rough calculations. Hsüan-Tsang calls this hill *Polo-ki-Pu-ti* or the Prāgabodhī. The pilgrim says that the hill stood on the other side of the Phalgu opposite the stūpa of the Kaśyapa brothers which were at a little distance to the south of the Gayā hill. There was a cave in this hill. This hill is nowhere referred to in Pāli or Sanskrit literature. Some scholars identify it with the Dhongra hill which is seven miles to the south-east of Gayā.[4] But the distance indicated by Fa-hsien and Hsüan-Tsang does not carry us so far. The hill was just to the east of the stūpa of the Kaśyapa brothers which were to the south of Gayā. The identification by Cunningham seems to be more plausible. So the position and description recorded by the pilgrims suggest its identification with the Morā Pahar of modern times which contains a cave or natural fissure about half way up the western slope and facing the Phalgu.[5]

There is no other hill in the locality which so clearly resembles the description of the pilgrims. Hence Cunningham seems to be correct in its identification.

BARABAR HILLS

There are two groups of hills, sixteen miles to the north of Gayā, locally known as the Barabar and Nāgārjunī hills. The whole group of hills is generally known by the more famous name of Barabar only.

These hills seem to have borne various names at different periods of history. Some of these names are known from the inscriptions which were inscribed in the hills themselves at different epochs. In the inscriptions of Aśoka and his grandson Daśaratha, these hills are called the Khalatika Parvata.[6] Though Patañjali[7] in his *Mahābhāshya* refers to the Khalatika

1. *Record of the Buddhistic Kingdoms* Ch. XXXI p. 75.
2. *On Yuan Chwang* Vol. II. p. 113.
3. A. S. I. Vol. III p. 106.
4. Imperial Gazetteer Vol. XII p. 198.
5. A. S. I. Vol. III. p. 106.
6. *Select Inscriptions* pp. 79-80.
7. I. 2.52. Khalati-kādishu vachanaṁ- khalatikādishu vachanaṁ-bhavati yuktavadhbhāvena.Khalatikasya parvatasyādūrābhavāni Vanāni *khalatikam vanāni*.

hill in this form, it would seem that this word is actually a prakritism connected with the root 'Skhal', to slip or 'to fall down'. At the top of the hill, there is a place still commonly called 'Pichhulia' meaning slippery. We can infer from Patañjali's reference that in the locality of the Khalatika parvata, there were forests which may have provided pasture land for the cattle of the neighbourhood. The animals in search of food may have regularly roamed over the hills, as they do even now, in such a large number that the hill was referred to as a "Vehicle for animals" (Goratha). In any case the *Mahābhārata*[1] mentions this hill as Gorathagiri and speaks of its beautiful trees and large number of animals. We are not sure how the word Goratha originated but it is not improbable that the word has some connection with the cattle and other animals, whether wild or domestic, which pastured on it.

The Hāthīgumphā cave inscription[2] of Khāravela states that the latter attacked the Gorathagiri, which seems to be no other than the Gorathagiri of the *Mahābhārata*. Beglar[3] and N. L. Dey[4] identify this hill with the Baithan hill, which lies five or six miles to the west of the Rājagṛha Valley. Beglar says that Baithan means the cow-pen and as such both these names Goratha and Baithan have the same meaning. He further points out that Rājagṛha cannot be seen from the Barabar hills as stated in the *Mahābhārata*. Beglar seems to be interpreting the lines of the Mahābhārata too literally. The author simply means to say that Kṛshṇa pointed out the site where the capital of Magadha stood, encircled by hills. So far as the actual city is concerned, it could be seen neither from the Barabar nor from the Baithan hill. We should not moreover forget the fact which we have pointed out elsewhere[5] that both the epics show only very hazy knowledge of Magadhan geography. The identification of Beglar and Dey cannot be accepted in the light of inscriptions discovered by Jackson[6] on the same hill. These inscriptions probably belong to the third century B. C.[7] and explicitly

1. II. 20. 27-32.
2. *Select Inscription* p. 208.
3. A.S. I. Vol. VIII p. 46.
4. G. D. A. M. I. p. 71.
5. Supra, p. 5.
6. J. B. O. R. S. Vol I. pp. 159-171.
7. Ibid.

mention the name Gorathagiri. In face of such strong evidence, there should remain no doubt about the identification of the Gorathagiri with the Barabar hill.

In an inscription of the sixth or seventh century A.D., the hill is called the Pravaragiri.[1] This might have been originally an epithet of the hill rather than the name itself. But it seems to have been the origin of the word Barabar. The derivation suggested by Cunningham from the compounding of *Vara* and *Avara* meaning great enclosure does not seem plausible, since there is nothing like an enclosure on the hill. We suggest that the original epithet of the hill *Pravaragiri* or *Pravara Parvata* was corrupted to Barabar by the influence of the common Persian word of the same spelling which is commonly used in Bihar even by the Hindus.

There are seven artificial caves in these hills. This is why the local people call the hills Staghara[2] or the seven houses according to Cunningham. Kittoe[3] explained the origin as Saptagarbha, 'seven wombs'. As this word was certainly used for caves, Kittoe may be right. However, 'ghara' is the normal Hindi equivalent of the Sanskrit *gṛha* and we, therefore, prefer Cunningham's etymology.

The caves have been excavated at different places in the hills. They are called the Karṇachaupara, Sudāmā, Gopīkā Kubhā, Lomasa ṛṣi, Viśvāmitra also called Viśvajhoparī, Vadathī-Kā-Kubhā and Vāpīyaka caves. Some of these caves are highly polished like other Mauryan remains. An inscription in the Sudāmā cave gives its name as the Nigrodha guha. The Karṇachaupara contains an inscription of the 19th regnal year of Aśoka. The Sudāmā cave and the Vishvamitra cave, each have inscriptions of Aśoka of his 12th regnal year. All these inscriptions record the dedication of the caves to the Ājīvika sect.

The Vāpīyaka Kubhā[4] is called by the same name in the inscription and there is another cave called Vedathīkā Kubhā. The Gopī cave contains an inscription of Daśaratha. On the western jamb of this cave, there is an inscription of the

1. A. S. J. Vol. I. P. 52.
2. A. S. I. Vol. I. p. 52.
3. J. A. S. B. Vol. XVI. pp. 401-16.
4. A. S. I. Vol. I. p. 49.

Maukhari family. We find a name 'Āchārya Śrī Yogānanda'[1] inscribed at several places in the caves. It seems that Yogānanda was a famous recluse in this area in the 7th or 8th century A.D.

We have not sufficient information as to how these caves were named. Some of these names seem to be of recent origin. It is possible, these caves may have been named after some particular characterstic or after individual ascetics who lived there at different times.

Although the Barabar hills stand in the neighbourhood of Rājagṛha they were far from the glory and power enjoyed by the Magadhan metropolis. Neither kings like Bimbisāra and Ajātaśatru, nor saints like the Buddha and Mahāvīra seem ever to have visited them. But the remains at Barabar bear testimony to the fact that it was a place where different sects—Ājīvikaism, Buddhism and Hinduism flourished at different periods. Jainism is the only sect which does not seem to have had any hold in this locality.

The ruins and the broken images in the Barabar hills and its surroundings show that at one time Buddhism had a stronghold in this area. But the place was probably first occupied by the Ājīvikas. This can easily be inferred from the fact that Aśoka, although he championed the cause of Buddhism, dedicated the Barabar caves to the Ājīvikas and not to the Buddhists. The Buddhists seem to have occupied the place later on.

From the 5th Century inscriptions of the Maukharis, we learn that these chiefs installed Hindu images of Kātyāyanī and other deities in the caves of the Barabar hills. From this time the Buddhists seem to have lost all their hold on this place. Fa-Hsien did not care to visit these hills. Hsüan-Tsang[2] simply refers to a hill which is most probably, the Barabar hill, but he does not give its name and describes nothing in detail, as he usually does in referring to Buddhist sites. If Śrī Yogānanda belonged to the seventh or eighth century A.D., it seems that Śaivism had by this time begun to gain a hold in this area. The ascetic offers his adoration

1. A. S. I. Vol. I. p. 49.

1. *On Yuang Chwang* Vol. II, p. 107.

to Siddheshvaranātha, who is still worshipped by people from far and wide as the presiding deity of the mountain.

A more important problem arises by Khāravela's invasion of the Barabar hills. As there is no doubt in the identification of the Gorathagiri referred to in his inscription, we cannot suppose that the invasion was made against another place. The Hāthīgumphā cave inscription states that Khāravela sacked the Gorathagiri and then terrorised Rājagṛha. What could have been the reason behind an invasion against a place such as the Barabar hill, which was never an important political centre ?

There were probably two reasons for this attack. The streams of different faiths had met at this place, only Jainism seems to have had no hold in this area and Khāravela was a Jain. It is possible that the Buddhist and the Ājīvaka ascetics did not allow the Jain saints to stay in the caves or otherwise worked against them. Therefore Khāravela attacked Gorathagiri and sacked it. This would be the first example of religious intolerance in the Indian history, if Khāravela attacked Gorathagiri with this motive.

We may, however, offer a further suggestion. The Barabar hills are natural fortifications. There are also some signs of brick walls. It is not improbable that the place was used as a cantonment and a garrison may have been stationed there to check any invasion from the south against Pāṭəliputra. Khāravela, therefore, thought it better to destroy the garrison and then to attack Rājagṛha.

KAUWĀḌOL

This is a group of hills, four miles to the south-west of the Barabar hills. Their Hindi name has the strange meaning of 'shaken by crows'. A large rock is on the peak of the hill. The people[1] of the locality say that there was formerly another rock placed on the peak in such a balanced way that it began to shake, if even a single crow sat upon it. This is simply hearsay. No one can say when the rock was on the peak. The story being an unconvincing one does not explain the origin of the name.

1. A. S. I. Vol. I. p. 41.

A little way up the hill there are remains of a large temple of stone. A few pillars are still there in dilipidated condition. The ruins of walls are also still to be seen. In the cell, there is a figure of the Buddha on a pedestal which bears an inscription of the usual Buddhist creed in Kutila character.[1]

We do not know if this place is referred to in any of our literature. Hsüan-Tsang[2], however, visited it. He says that he went to Śīlabhadra monastery, 20 *li*, to the south west of the Guṇamatī monastery. The latter is identified with Dharawat[3] a village in the locality of the Barabar hills. The Kauwāḍol is the only isolated hill in this area which has ruins of a monastery and therefore seems to be the site of the Śīlabhadra monastery. Cunningham seems to be right in this identification. Hsüan-Tsang says nothing about Śīlabhadra, with whose name this monastery was associated. Had he been the famous Śīlabhadra of the Nālandā University under whom the pilgrim had studied, he would have mentioned the fact that the monastery was named after his teacher. But as he keeps silent, it is probable that the founder of the monastery was someone else.

GURPA HILL

This stands 25 miles to the east of Gayā. Neither Sanskrit nor Pāli literature speaks about it. But the Chinese pilgrims refer to this hill. Fa-Hsien[4] calls it Chi-tsu which Beal translates as the Kukkuṭapādagiri. He places it 3 li south of Bodha Gayā. Hsüan-Tsang[5] places it 100 *li* east of the Mohana river. He says that it was also called Lang-chih (wolf's traces). The pilgrims agree that the hill stood amidst dense forest and had three peaks. They associate the hill with Mahākaśyapa, the disciple of the Buddha, who is said to have entered into Nirvāṇa at the top of this hill,

The identification of this hill is a matter of controversy among scholars. Cunningham[6] identified the Kukkuṭapādagiri or Gurupādagiri with the modern Kurkihara near

1. A. S. I. Vol. VIII. p. 40.
2. *On Yuan Chwang* Vol. II. p. 109.
3. A. G. I. p. 522.
4. *Record of the Buddhistic Kingdoms* Ch. XXXIII p. 82.
5. *On Yuan Chwang* Vol. II. p.143.
6. A. S. I. Vol. I. p. 15.

Wazirganj in the district of Gayā. He thinks that the hill which stands to the north of the village should be identified with three peaked hill. Stein[1] identified this hill with the Śobhanātha hill, two miles south of Punwa in the same district. R. D. Banerjee[2] identified the hill with the modern Gurpa hill, which stands near the station of the same name on the Gayā-Calcutta line, in the district of Gayā. This place is still full of forest and a wild rivulet flows through it. The hill is very steep and has three peaks. There is a cleft on the top of the hill, which is probably that recorded by Hsüan-Tsang as opened by the stick of Mahākaśyapa. There are still remains[3] of a shrine of ancient large bricks which was probably a stūpa, on the top. There are several inscriptions found in this hill bearing the usual formula of the Buddhist creed.[4]

The Gurpa hill is still a place of worship. The people assemble there in the beginning of the rainy season to offer their adoration to the Gurpāsvāminī, the presiding deity of the hill.

Both Kurkihar and the Śobhanātha hill, no doubt, contain Buddhist antiquities, but they do not resemble the site as indicated by the pilgrim. The names Kurkihara or Śobhanātha hills do not seem to have the least affinity with the word Kukkuṭapādagiri. The name Gurpa seems to be an abbreviation of the word Gurupādagiri. The hill was known by this name, probably because it was sanctified by the holy feet of Mahākaśyapa.

We, therefore, fully agree with Banerjee's identification of the Kukkuṭapādagiri with the Gurpa hill.

KAIMUR RANGE

This range extends from Mirzapur to Sahasram in the Shahabad district. The ancient name of the country along which this chain of hill extends was probably Kairadeśas from a daitya of that name known to tradition as its king.

1. I.A. (1901) p. 88.
2. J. A. S. B. (1906) pp. 77-83.
3. J. A. S. B. (1906) p. 81.
4. Ibid. pp. 81-82.
5. J. A. S. B. (1877) pp. 16-36.

It is probable that the name might have originated from Kārusha, a more ancient name of this country. From Kair, the hill took its name Kaimura.

There are several shrines of Śakti on the summits of this range. It appears the area abounded in Śakti-worshippers. In one of the shrines called Tārāchaṇḍī, there is 12th century inscription[1] of Pratāpadhavala Aila. He is probably the same as Pratapadhavala Deva of the Rohtasgarh inscription.[2] We have no reference to this dynasty anywhere else.

ROHTAS

This hill is in the southern part of the district of Shahabad. It is a very small hill and contains the ruins of a fortress for which it is known as the Rohatasagadha. The fortress has been used from time to time by the local rulers for their defence purposes. The importance of the fortress was very high as it stood on the border of a region which was inhabited by wild tribes and hence there was a constant fear of attack from that side. The local tradition describes the construction of this fortress to Rohitaśva, the son of famous Hariśchandra of the solar dynasty. We are not sure of the date when the fort was built.

The hill is known as the Lohitagiri in Sanskrit literature. It was also known as Gopādri and Gopāchala.[3] Several inscriptions have been discovered in this hill. One[4] of them refers to Śasāṅka as *sāmanta*. This place was probably the early seat of his power. We find another inscription belonging to Pratāpadhavala-deva of the 12th century, who was probably a local chief and seems to have extended his power to the adjoining areas.

MANDĀRA

This hill stands 30 miles to the south-east of Bhagalpur proper. It is to the east of the river Chandanā. There are numerous architectural and sculptural remains which show the importance of the hill and the antiquity of its surroundings. The hill is only 700 ft. high, and all around the middle,

1. J. A. O. S. VI pp. 547-59.
2. E. I. IV. p. 310.
3. G. D. A. M. I. p. 71.
4. C. I. I. Vol. III. p. 283.

there is a groove which is said to be the impression of the coil of the snake Vāsukī during the ocean churning, when Viṣṇu bore its weight in the form of a tortoise.[1] On a lower level, there are ruins of a temple which was probably that of Madhusūdana.[2] On the western side of the hill, in a dark cave, there is an image of Nṛsiṁha carved in the rock, and near it is an image of Vamanadeva and Madhusūdana.[3] On its eastern side at the foot of the hill, there are extensive ruins of buildings. A stone structure at present called Nātha-thāna seems to be a Buddhist monastery which probably later came under the control of the Hindus. There are many tanks, some of which are dry at present. One of the tanks was caused to be excavated by Koṇa Devī,[4] the wife of Ādityasena of Magadha. This shows that in the seventh century A.D., Aṅga formed a part of the kingdom of the Guptas of Magadha.

The name Mandāra seems to be very ancient. The *Kūrma*, *Vāmana* and the *Vārāha Purāṇas* recognise the hill by this name. The *Mahābhārata*.[5] no doubt mentions a hill of the name, but it seems to be another Mandāra, somewhere in the Himālaya range. The Mandāra was probably known to Megasthenes[6] as the Mount Maleus. The statement is so meagre and uncertain that nothing can be said definitely.

Though there are many Buddhist remains and sculptures on it, this hill is hardly referred to in the Buddhist literature. On the other hand, the Hindu scriptures are full of allusions to this hill. It seems to have possessed a sanctity like that of Gayā in the Hindu scriptures. Both these places are associated with the names and deeds of Viṣṇu. It is possible that at first the Hindus had their stronghold on this hill and that the Buddhists temporarily established themselves there later, but were ousted by the Hindus again.

There is nearby a tank called Pāpaharaṇī[7] which implies

1. *Kūrma Purāṇa* Ch. I; *Vāmana Purāṇa* Ch. 90.
2. *Garuḍa Purāṇa* Part I. Ch. 84.
3. J. A. S. B. Vol. XX p. 272.
4. C. I. I. III. p. 211.
5. Anuśāsana Parva Ch. XIX; Vana Parva, Ch. 162.
6. *Indika* X. Pliny.
7. A. S. I. Vol. VIII. p. 130.

that a bath in this tank absolves a man of his sins. It is said in local tradition that a certain Cholarājā was cured of his leprocy by bathing in this tank. He made his capital at this place and beautified it with bazaars and roads worthy of a capital. But later on the town was destroyed by Kālā Pahāḍa, a fanatical Muslim convert.

We should not put much reliance upon such legendary accounts, but it is not impossible that a miner Chola prince may have come to this place in his wanderings and temporarily established himself as the king in this locality. This incident may have happened in the tenth or eleventh century A.D. when the rulers of southern India were making continuous invasions against northern India. We find the names of Magadha, Aṅga, Vaṅga, Rāḍha among the territories ravaged by the Chola kings. We find a similar case in the Sena dynasty whose ancestors came from the Carnatic[1] and established their kingdom in northern India. Therefore it is not improbable that an adventurous prince of the Chola dynasty came to Aṅga at the end of the Pāla dynasty and established himself as King.

This Chola rājā was probably a local chief and his dynasty came to an end with himself. We have no record of any other Chola king in Aṅga.

The place exhibits the signs of Muslim vandalism. It is said that Mandāra was invaded probably in the 15th century A.D. by Kālā Pahāḍa,[2] the fanatical general of Sultan Sulaiman Karrani of Bengal. His name is so notorious for the destruction of Hindu and Buddhist shrines that ravages rendered at any place in northern India are ascribed to him. We can simply say that some Muslim fanatic brought an end to this hilly town.

ANTARGIRI AND BAHIRGIRI

These names show that they are mountains, but in the *Mārkaṇḍeya Purāṇa*,[3] they have been designated as the peoples living in the eastern region. The *Matsya Purāṇa*[4] refers to them in the singular as the Antargiri and Bahirgiri. As

1. E. I. Vol. I. pp. 305-15 (Deopara Inscription).
2. *History of Bengal* Vol. II pp. 178, 183, 193 etc,
3. Ch. 57.
4. Ch. CXVII.

they are mentioned between the Mudakaras and Pravaṅgas, Pargiter[1] identifies the Antargiri with the people living in an area encircled by the modern Rajamahal hills and the Bahirgiri with those who lived on the outskirts of the hill.

So far as the peoples are concerned, they may be two different peoples, but the hill will be the same.

The *Mahābhārata*[2] refers to the Antargiri and the Bahirgiri being conquered by Arjuna. In this context, they seem to have been living somewhere in the eastern part of the Himalayas. It appears there were no hills of these names and the terms were applied to the peoples only.

The Purāṇic chroniclers and compilers of the *Mahābhārata* probably had no idea of the geography of the eastern region. So in the present state of our knowledge, we cannot locate these hills accurately.

PATHARGHATA

This hill is in the Bhagalpur district on the southern bank of the Gaṅgā. The place abounds in ancient ruins. This hill is probably the Śilāsaṅgama[3] which is an abbreviation of the Vikramaśīle Saṅghārāma according to Mr. N. L. Dey. But we cannot say how Mr. Dey got the idea of Śilāsaṅgama. The Vikramaśīla university was situated in the neighbourhood of this hill. We shall deal with this place later on in detail.

KALUHA PAHAR

This hill stands in the Chatra sub-division of the Hazaribagh district, 26 miles to the south of Bodh Gayā. It stands on the eastern bank of the Lilajan. There are extensive ruins on the top of this hill. A large number of broken images are found there. N. L. Dey[4] says that he found an old wall running from the south to the north on the western foot of the hill. There was a door also in the wall. On the top, there is a temple of Kuleśvarī Devī, which is said to have been built by Rājā Chandraketu of Dantar. We know nothing about the date or reign of the King. According to Dey[5], the images

1. *Mārkaṇḍeya Purāṇa* p. 325.
2. II. XXVII. 3.
3. G. D. A. M. I. p. 185.
4. J. A. S. B. LXX pp. 31-37.
5. J. A. S. B. LXX pp. 31-37.

on the top of the hill are mostly Buddhist excepting a statue of Parśvanātha, the 23rd Jain Tīrthaṅkara. But Stein[1] thinks that the sculptures on the hill, whether detached or carved in rocks, are figures of the Tīrthaṅkaras.

In ancient times this part of the country was covered with thick forests, and we do not find the Buddhists generally occupying such areas. Moreover places to the south of Magadha are generally associated with the Jains rather than the Buddhists. It is, therefore, possible that this place may have been a stronghold of the Jains.

Dey[2] identifies this hill with the Makulaparvata of the Burmese annals, where the Buddha is said to have passed his sixth rainy season. In his opinion, the letter 'ma' was dropped and in course of time 'Kula' was corrupted into Kaluha.

According to *Śrī Tīrthamālā Amalokaratna*,[3] the name of the place in the śāstras is Bhaddalapuranagara, where Śītalasvāmin, the tenth Tīrthaṅkara, was conceived, born, received initiation and attained enlightenment.

The identification of this hill with the Makula Parvata does not seem plausible in the face of the phonetical changes. Stein[4] seems to be right in its identification with the Kolāhala mountain of the Purāṇas.[5] This Kolāhala mountain has been identified with the Kowakol in the Gayā district by Beglar.[6] But the Kowakil is a small hill and possesses nothing to make it famous enough to attract the attention of the Purāṇic chroniclers.

PĀRASNĀTH HILL

This stands in the Giridih sub-division of the Hazaribagh district. The hill has been named after the famous Jain Tīrthaṅkara Pārśvanātha, who is said to have lived 250 years before Mahāvīra. The hill seems to have been an abode of Jain ascetics from very early date and no less than nineteen Tīrthaṅkaras out of the twenty-four are said to have entered

1. I. A. Vol. XXX. p. 54.
2. J. A. S. B. LXX. pp. 31-37.
3. In Indian Antiquary Vol. XXX, Stein writes that the text was published in 1883 but no copy was availbale to him.
4. I. A. Vol. XXX. pp. 90-95.
5. *Mārkaṇḍeya Purāṇa* Ch. 57.
6. A. S. I. Vol. VIII p.

Nirvāṇa on this hill. In the *Kalpa Sūtra*[1] this hill is called the Sameta-Śikhara. In other Jain works, the hill is known as the Samidagiri[2] and the Mallaparvata.[3] The word Samidagiri is a corruption of Samādhigiri, a name given because the nineteen Tīrthaṅkaras had attained Moksha on this hill.

B. C. Law[4] identifies this hill with the mount Maleus of the Greeks. The Greeks do not mention the locality where the hill stood. From their statement it can be gathered that the hill was somewhere near Pāṭaliputra. Its name is more similar to Mandār, so in this position no possible conclusion be arrived at.

1. S. B. E. Vol. XXII p. 271.
2. G. D. A. M. I. p. 176.
3. Ibid.
4. *Mountains of India* p. 16.

CHAPTER IV

THE RIVER SYSTEM OF ANCIENT BIHAR

North Bihar has many rivers and innumerable rivulets. The main rivers rise from the Himalayas, flow to the south and south-east, and fall directly or through a larger river into the Gaṅgā. The small streams are generally the off-shoots of big rivers and empty their water with other tributaries into the same river in its lower course. The most important rivers of this tract are the Sarayū, often known as the Ghāgharā, Gaṇḍakī, little Gaṇḍaka, Bāgmatī, Kamalā, Kośī, Panara, Mahānandā and above all the Gaṅgā which touches the south or south-western border of most of the districts of north Bihar. Besides these big rivers there is a net work of streamlets which overflood the whole of north Bihar during the rainy season and cause havoc in the life of the people. Among these are the Gharahi, Khanwa, Lalbegi, Dhanauti, Tiljuga, Karai, Lakhandi, Adhawara, Baya, Lalbakya, Bhurengi, Balan and the like. But these rivers are hardly referred to in ancient Indian literature.

North Bihar consists of alluvial soil, hence the land is soft. This is the reason why we find the rivers esasily changing their courses. The most notorious for this is the Kośī which every year renders thousands of people homeless and washes away lakhs of property. Unfortunately changes of the courses of rivers have been hardly marked by ancient Indian scholars. Either they were indifferent to these physical changes or they had not developed their geographical knowledge.

The most important river, mentioned for the first time in Vedic literature[1] in connection with the Videhas, is the Sadānīrā, which means a river always full of water. This river formed the boundary line[2] between Kosala and Videha. Scholars are not unanimous in identifying it. It is generally

1. Sat. B. 1.4; 1-14.
2. Ibid.

identified with the Gaṇḍakī[1] with or the Rāptī,[2] while some identify it with the Kāratoyā,[3] which flows through northern Bengal. Pargiter supports the theory of Oldenberg, who believed it was the Rāptī, quoting a verse from the *Mahābhārata*,[4] where the Gaṇḍakī and Sadānīrā are mentioned separately. It is possible however that the word Sadānīrā was used as an epithet of the Gaṇḍakī. If we accept the view of Oldenberg, that it was the Rāptī, we shall have to presume that the boundary of Videha extended much farther west than in later times and at the same time we shall have to locate the Malla territories between Kosala and Videha. But the site of Kusīnārā of the Buddhist texts, which was the chief city of the Mallas, is fairly certain, and is well to the east of the Rāptī in territory which on Oldenberg's assumption would be part of Videha. Moreover, the people at present occupying the area which lies to the west of the Gaṇḍakī, which falls into the Gaṅgā just opposite to Patna, are quite different in dialect, spirit and taste from the people living to the east. In Buddhist literature the Sadānīrā is hardly referred to, and the Greek historians are quite silent about it.

The Rāptī at present flows past Sahet Mahet which is taken as the site of ancient Śrāvastī. If this is the river referred to in the *Śatapatha Brāhmaṇa*, it was known to the Buddhists as the Ajiravati, and not as the Sadānīrā. The identification of the Sadānīrā with the Kāratoyā is now rejected by all authorities, since it places it far too much to the east.[5]

The reference in the *Mahābhārata* which mentions the Sadānīrā as distinct from the Gaṇḍakī may be accounted for either by suggesting inadequate knowledge on the part of the compiler or by proposing that, writing at a later time, he had distinguished the Gaṇḍakī and the little Gandak Sadānīrā is an epithet which may be applied to many rivers in the course of centuries and is very appropriate to the Gaṇḍakī, which has always been looked on as the eastern boundary of Kosala.

1. Weber—Indische studien pp. 112, 181.
2. Oldenberg—*Buddha* p. 398.
3. Imperial Gazetteer Vol. 15, p. 24.
4. II. 20. 27. Gaṇḍakīm cha mahāśonaṁ Sadānīrām Tathaivacha Ekaparvtake nadyaḥ Krameṇaitya vrajanta te.
5. *Mārkaṇḍeya Purāṇa* p. 294.

With all these considerations in view, we think Weber is right in identifying this river with the Gaṇḍakī of modern times.

GAṆḌAKĪ

This is an important river of north Bihar. It rises from the spurs of the Himalayas and flows across the district of Champaran, Saran and Muzaffarpur.

The Gandak has several streams in the Nepalese Terai which unite at Tribenī above the Saran district. Brian Hodgson[1] wrote about the Gandak in 1849 that "in the basin of the Gandak we have successively from the west, the Barigar, the Nārāyaṇī, the Sweti Gaṇḍakī, the Marsyangdi, the Darandi, the Gandi and the Trisul." These are the seven streames from which people commonly call it the Sapta-Gaṇḍakī. We are not sure if the river has actually these seven streams at the present time, for sometimes it happens that the old bed of a river is listed as a flowing stream. In ancient India people seem to have had a fancy for describing rivers as having seven streams. The Indus[2] is referred to as possessing seven mouths and the Kośī, as we shall see, is also said to have seven streams.

The river still bears some of Hodgson's names at different places in its course. In the Muzaffarpur district it is known as the Nārāyaṇī and Śāligrāminī. This river flowing through the Saran district falls into the Gaṅgā opposite Patna; another river of the same name flowing through the districts of Champaran, Muzaffarpur, Darbhanga and Monghyr falls into the Gaṅgā opposite Monghyr town.

The Gaṇḍaka is mentioned for the first time in the *Śatapatha Brāhmaṇa*,[3] if as we believe it[4] is to be identified with the Sadānīrā of the same work. The *Mahābhārata* often mentions this river as a large one, in connection with the conquest of the eastern region by Bhīma. It is also referred

1. J. A. S. B. (1849) Part II, pp. 761—87.
2. *Select Inscriptions* p. 276.
3. Śat. B. 1-4. 1-14.
4. See above p.

to as a place of pilgrimage,[1] but it is surprising that in the sister epic, the *Rāmāyaṇa*, the river is not mentioned in the list of the rivers of northern India. In this text, there is mention of a river Kālīmahī, which may be the distant echo of the name of the Kālī-Gaṇḍaka, one of the three principal affluents of the Gaṇḍaka at its rise.

The Buddhist[2] literature mentions five rivers called Mahāgaṅgā which issued forth from the Himalayas—they are the Gaṅgā, Yamunā, Achiravatī, Sarabhu and Mahī. The identification of the river Mahī is still very doubtful. The *Mārkaṇḍeya Purāṇa*[3] mentions a river of the same name emerging from the Pāriyātra hill. But that river is not a tributary of the Gaṅgā, nor does it rise from the Himalayas. We do not find any other river of such a distant place included in the list. We think that the Mahī of the Buddhist literature was the river Gaṇḍakī. The present-day Mahī is a small tributary of the Gaṇḍakī, retaining the old name of the parent river. It flows through the Saran district. From the geographical data of the early Pāli scriptures, it would seem that this was the only important river other than the Gaṅgā with which the early Buddhists were much acquainted, but it has been given no place in their literatue. Fa-Hsien[4] tells us that a journey of four *yojanas* to the east from Vaiśālī brought him to the confluence of five rivers and then crossing the river (Gaṅgā) and going south for one *yojana*, he arrived at Pāṭaliputra. But the present geographical position of the rivers does not confirm his statement.

The passage apparently denotes the place where the fifth and the last river 'Mahī' joined the Gaṅgā opposite the confluence of the Soṇa. If Fa-Hsien actually meant the confluence of five rivers, we can assume that the Sarayū fell into the Gaṅgā to the east of the place where it joins the Gaṇgā at present.

In this way the Gaṅgā, Mahī (Gaṇḍakī), the Soṇa, and the

1. Mbh. III. 84. 114.
2. S. N. A. II p. 439; IV. p. 101; V. p. 22.
3. Ch. 57.
4. *Records of the Buddhistic Kingdoms*; Ch. XXIII.

Sarayū together formed a confluence of the five rivers and Fa-Hsien did not go to the east but to the west of Vaisāli. It is therefore possible the *Rāmāyaṇa* mentions this river under the name of *Kālīmahī*.[1] The *Mārkaṇḍeya Purāṇa*[2] explicitely mentions the Gaṇḍakī rising from the Himālayas. The river is said to have been formed from the sweat of the cheeks (gaṇḍa) of Viṣṇu[3] when he performed austerities near its source. Megasthenes knew it as a tributary of the Gaṅgā and called it Condochates.[4]

Artemidoros[5] speaks of a certain affluent of the Gaṅgā as breeding crocodiles and dolphins. He named it *Oidenes*. At the present time the Gaṇḍaka is the only tributary of the Gaṅgā which breeds crocodiles. The Purāṇic tale of *Gajahrāha* (fight between and crocodile) is said to have taken place at its junction with the Gaṅgā. We, therefore, think that the *Oidenes* of Artemidoros is no other than the Gaṇḍaka. The *Abhidhānachintāmaṇi*[6] calls the river by its present name.

SARAYŪ

A river Saryū is mentioned in the *Ṛgveda*,[7] once in association with the Sarasvatī and Sindhu and again with the Rasā, Amitabhā and Kubhā. But scholars have grave doubts that the Vedic seers actually meant the modern Saraju which flows in the eastern part of India. Zimmer[8] locates the Vedic Sarayū in the Punjab and Hopkins[9] in the far-west beyond the Sindhu. Ludwig identified it with the Kurram while Vivien-de-St. Martin was inclined to identify it with the united course of the Sutlej and Bias. The Ṛgvedic Aryans had probably no knowledge of the modern

1. Kishkindhā Kāṇḍa, 40, 20.
2. Ch. 57.
3. *Vārāha Purāṇa*, Ch., 144.
4. *Indika*, Arrian, Ch. IV, Maccrindle, p. 191.
5. Ibid., Strabo, XV, 72; Maccrindle, p. 77.
6. Ch. IV., 353.
7. IV. 30. 18; V. 59. 9; X. 64. 9.
8. Altindisches Leben 17, 45.
9. *Religions of India*, p. 34.

Ghaghara or Sarju with which the Sarayū of later Sanskrit literature is to be identified, for the hymns seldom mention even the Yamunā and Gaṅgā, which were nearer the centre of Vedic culture. But the post-vedic literature shows the definite knowledge of the Sarayū. Pāṇini[1] was acquainted with the river. In the Buddhist literature it is spelt 'Sarabhu'[2] The *Rāmāyaṇa*[3] mentions the Sarayū in the list of the rivers of northern India. Kālidāsa has alluded to this river many a time in the *Raghuvaṁśa*. He has described its confluence with the Gaṅgā, which lies at present in the Bihar state, as very sacred.[4] During the age of the *Rāmāyaṇa*,[5] the Sarayū joined the Gaṅgā opposite modern Buxar, which is located as the hermitage of Viśvāmitra. It seems to have shifted its course farther east in later times.

Megasthenes[6] mentions two rivers called Sittokatis and Solomattis which have not been certainly identified. He says that these rivers fell into the Gaṅgā and were navigable throughout the year. The rivers mentioned by Arrian on the authority of Megasthenes are not in order from west to east. If we take them in order, the rivers Sittokatis and Solomattis should be located somewhere in the eastern part of Bihar. Benfey[7] identifies the Solomattis with the legendary Sarasvatī which was thought to join the confluence of the Gaṅgā and Yamunā at Allahabad. But we know certainly that the Sarsvatī does not flow in this area. Cunningham[8] in one of his maps identifies the Sarju with the Solomattis. He is probably right in his identification as there is some similarity in names, the river is navigable throughout the year, and it is a tributary of the Gaṅgā. Ptolemy[9] names a river 'Sorabos', which is identified by all scholars with the Sarayū.

1. VI. 4. 174.
2. S. N. A. II. p. 439.
3. Bāl, Ch. 24.
4. *Raghuvaṁśa* 8. 95.; 14. 3.
5. Bāl, Ch. XXIV.
6. *Indika*, Arrian, IV; Maccrindle, p. 191.
7. I. A., Vol. V. p. 331.
8. A. G. I., to face page 445.
9. *Ancient India*, Ptolemy, VII, 28; Maccrindle, p.. 99.

Megasthenes[1] also mentions a river Agaroṇis which Rennell[2] identifies with the Ghāgharā, another name of the Sarayū. It would be but natural for an alien to take the two words as names of two different rivers, especially when he was not very familiar with the language of the people he was dealing with. Megasthenes therefore took Agaroṇis and Solomattis as names of two different rivers. The name Ghāgharā seems to have originated from the Sanskrit word 'Gharghara' a gurgling sound of water which the river is supposed to produce. This river is sacred to the Hindus and Buddhists alike.

VEGAVATĪ

The Jain Literature[3] mentions a river Veyavaī which seems to be the Sanskrit Vegavatī. The river is said to have been flowing near the village of Aṭṭhigāma.[4] Martin[5] identified it with the Gaṇḍaka. But we should not forget that in the Muzaffarpur district, there is a small river called Bāyā. The Vegavatī is probably the ancient name of the Bāyā. The modern name of the river seems to have been derived from the Prākrit word Veyavaī.

BĀGMATI

The Bāgmatī rises in the Mahāvrata range[6] of the lesser Himālayas and flows to the south through the Darbhanga district. It formerly joined the little Gaṅḍaka at Rosera and now it joins the river a little lower at Tilkeshwar together with the Tiljuga river. Thus the Bāgmatī falls into the Gaṅgā through the Burhi Gaṇḍaka.

This river does not play any important part in ancient Indian literature, but is casually referred to in Sanskrit. In the *Mithilā khanda* of the *Bṛhad Viṣṇu Purāṇa*, the author mentions the river as Bāgvatī,[7] but we are not sure of the date

1. *Indika*, Arrian, IV; Maccrindle, p. 191.
2. Ibid., Maccrindle, p. 194 (footnote)
3. *Life in Ancient India as depicted in the Jain Canons*, p. 257.
4. Ibid., p. 257.
5. *Eastern India*, Vol. II, p. 9.
6. Himalaya Mountains and Tibet, Part III, p. 148.
7. *History of Tirhut*, p. 2 (foot note)

of the composition of this text. It seems to be a work of later centuries.[1] The *Svayambhū*[2] and the *Vārāha*[3] Purāṇas call it the Vāgmatī. In the *Purushaparīkshā*,[4] a 14th century work, Vidyāpati names the river Bāghvatī. The *Majjhima Nikāya*[5] mentions that the Bāhukā, Sundarikā, Sarasvatī and the Bāhumatī were rivers while Gayā and Prāyaga were tīrthas only. These rivers are not in any systematic order. The Bāhumatī is probably the Vāgmatī of Sanskrit, since the names are similar. It is called the Bachamati[6] also in Buddhist literature, because it was created by the word uttered by the Buddha Krakuchhanda when the latter visited Nepal with his disciples from Gauḍa-deśa. The Buddhist legend and the *Bṛhadviṣṇupurāṇa* show agreement in the traditional origin of the name of the river. The *Udāna*[7] mentions a river Vaggumudā which flowed to the east of the Vajjī territory. This Vaggumudā seems to be the Vāgmatī of present time. The different names of the same river in the Buddhist literature shows how the name was changing from time to time. The Bāghavatī, the name given to this river by Vidyāpati seems to have some connection with the word *Vyāghra* (tiger); tigers are found in abundance on its banks in the Nepalese Terai.

Megasthenes[8] mentions a river Kakauthis which Lassen identifies with the Kakuthā of the Buddhist[9] literature. The Sanskrit word Kākustha means 'palate', a word which has some affinity with 'speech' or 'sound'; we have seen that a Buddhist legend and the *Bṛhadviṣṇu Purāṇa* give legendary accounts of the river Bāgmatī arising from the speech of a divinity. Thus the river Kakauthis may perhaps be identified with the Vāgmatī. The *Mahāparinibbāṇa Sutta*[10] however, specially mentions this river in the vicinity of Kuśīnārā,

1. Ibid.
2. Ch. V.
3. Ch. 215.
4. Labdhasiddhi kathā-verse I, Vagvatyām Bhavadevasingh nṛipatiḥ etc.
5. Vol. I. p. 39.
6. G. D. A. M. I; p. 15. Dey does not give the original reference.
7. III. 3.
8. *Indica*, Arrian, IV, Maccrindle, pp. 191-92.
9. D. II. p. 129; *Udāna* 8.5.
10. Ibid.

about whose location we have no doubt. Cunningham thus seems to be right in identifying the Kakuthā with a small stream Barhi in the Gorakhapur district. Carlleyle identifies this river with the Ghaghi, another stream which flows through the same district. We think that, on the evidence of the *Mahāparinibbāṇa Sutta*, the Kakuthā should be identified with the Barhi which flows in the neighbourhood of Kuśīnārā.

KAMALĀ

The Kamalā is always associated with its tributary the Tiljuga and many small streams. They water the Madhubani sub-division of the Darbhanga district. In its lower course the Kamalā is called the Ghaghari. The Kamalā receives two of the seven branches of the Kośī and falls into the Gaṅgā at Karagola to the south of Purnea.

We hardly find the river mentioned in early Sanskrit and Buddhist literature, but the *Bṛhad-viṣṇu Purāṇa* alludes to this river flowing through the heart of Mithilā.[1] We are not certain that the Greek geographers had any knowledge of the Kamalā, but the Omallis of Arrian,[2] which has not been satisfactorily identified, may be the Kamalā, as the latter syllables of the two names are somewhat similar.

KOŚĪ

The Kośī has long been the most important river of north Bihar. It rises in the Himālayas and enters the plain at Varāhakshetra, which is a place of pilgrimage for the Hindus. It flows to the west of the district town of Purnea, and its main stream unites with the Gaṅgā near the Maniharighat.

The Kośī is a most notorious river for changing its course. There is perhaps no river in India which has changed its course so frequently as the Kośī has done. It can be compared with the rivers of China, which suddenly wash away large tract of land. Probably the river formerly flowed farther east than where it flows at present.

Hamilton,[3] in the first decade of the nineteenth century, wrote about this river that "the Pundits inhabiting its

1. *History of Tirhut*, p. 2 (foot note).
2. *Indika* (Arrian) Ch. IV. Maccrindle p. 191.
1. *Eastern India* Vol. III. p. 15.

banks allege that in the times of remote antiquity, the Kusi passed southwardly where Tajapur is now situated and from there towards the east until it joined the Brahmaputra, having no connection with the Ganges", and he further said, "the opinion seems highly probable. I think it not unlikely that the great lakes north and east of Maldah are remains of the Kusi united to the Mahananda."

Rennell[1] wrote of changes in its course in his time (1787). He stated, that the Kośī at no distant time previously flowed past the state of Purnea and fell into the Gaṅgā 45 miles below its present junction. He also said that the Kośī formerly emptied its water in the Brahmaputra.

Hiüen-Tsang[2] had to cross a large river on the way to Kāmarūpa. Cunningham[3] identified this river with the Tistā but the latter is not large enough to be worth mentioning. It is not improbable that the river was the Kośī. In medieval times, the Kośī flowed near Gaur, and owing to its flooding, the Musalman rulers had to desert the city in favour of Rajmahal.[4] The dead current in that area is still known as 'Marā Kośī'.

Fergusson,[5] referring to the period when the combined Kośī and Mahānandā flowed through the Ursagar says; "That this should have occurred within the very limited range of traditions of lower Bengal, induces me to suppose that the beginning of the Christian era is the highest antiquity that can be ascribed to such a state of things. It may be much later."

Thus we see that the Kośī has covered a wide range of courses from eastern Bengal to the eastern part of north Bihar and is still tending to change its course to the west. There are several streams which join the Kośī and they together with the main branch are called the Saptakośī The streams from east to west are the Tambar, Tamra, Aruṇa or Eran, Dūdha Kośī, Likhu Kośī, Tambra Kośī and the Bhotia Kośī.

1. *Memoir of A Map of Hindoostan* p. 265.
2. *On Yuanchwang* p. 185 (Vol. II).
3. A. G. I. p. 501.
4. J. A. S. B. (1895) Part I. pp. 10-11.
5. Quoted in the J. A. S. B. (1895) pp. 1-24.

A Jātaka[1] story tells that a truthful Brāhmaṇa was born in the Himālaya country in a lovely spot on the bank of the Kauśikī, a branch of the Gaṅgā. It can be gathered from the same work[2] that there grew fruit trees of several kinds like rose apples, bread fruit, dates and figs on its banks. We can infer from this story that at that time the Kośī brought silt which made its banks fertile and that its currents were not then so swift as to wash away the soil. The condition of the territory watered by the Kośī is quite changed at present. The area it flows through has become quite barren. We find no trace of trees on its banks, but only heaps of sand.

This change may have occurred owing to de-forestation in its catchment basin in recent years. It is probable that for this reason it now carries more silt and sand, which it deposits in its bed along the banks, devastating large areas. The Kośī has a large mountainous course and collects the water of a large area, but its present course through the plain before it reaches the Gaṅgā is comparatively short. Therefore it is obliged to deposit its load of silt over a short distance. This intensifies the frequency of flood as well as the depositing of sand.

The *Rāmāyaṇa*[3] includes the Kauśikī in the list of rivers of northern India. It says that the river was named after Kauśikī who was the sister of the sage Vishvāmitra. It is not unnatural to imagine that the sister of Vishvāmitra was a lady of quick temper like her great brother. So the origin of the river has been most suitably associated with Kauśikī. The *Mahābhārata*[4] mentions a king of Kauśikī Kachha, the region of the Kośī river whom Bhīma conquered.

The *Mārkaṇḍeya Purāṇa*[5] refers to its rise from the Himālayas and calls it the Kauśikā. In the *Kumārasaṁbhava*[6] Kālidāsa alludes to the waterfall of the Kośī. He probably had in mind Vārāhakashetra where the Kośī enters the plain.

This river is probably mentioned under the name of

1. J. V. 511- p. 6.
2. Ibid.
3. Bal. Ch. 34.
4. II. 30. 22.
5. Ch. 57.
6. Ch. 6. 33. Mahākośīprapāte sminsaṅgamah punareva nah.

Kauśika in the Nidhanpur[1] Copper Plate of Bhāskaravarman. K.L. Barua[2] identifies this river with the modern Kośī while Dr. Bhandarkar[3] and J. C. Ghosh[4] are of the opinion that the river mentioned in the plate is the Kusiara which flows through the Sylhet district. But their arguments have been very thoroughly contradicted by Dr. P. C. Chaudhary[5] who has shown that the lands granted to the donee lay to the east of the Kośī and are to be identified with the places in the Jalpaiguri district. It is thus clear that in the early part of the seventh century A.D., the Kośī flowed through north Bengal.

The Kosoamos of Arrian[6] and the Cosoagus[7] of Pliny are generally identified with the modern Kośī, but Schwanbeck says that those words represent the Sanskrit *Kosavah* which is an epithet of the Sona. Arrian places this river between the Erranoboas and the Sonus, therefore, according to Schwanbeck, it may have been a branch of the Soṇa. As far as the order of enumeration is concerned, we can say with confidence that Arrian muddled up the names of these rivers. He mentioned as two separate rivers the Erranaboas and the Sonus which are alternative names of one and the same river. Moreover the name Kosoamas is more similar to Kauśikī than to *Kosavoh*. Therefore, we support the usual identification.

There is still a large number of rivers which have not been described. Most of them are so small that we hardly find them mentioned in ancient Indian literature. In epigraphy too, they have not been referred to. One of them, however, the Mahānandā, is definitely an important river. It forms at present the boundary between the states of Bengal and Bihar. But ancient Indian literature is quite silent about it, and we can give no explanation of this strange fact.

1. E. I. XII p. 65; XIX. p. 115.
2. *Early History of Kamarupa* p. 51.
3. I. C. Vol. I. p. 137.
4. I. H. Q. Vol. VI. p. 642.
5. History of the Civilization of the People of Assam up to the 12th Century A.D., unpublished doctoral thesis, London 1953. p. 250.
6. *Indika* Ch. IV. McCrindle p. 191.
7. Ibid. p. 192. (Foot note)

GAṄGĀ

The Gaṅgā is the most sacred river of India. It is held in such high esteem by the people that any holy river in any part of the country is given the name Gaṅgā. This river enters Bihar in the Shahabad district and leaves the state passing through the Santhal Parganas district. The width of the Gaṅgā in this state is broader than in any other part of its whole course. It divides the state into two parts, north Bihar and south Bihar. The northern bank of the Gaṅgā in this state has always been deemed very sacred. The reason for this is not far to seek. The area to the north of the Gaṅgā is generally known as Mithilā, which has been a stronghold of orthodox Brāhmaṇism from very early times, while south Bihar was the birth-place or rather the cradle-land of Buddhism. It is true, the Lichchhavis of north Bihar were deeply under the influence of Buddhism, but there Brāhmaṇism never totally lost its ground and soon again asserted itself. The case in south Bihar was quite different. It remained the stronghold of Buddhism till the end of the twelfth century and the universities such as Vikramaśīla and Nālandā, which were centres of Buddhism, flourished on its soil. Therefore, it can be naturally concluded that, after the disappearance of Buddhism from the land, the Paṇḍitas of Mithilā eulogized their own land, while the voice of Magadha was hushed in dead silence. In Buddhist and Jain literature we do not find any such distinction. Moreover, the land up to Kajangala was included in the Majjhima desa[1] (Middle land), which was deemed highly sacred by Brāhmaṇic scholars.

However, we can suggest another explanation also. The germ of this difference seems to be more political than religious. There was a great deal of difference in the administrative systems of the two regions, which, although so near geographically, were originally separate. The states in north Bihar were tribal republican in their character, while Magadha always had a centralised administration under a monarch; What was once an administrative difference, was gradually and steadily given the support of religion, which still persists.

The course of the Gaṅgā has not changed much in Bihar,

1. *Vinayapiṭaka*, I, 197.

but we have a few literary references which show that the river has shifted its course a few miles way from its old bed. From the itinerary of Hsüan-Tsang,[1] it seems that the course of the Gaṅgā was much nearer to Arrah than it is at the present time. Similarly in the 14th century A.D., the Soṇa fell into the Gaṅgā at Maner,[2] while in our day the Gaṅgā flows more to the north. The Jātakas[3] tell us that the city of Champā stood on the junction of the Gaṅgā and the Champā. If the identification of Champā with the villages of Champanagar and Champapur is correct, we can say that the Gaṅgā has gradually shifted to the north from its ancient bed for about 30 miles. However, such slow changes in the course of a big river like the Gaṅgā have comparatively little importance. We have no definite evidence of sudden and disastrous changes of the Gaṅgā as we find in the case of the Kośī, Gaṇḍaka etc.

The rivers of south Bihar are different in nature from those of north Bihar. All are hill streams and for the most part of the year there is little water in them excepting the Soṇa. Most of the rivers rise from the table land of Chhotanagpur and flow in different directions. The soil of the land is very hard, hence the rivers generally do not change their courses so frequently as they do in north Bihar. The number of the rivers on this side of the Gaṅgā is greater than that of those on the north, but the majority of them are too small to be worth mention. The rivers such as Karmanāśā, Soṇa, Punpun, Morahar, Phalgu, Pañchānan, Sakari, Tilaiya, Lilajan, Mohana, Kiyul, Chandan and the like flow from the south to the north and empty their water into the Gaṅgā. Other rivers such as the Barakar, Damoder, Svarṇarekhā, Koil, Baitarṇī, Mayurākhshī, Ajayā etc. rise in the highlands of Chhotanagpur and flow to the south—south-east and west.

Some rivers are mentioned in ancient Indian literature as flowing through Magadha, but we are quite at a loss about the rivers of ancient Jhārkhaṇḍa, the Chhotanagpur area of our days. As these are is full of forests and hills and the land

1. *On Yuan Chwang.* p. 60. (Vol. II).
2. See below p. 110.
3. J. Vol. II, (Champeya Jātaka) pp. 454 68.

is not fertile, people had no interest in exploring the area; hence there was little human intercourse in early days and its original inhabitants are evidently primitive. It is, therefore, natural that the rivers of this region have been seldom referred to.

KARMANĀŚĀ

The Karmanāśā rises in the Vindhyā hills and falls into the Gaṅgā near Chausa. The river forms the western boundary of the Bihar state. The Purāṇic[1] traditions speak of its origin from the mouth of Triśaṅku, whom Viśvāmitra tried to send to heaven in his corporeal form, but who was thrown back by the gods. For this reason the Karmanāśā is still regarded as an accursed river. It is believed that one who passes through its water is deprived of his religious merit. The *Mārkaṇḍeya*[2] *Purāṇa* speaks of a river Karmoda. The *Vāyu*[3] and the *Vārāha*[4] *Purāṇas* mention the Kāratoyā in the same context. But a river rising from the Vindhyā mountains cannot be identified with the Kāratoyā, which flows through north Bengal from north to south. It may be the Karamoda, which later on became the Karamanāśā of our days.

Arrian[5] mentions a river Kommenases which Rennell[6] and Lassen identified with the Karamanāśā. Cunningham[7] supports them in one of his maps. The Greek name seems quite applicable to Karmanāśā and we accept the identification. It is really surprising that the Buddhist literature is quite silent about this river.

SOṆA

The river Soṇa takes its rise in the Mekal hills of the Jabbalpore district, flows to the north and north-east for about 400 miles, and falls into the Gaṅgā, at present at a distance of more than twenty miles to the west of Patna near a village called Hardichhapra. This is one of the largest rivers

1. *Vāyu Purāṇa*, Ch. 88, 113.
2. Ch. 57.
3. Ch. 45. 100
4. Ch. 85.
5. *Indika.* (Arrian) Ch. IV. Mccrindle p. 191.
6. *Memoir of A Map of Hindoostan* p.
7. A. S. I. Report, Vol. I, to face p. 1.

of India, the third largest according to the Greek historians. But their statements seem to be based on inaccurate information because there are many rivers in India which are larger than the Soṇa. The river is navigable through-out the major part of the year. It receives several tributaries on both banks and hence it grows wider as it proceeds. The river has changed its course several times, but the changes have not been so frequent and rapid as in the case of the Kośī.

Some scholars have tried to trace the old bed of the Soṇa from time to time and have arrived at certain conclusions which further research has shown to be not wholly correct. Beglar[1] believed that during the age of the *Rāmāyaṇa*, the Soṇa took a north-eastern course from the Sonbhadraghat, which is in the south-western part of the Gayā district, there joined the Punpun, and the united stream fell into the Gaṅgā near Fatuha. He believed that the Soṇa flowed through the same bed till the Buddha's nirvāṇa. Major Rennell[2] observed that "the ancient bed of the Soane is yet traceable on the south of Patna and seems to have led into the Ganges near Fatuah." J. B. Elliot[3] observed that "formerly the course of the Sone turned eastward from near Sydabad, whence it proceeded by Ghorhutta and Bikrampur to Nowatpoor thence via Moorgiachach, Mooradpoor, Danapoor, Ghosunda, Koorjee and Khagaul to Phoolwaree. From the latter town it flowed past Khwajapoor, Sheikhpoora and Dhukurpoor to Meethapoor, whence in two streams (jurrah) it fell into the Ganges near Bankipoor at the Takia of Shah Rookum Phulwari. From Phoolwaree, a small stream (Sota) flowed to the eastward and from opposite Meethapoor proceeding in a south-easterly direction, it finally united with the Ganges near Fattoha (Fatwa). In the time of Mukhdoom Shah Shurufoodeen Ahmad Yahea Muneree (from which a period of upward 470 years reckoning to the end of 1257, Hijaree has elapsed) the main stream of the Sone taking its course to the west of the town Muner united with the Ganges near that place and the eastern course with the

1. A. S. I. Report Vol. VIII. pp. 6--33.
2. Memoir of A Map of Hindoostan p. 53.
3. J. A. S. B. (1845), Part I, p. 138.

Sota became dry." Maxwell[1] found a small stream to the south of the city making its exit into the Ganges through the arch of an old bridge about 3½ miles above Fatuha, and believed that this was an earlier course of the Soṇa.

All these scholars recorded their observations in the eighteenth and the nineteenth centuries, when they were not sure of the exact location of Pāṭaliputra. Beglar's remark that the Soṇa continued to flow through the Punpun and fell into the Gaṅgā near Fatuha from the time of the *Rāmāyaṇa* to the Buddha's nirvāṇa is not supported either by the *Rāmāyaṇa* or the Buddhist literature. A big river such as the Soṇa cannot have flowed into the Punpun which is too small to carry the whole volume of water of the Soṇa. If it had ever been the case, it must have occured in the prehistoric period of which we have no record.

The excavations begun under Dr. Spooner and continued from time to time by other scholars have proved finally that the site of ancient Pāṭaliputra extends from the modern village of Kumrahāra to Patna city.[2] From the *Mahāparinibbāṇa Sutta*,[3] we learn that Ajātaśatru built a fortress on the Gaṅgā to check the inroads of the Lichchhavis which later on grew into the famous town of Pāṭaliputra. Had the Soṇa fallen into the Gaṅgā near Fatuha, as Rennell and Beglar believed, Ajātaśatru would have preferred to construct the fort at Fatuha, because in doing so he might have escaped the trouble of crossing a big river like the Soṇa. From the evidence furnished by the *Mahābhāṣya*[4] and Megasthenes,[5] we know certainly that Pātaliputra was on the confluence of the Soṇa and the Gaṅgā. Therefore it is almost certain that in the time of the Buddha and later, the Śoṇa united with the Ganges to the west of modern Patna. Our conclusion is supported by the *Mudrārākṣasa*[6], where we find king Parvateśvara, who came from the west

1. J. A. S. B. (1845) Part I, p. 138.
2. The extent of the city recorded by Megasthenes will naturally cover the area of Patna city, which is only 3 to 4 miles from Kumhra. A portion of an Aśokan pillar has been unearthed there during the excavations in 1956.
3. Dh. A. II. p. 866 ff.
4. II. I.
5. *Indika*, Frag. XXV, Strabo, XV.
6. Act. IV, Sc. II. Verse 16.

or north-west, saying that his elephants and chargers will drink the water of the Soṇa and then level the walls of Pāṭaliputra. It is possible that a small and insignificant stream of the Soṇa flowed to the south of Pāṭaliputra in later centruries and gradually dried up, as recorded by Elliot. If there is any sand of the Soṇa in the soil of Pāṭaliputra, we can infer that it was owing to a flood which deposited sand in that area. Had the Soṇa flowed through the site of modern Patna, we should have discovered large beds of sand during excavations. The absence of such beds proves that at no period of history did the main stream of the Soṇa flow to the south of Pāṭaliputra to unite with the Gaṅgā at Fatuha.

The *Mahābhārata*[1] mentions the Soṇa and Mahāsoṇa among the rivers crossed by the Pāṇḍavas and Kṛishṇa on the way to Rājagṛiha, the former river in association with the Gaṅgā, and the latter between the Gaṇḍakī and Sadānīrā. The Soṇa even at present is called a 'Nada' owing to its width. Hence we think that the Soṇa and the Mahāsoṇa are one and the same river. Supposing the Pāṇḍavas had crossed all the rivers as described in the *Mahābhārata*, with which large river, other than the Soṇa, is the Mahāsoṇa to be identified ? Moreover, we have shown that the Gaṇḍakī and the Sadānīrā are one and the same river.[2] The Pāṇḍavas are said to have crossed the Soṇa again after crossing the Gaṅgā. In view of these repetitions and the jumbling up of river names it is evident that the compiler of the epic had an imperfect knowledge of the geography of many parts of India. He simply set out to show his acquaintance with the names of the rivers of which he had heard from tradition. We should not rely much upon such descriptions.

At the time of the compilation of this part of the epic, some water of the Soṇa probably flowed through the modern *Banas*, a small river to the west of the town of Arrah. In the *Mahābhārata*[3] a river named Parṇaśa is mentioned on the occasion of the royal sacrifice after the digvijaya of the Pāṇḍava brothers. The *Vāyu Purāṇa*[4] mentions a river Varṇaśā.

1. II. 20. 27-29.
2. See above p. 89.
3. II. 9. 21.
4. Ch. 45. 97.

We think that Parṇaśā or Varṇaśā is the name of the modern Banas, but it is too small a river to be mentioned in the list of the rivers at the time of the royal sacrifice unless it was a somewhat large river in former times. We shall not be far from truth in supposing that the Banas received some water from the Soṇa, through some channel not known at present.

The *Rāmāyaṇa*[1] names the river Soṇa. N. L. Dey[2] is of opinion that at the time of the Rāmāyaṇa, it flowed past the eastern side of Rājagṛiha. The river mentioned in the *Rāmāyaṇa*[3] as flowing past Rājagṛiha is the Sumāgadhī for which Magadha was famous. We cannot see how Dey identified the Sumāgadhī with the Soṇa unless from the fact that the *Rāmāyaṇa* looks on the former as the chief river of Magadha other than the Gaṅgā. The Soṇa being in fact the largest river, he may have decided that they were identical. But the present course of the Soṇa is so far from Rājagṛiha that such a change in its course seems quite impossible. From the Buddhist[4] literature, it is not clear whether the Sumāgadhī was a river or a pond. Buddhaghoṣa[5] describes it as a pond.

The *Mārkaṇḍeya Purāṇa*[6] refers to the Soṇa. Kālidāsa[7] mentions the big waves of the Sona when it empties its water into the Gaṅgā.

The river has another name in the *Amarakosha* where it is called the Hiraṇyavāha, perhaps either because its sand was of golden colour or because the river brought gold dust in its flow. Beglar[8] identifies the Hiranyāvaha with the Gaṇḍakī. But Bāṇa[9] explicitly mentions the Hiraṇyavāha as another name of the Soṇa. This is confirmed by the *Abhidhānachintāmaṇi*[10] also

The Greek historians mention both the Erranoboas and the Sonus, which has led to confusion in identifying the river.

1. Kiṣkindhākāṇḍa, Ch. 40. 21.
2. G. D. A. M. I. p. 188.
3. Bāl. Ch. 32. 9.
4. D. Vol. III, p. 39.
5. D. A. III. p. 835.
6. Ch. 57, p. 295.
7. *Raghuvaṁśa*, VII. 36.
8. A.S.I. Report Vol. VIII pp. 6-33.
9. *Harṣacharita*, p. 19.
10. IV. 156.

Megasthenes[1] tells us that Pāṭaliputra was on the banks of the Ganges and Erranoboas. Elsewhere he mentions a river Sonus. Ptolemy[2] refers to a river Soa. The Erranoboas must be identified with the Hiraṇyavāha which is definitely the Soṇa of our days. There is little difference between the words Sonus and Soa. The question arises whether the Sonus and the Erranoboas were two different rivers. It is possible that Megasthenes had heard both names and believed that they referred to different rivers, as he was a foreigner and probably did not follow Indian languages well. If we take the Sonus as a branch of the Erranoboas, we should assume that both the rivers joined the Gaṅgā to the west of Pāṭaliputra. Had there been a stream of the Soṇa flowing to the south of Pāṭaliputra, as suggested by J. B. Elliot,[3] Megasthenes would not have left it unmentioned, since he describes an artificial moat full of water round Pāṭaliputra and the so called Sonus would have formed a natural one. No doubt some sandy beds have been found at Kumrahara during excavations,[4] but it is possible either that they were deposited there owing to the flood in the Soṇa or that the Punpun once flowed through the area and later receded farther south. We think that the confusion of the Erranoboas and the Sonus has arisen owing to a misunderstanding on the part of Megasthenes. The river is the Soṇa of our days.

PUNPUN

The Punpun rises in the high lands of Madhya Pradesh and like the Soṇa flows to the north and north-east. It unites with the Gaṅgā near Fatuha in the district of Patna. The bed is almost dry except in the rainy season, but a thin current flows throughout the year, unlike other rivers of South Bihar.

The Punpun is scarcely mentioned in literature. The *Mahābhārata* and the *Rāmāyaṇa* are totally silent about this river. The Buddhist literature too do not refer to it. We

1. *Indika*, Frag. XXV, Strabo XV.
2. *Ancient India* (Ptolemy) VII, 28. McCrindle, p. 99.
3. J. A. S. B. (1845) pp. 137-54.
4. This is based on my personal observation during excavations at Kumhra in 1952-53, in which I had taken part. The report has now been published by the K. P. Jayaswal Institute, Patna.

find the river mentioned in the *Vāyu*[1] and the *Padma Purāṇas* in connection with the *Gayā Mahātmya* as the Punaḥpuṇā (again and again) of which Punpun is a colloquial form. The river might have been called by this name for the simple reason that it was frequently in flood, as it is at present, or because it never dried up as reported above. The Purāṇas take the word Punaḥpunā in a spiritual sense, and state that sins are removed again and again after offering oblations to the Pitṛs in this river.

Wilford[2] states that this river is called the Māgadhī or Kīkaṭī because it flowed through the country of Magadha or Kīkaṭa. He gives no original sources mentioning such rivers and we do not see reason enough to support the view that the Punpun was ever known by these names. A large number of rivers flow through Magadha and thus why should this alone be called by these names ? No doubt, the *Rāmāyaṇa*[3] mentions Rājagṛha situated on the bank of the Sumāgadhī but Buddhaghoṣa[4] says that this was a pond. The name Kīkaṭī is not supported by any independent source.

During recent excavations at Kumrahara, sand has been found which seems to have been deposited in the vicinity of Pāṭaliputra by flood of the Punpun, unless the river itself flowed through that area in the post-Mauryan[5] times, and the sand is the evidence of an old bed of this river which receded farther south in later days. As the layer of the sand was very thin, however, the former alternative seems to be better. The Greek historians have not referred to this river or, if there is any reference, it is under a different name which has not as yet been identified.

PHALGU

The Phalgu arises from the union of the two rivers, Lilajan and Mohana, which issue from the high lands of Chhotanagpur. The rivers unite roughly two miles above Gayā

1. Ch. 108. 73.
2. Asiatic Researches Vol. XIV. pp. 373-470.
3. Bal. 32. 9.
4. D.A. III. p. 835.
5. It is based on my personal observation during excavations of 1952-53.

and then the combined streams flow under the name of the Phalgu. Near the Barabar hill, the river bi-furcates into two branches, which in union with other small rivers at the end of their journey are known by the name of the Harohar. This river falls into the Kuyul near Monghyr.

Cunningham[1] in one of his maps has shown that the Phalgu too, has changed its course. From the Barabar hill the river flowed north-east by the famous village of Tailadhaka. But now it flows two miles west of that village. The old bed of the Phalgu is still visible at Tailadhaka and in its neighbouring areas.

In the *Vāyu Purāṇa,*[2] several rivers and streams are mentioned at Gayā, namely the Mahānadī, Madhukulyā, Vaitaraṇī, Ghṛitakulyā, Madhuśravā and Devikā. The Mahānadī is probably the Phalgu as it is said to flow just to the east of Gayā[3]. Elsewhere the *Vāyu Purāṇa* identifies the Devikā with the Mahānadī and the latter itself is no other than the Phalgu according to the same work.[4] This is supported by the *Mahābhārata.*[5]

The Madhuśravā and the Ghṛitakulyā are insignificant streams. They rise from the local hills and merge into the Phalgu. They are so unimportant that they have no popular names, but they are remembered by the Gayā Brāhmaṇas.

The river Phalgu is sacred to the Buddhists and the Hindus alike. Even before the Buddha, it seems to have been sacred river, for the Kaśyapa brothers are said to have performed their sacrifices on its banks.[6] According to the *Udāna*[7] a large number of matted-hair ascetics assembled on the banks of the Phalgu every year in the first eight days after the termination of the winter at the close of the month of Māgha. A large number of pilgrims went there from different parts of the country.

The Phalgu is known in Buddhist literature by the name

1. A. S. I. Vol. I, to face p. 3.
2. Ch. 109. 16, 17.
3. Ibid.
4. *Vāyu Purāṇa* 110. 6.
5. *Vanaparva*, 85, 12. Sa cha puṇyajalātatra Phalgunāmā mahānadi.
6. *Udāna* p. 6.
7. Ibid.

of Nairañjana, which is remembered in the modern name of Lilajan, the Phalgu's chief tributary. It was on the bank of this river that Gautama achieved enlightenment and became Buddha.

Megasthenes[1] mentions a river 'Magon'. Mannert identified this with the Rāmagaṅgā, but McCrindle prefers to identify it with the Phalgu or the Mahānadī, which he calls Mohana, the name of one of its tributaries. The Mohana alone is not a famous river. It is more probable that the Greek 'Magon' is derived from the word Mahānadī which is an epithet of the Phalgu at Gayā.

The rest of the rivers—the Sakari, Tillaiya, Paimara, Panchanana, Kol, Damodar, Svarṇarekhā, Barakar and the like are scarcely mentioned in the literature. Some of them, however, have been mentioned in geographical works of later centuries.[2]

SAKARI

The Sakari rises in the high hills of Chhotanagpur and flows through the Hazaribagh, Gaya, Patna and Monghyr districts. At the end of its course, it joins the combined streams of the Harohar and falls into the Kiyul.

The Sakari flows at some distance to the east of Rājagṛha. But it has long been shifting its course to the east and hence in the remote past this river may have flowed past the city of Rājagṛha.[3] The *Rāmāyaṇa*[4] mentions a river Sumāgadhī as flowing through Rājagṛha. But it was a pond according to Buddhaghoṣa.[5] If it were a river, it is not improbable that the modern Sakari is the Sumāgadhī of the *Rāmāyaṇa*, because there is some similarity of sounds in the names.

Cunningham[6] says that the river Śuktimatī derived its name from the Suktimal mountains, in which it had its source.

1. *Indika*, Arrian, IV, McCrindle, p. 191.
2. Asiatic Researches, Vol. XIV, pp. 373-470.
3. A. S. I., Vol VIII, p. 127 (Foot-note).
4. Bāl., 32. 9.
5. D. A. III, p. 835.
6. A. S.I. Vol. XVII, p. 60.

He asserts that the river is the same as the Mahānadī, Beglar[1] agrees with Cunningham so far as the source of the Śuktimatī is concerned, but he identifies it with the Sakari.

The serious difficulty about the identification is that no Purāṇa mentions the Śuktimat mountain as the source of the Śuktimatī. The *Mārkaṇḍeya Purāṇa*[2] clearly points to the Vindhyā mountains as the source of this river. Pargiter, therefore, identifies the modern Sakari with the Sakuli of the *Mārkaṇḍeya Purāṇa* rising from the Vindhyā mountains. He however gives no argument on which to base his conclusion.

About the Śuktimatī, the *Mahābhārata*[3] says that the Śuktimatī flowed near the Chedi capital, which is identified with Tripurī in the Jabbalpur district.[4] But Beglar states that "there is no river at all approaching in name or features the Śuktimatī as described in the *Mahābhārata* flowing past it, for the Narmadā is evidently not the Śuktimatī."[5]

He further says that according to the Purāṇic tradition, the Chedi kingdom was divided among the five sons of Vasu, one of whom had become the king of Magadha. On this basis he suggests that near the source of the Kiyul and the Sakari, there may have been the Chedi capital through which the Sakari flowed. But this seems to be a far fetched imagination which cannot be proved successfully. The legendary families of the Purāṇa must represent chiefs of the remote past and the geographical data have been much adopted in later times. The only important Chedi kingdom in historical times was that of the Kalachuris of Tirpurī, and it seems impossible to believe that any part of their kingdom can be referred to in our province.

The Mārkaṇḍeya Purāṇa no doubt describes the Vindhyā as the source of the Śuktimatī, but this may be owing to the mistakes of the copyists. The Śuktimat range, according to the *Mahābhārata*, lay in the eastern region which was conquered by Bhīma. We think that the spurs of Chhotanagpur may be identical with the Śuktimat range, as no other mountain

1. Ibid Vol. VIII, p. 125.
2. Ch. 57.
3. I. 63. 29-38.
4. J. A. S. B. (1895) p. 249.
5. A. S. I. Vol. p. 125.

in the eastern part of the country can be identified with it, as we have shown.[1]

The *Bhāgavata Purāṇa*[2] mentions a river Śarkarāvata which, N. L. Dey[3] identifies with the Sakari. He seems to be correct on the basis of similarity of names, but Purāṇic data are so confused that it is difficult to arrive at any definite conclusion.

Megasthenes[4] mentions a river Sittokatis as a tributary of the Gaṅgā. This is very similar in sound to the Śuktimatī, especially in a Prakritic form such as Suttimatī.

PANCHĀNAE

The correct name of this river is Pañchānana which means a river having five mouths. The river is formed of five streams which meet a few miles south of Rājagṛha and flow to the east of the site under this name. This river through many branches joins the Harohar and falls into the Gaṅgā.

The *Saṁyutta Nikāya*[5] mentions in passing reference a river Sappiṇī. The *Aṅguttara Nikāya*[6] informs us that from the Gṛdhrakūṭa hill near Rājagṛha once Buddha went to the bank of the Sappinī to meet some wanderers. The name seems to be the Sanskrit Sarpiṇī or snake. The snake is sinuous and supposed to have more than one tongue. The Pañchānana too, has several branches and is very winding in its course; hence we think that this river is the Sappiṇī of the Pāli texts. We have found no references either to the Sarpiṇī or Pañchānana in Sanskrit literature.

KOIL

The Koil rises in the hills of Chhotanagpur and flowing through the Palamu district falls into the Soṇa. Its Sanskrit name is Kokilā. Wilford[7] mentions a river of this name which, he says, is called the Vaitarṇī in its lower course. We have not found any reference to this river in ancient Indian literature.

1. See above p. 49.
2. V. 18. 19.
3. G. D. A. M. I. p. 182.
4. *Indika*, Arrian IV, McCrindle, p. 191.
5. S. Vol. I, p. 153.
6. A. Vol. I, p. 185, Vol. II p. 29. 176.
7. Asiatic Researches XIV p. 402.

SUVARṆAREKHĀ

The river rises from the hills of Chhotanagpur and flows past the well-known modern town of Jamshedpur and through northern Orissa. According to Wilford it was also known as Hiraṇyarekhā,[1] both names meaning a golden streak. He thinks that the Suvarṇarekhā and the Śuktimatī are one and the same river, while we have shown that the Śuktimatī is the Sakari of our days.

The *Mārkaṇḍeya Purāṇa* does not refer to this river. The name shows that the river brought gold dust in its flow and this belief still persists among the local people.

AJAYĀ.

This river flows through the Santhal parganas and falls into the Gaṅgā in the district of Burdwan. Its correct Sanskrit name seems to be Ajayavatī or Ajayamatī. The river is not very important and the Purāṇas do not seem to refer to any river of this name. Dey[2] and Wilford[3] referred to this river as mentioned in the *Gālava Tantra* as Ajayā, Ajayee, Ajasa, but the text referred to by Wilford is not obtainable. Megasthenes[4] mentions a river Amystis which seems to bear a slight similarity to the name Ajayamatī. Dey and Wilford agreed to this identification. Arrian says that this river flowed past the city of Katadupa, i.e. Katadvīpa.[5] At present this place is known as Kaṭawā.

DĀMODARA

The Damodar rising in the southern part of the Chhotanagpur, flows through the Hazaribagh and Manbhum districts and enters the state of West Bengal. This river is sometimes locally known as Damodā or Damodī.[6] Wilford identifies Damodar with the Vedasmṛti or the Vedavatī

1. Ibid. Wilford does not mention the original source where he found this river mentioned.
2. G. D. A. M. I., p. 3.
3. Asiatic Researches, Vol. XIV, p. 402.
4. Indika, Arrian, Ch., IV. McCrindle, p. 191.
5. Ibid.
6. Asiatic Researches, Vol. XIV, p. 402.

of the *Kshetrasamāsa*, one of his unpublished sources. He says that the Damodara is known by the name of the Devānanda in its upper course.[1] There is much similarity between the words Devānanda and Andomatis of Arrian.[2] But Arrian says that the Andomatis and the Cacuthis rose from the country of the Mandiadini which Wilford[3] thinks should be Mandabhāgya (unfortunate) or Manda-dhānya (poor in corn). The Chhotanagpur area may have been known as country of Mandabhāgya or Mandadhānya in ancient time as the whole tract was full of forest and rocks, but it is very difficult to identify the Cacuthis, (Kakauthis), which is generally identified with the Buddhist Kakuthā or the modern Barhi, a small river in the Gorakhapur district. Seeing this difficulty Wilford[4] identified Cacuthis with the Punpun, which does not seem probable. Arrian did not properly understand the geography of this part of the country and thus he has probably made several mistakes.

BARAKAR

The Barakar rises in the hills of Chhotanagpur and flows through the district of Hazaribagh. It passes into the state of West Bengal at a place called by the name of this very river in the Grand Chord railway line. The river is mountainous like other rivers of this area.

A river Ṛjupālikā is mentioned in the *Kalpasūtra*[5] in the Prākṛit form of its name—Ujjuvāliyā. The text says that Mahāvīra arrived here from Majjhimapāvā and attained Kaivalya or full spiritual emancipation on the bank of this river in the township of Jṛimbhikagrāma.

J. C. Jain[6] thinks that the place must be located somewhere near modern Pāvāpurī, in the Patna district. Muni Kalyāṇa-Vijaya[7] identifies it with the Jambhigaon on the Damodara. Mrs S. Stevenson[8] says that "Mahāvīra stayed

1. Ibid.
2. Indika, Arrian, Ch. IV. McCrindle, P.191.
3. Asiatic Researches Vol. XIV. p. 403.
4. Ibid.
5. *Kalpasūtra* (S. B. E. XXII) p. 263.
6. *Life in Ancient India As Depicted in the Jain Canons.* p. 289.
7. S.B.M., pp. 370, 357.
8. *The Heart of Jainism*, p. 38.

in a place not very far from Pārasnātha hills called Jṛimbhika-grāma". This river is sometimes spelt Ṛjukulā or Ṛjuvalikā.[1] The *Kalpasūtra* is quite silent about the village and the river flowing thereby. N. L. Dey[2] says that, in a modern temple on the bank of the Barakar, eight miles away from Giridih, there is an inscription which seems to mention the name of the river Ṛjupālikā. The inscription was probably taken there from the original temple which was probably in Jṛimbhika-grāma.

It is not necessary that the river and the village should be in the neighbourhood of Pāvāpurī. At present, there is no river in the locality of Pāvā which can be identified with the ancient Ṛjupālikā and Pāvā itself was not very famous before the death of Mahāvīra. It is, therefore, not improbable that when Mahāvīra attained enlightenment he was wandering in the locality of the Pārasnātha hill which was a sacred place owing to the tradition of the death of Pārśvanātha there.

At present Jambhigaon is on the Damodara river but we do not find any similarity between the name Damodar and Ṛjupālikā. So we are not sure of the location of this river nor we can say how this word could be changed into Barakar, on whose bank the inscription has been found.

CHĀNDAN

The Chāndan rises in two streams in the north-west of the Santhal parganas and flows to the north. It falls into the Gaṅgā to the east of Bhagalpur proper, between Barari and Ghoghari. The river seems to have been given different names at different periods of history. It was known by the name of Mālinī[3] and Chandanā.[4] The latter name seems to be more famous as it still survives in the form Chāndan. It is known by the name of Champā[5] in the Buddhist literature. The *Rāmāyaṇa* does not mention this river at all. In the *Mahābhārata*[6] it is referred to several

1. Ibid.
2. G. D. A. M. I. p. 168.
3. *Abhidhānachintāmaṇi*, IV-42.
4. *Vāyu Purāṇa* , 108-79.
5. J. IV. 454. (Champeya Jātaka).
6. II. 20. 28.

times. The river formed a part of Jarāsandha's territory which he offered to Karṇa. In the same work it is called the Māla.[1] The name seems to be a shorter form of Mālinī or a discrepancy may have crept in owing to the mistakes of copyists. Kṛishṇa with Arjuna and Bhīma is said have crossed the river on the way to Rājagṛha from Kurukshetra. This river is placed with the Charmaṇvatī in north Bihar. The author seems to have had no knowledge of the geography of this part of the country. Kṛishṇa and the Pāṇḍavas would never have had to cross the Mālinī on the way to Rājagṛiha.

Kālidāsa[2] mentions a river Mālinī in the *Abhijñāna Śākuntalam* but this seems to be a different river near Hastinā-pura. The river Chandanā or Champā formed the eastern boundary of Magadha. On its bank[3] lived probably a wild tribe of Nāgas who helped Bimbisāra in conquering Aṅga.

The Purāṇas call[4] it Chandanā and deem it an important river. The *Abhidhānachintāmaṇi*[5] calls it by both the names— Champā and Mālinī.

According to the *Kshetra Samāsa*,[6] this river is called Sulakshiṇī or Chandrāvatī. According to the *Jinavitasa*,[7] this river is named Araṇyavāha or the torrent through the wilderness. It seems that names such as these were not those by which the common people knew the river but were appelations given to it by scholars.

MAHĀNADA

This is a small river which flows through the Bihar Sharif sub-division. At present the river is known as Mahana which shows that in ancient time its correct name was Mahānada or Mahānadī. Our attention has been drawn to a stone bowl from this region with an inscription, which is still unpublished.[8] On the basis of paleography, the inscription seems to belong

1. Ibid.
2. Act VI, Verse 17.
3. J. IV. No. 454.
4. *Vāyu* 108. 79; 45. 97. Kāverī Sindhunīrā cha Chandanā cha saridvarā.
5. Ch. IV. 42.
6. Asiatic Researches XIV p. 401.
7. Ibid.
8. We are indebted for this information to Mr. C. S. Upasak, who is at present working on the full interpretation of the inscription.

to the early Christian era. The inscription throws some light on this river. It records what appears to be a Jain donation at a place on this river 'Mahānadaka Phagunadke'. This phrase can be explained in two ways; the great Phalgu nadī or the Mahānada which is a branch of the Phalgu. The first explanation is not tenable in the light of the fact that we have no record of the Phalgu so far to the east as Bihar Sharif while it is possible that the Mahānada may have received some water from the Phalgu through some channel no longer in existance. At present, there is no connection between these two rivers and we are not in a position to hazard any supposition.

NARDARIKĀ

The Nālandā[1] inscription of Yaśovarmadeva mentions a river named Nardarikā. Hirananda thinks that it might have been a streamlet or lake at Nālandā. Its situation is not at all clear from the inscription. Hence we cannot locate this stream.

1. E. I. Vol. XX pp. 37-46.

CHAPTER V

REGIONS AND DISTRICTS

The modern state of Bihar consists of four administrative divisions—Tirhut, Patna, Bhagalpur and Chhotanagpur—but physically the state is divided into two broad divisions by the river Gaṅgā. The land on the left bank of the Gaṅgā is fertile and soft while that on the right bank is full of rocks and is shallow and unproductive. The land to the south of the Gaṅgā may again be divided into two parts. The Patna division and a part of the Bhagalpur division have plain and fertile land with a few ranges of hills here and there. But the area to the south of Patna and Bhagalpur divisions consists of the high plateaus of Chhotanagpur, full hills, valleys, rivers and forests. Thus the state of Bihar has actually three broad physical divisions—North Bihar, South Bihar, and Chhotanagpur.

This state is bounded on the north by the Nepalese Terai, on the east by the state of West Bengal, and on the south by the state of Orissa, while the states of Uttar Pradesh and Madhya Pradesh are to the west of this state.

The modern divisions of India into different states have been created for administrative facility. But the case in ancient India was altogether different. There was a large number of states, smaller or bigger, most of which were originally known by the names of the tribes inhabiting them. There was no state such as modern Bihar. The very name of this state is an artificial one. We do not find any reference to the name Bihar in Pāli or Sanskrit literature. The name[1] was applied to the adjoining tracts of the modern small town of Bihar Sharif for the first time during the invasion of Bakhtiyar Khilji. The invader found a large number of the Buddhist vihāras or monasteries in this district, so he named the whole area as Bihar. The town itself was named Bihar after

1. *History of Bengal*, Vol. II p. 3.

the sack of the Odantapura Mahāvihāra which is located at this site.[1] The town of Bihar Sharif became an administrative centre during the Muslim rule, and with the expansion of their conquests the whole land to the north and the south of the Gaṅgā came to be known by this name after the place from which the whole region was governed. The Chhotanagpur area remained a separate unit under the name of Jhārakhaṇḍa. Bihar was definitely recognized as a province during the reign of Akbar, and the district of Champaran,[2] which lies in the extreme north of this state, was a sarkar in its jurisdiction. We do not know that was the position of Chhotanagpur during the Muslim rule. It may have formed a part of either Bihar or Jajnagar (Orissa). Thus we see that Bihar as the name of this state is not an ancient one.

In ancient times, the area now falling under the jurisdiction of Bihar comprised several states—some as a whole and some in parts. The states of Mithilā (Videha), Vaiśālī (Lichchavi), Magadha and Aṅga definitely formed parts of Bihar as a whole, while portions of the states of the Mallas, Kosala and Vaṅga were also contained in its territory.

Chhotanagpur, as said above, is now a part of Bihar, but it is a modern name and we hardly find any reference to this region in ancient literature. If there is any name at all, which signifies this tract of land it does not throw any light upon its history and hence we are quite in dark about it.

Let us discuss these ancient states one by one and mark the changes that took place in the course of centuries.

VIDEHA

Of all the ancient states which existed in the region of modern Bihar, the land of the Videhas was the first to come into contact with Aryan civilization. The *Ṛgveda* does not mention the Videhas, but we find a casual reference to the Videhan country in the *Śatapatha Brāhmaṇa*.[3] The text relates that Māthava Videgha, accompanied by his priest Gotama Rāhugaṇa, proceeding from the bank of the Sarasvatī, came to the Sadānīrā, the land beyond which was

1. See Supra p. 219.
2. *Ain-i-Akbari*, pp. 152, 155.
3. S. B. 1. 4., 1. 10.

not touched by the sacrificial fire and so was uninhabited by any Brāhmaṇa. The fire god, Agni promised to live there, but not in physical form. Then Māthava Videgha cleared the jungle, dried up the marshes and established his kingdom. Dr. Raychaudhuri[1] thinks that this is the land referred to in the *Mahābhārata*[2] as Jalodbhava or 'reclaimed from the swamp'. But in our opinion, as we shall show, this epithet has been applied to the territory which comprises the modern districts of Saharsa and Purnea and the eastern part of Darbhanga.[3] This region has been called Aṅguttarapa in the Buddhist literature.[4]

Whatever the truth behind the Vedic narrative, it is clear from the story that Māthava was the leader of the first immigrants to spread Aryan culture in that part of India and so it was after him that the territory was known as Videha.

The name Videha is evidently a form of the chieftain's name 'Videgha' and the story of Agni's promise to live there in disincarnate form is probably a late tradition developed after the region got its name on the basis of a false etymology (*Vi-deha*, "deprived of a body").

The boundary of Videha is a matter of controversy among scholars. We have no authoritative source from which we can ascertain its northern, eastern and southern limits. As there is no mention of a state to the north of Videha, it is possible that the modern Nepalese Terai formed its northern boundary. On the east, the Kośī is the only natural boundary. The Videhas may have spread up to this river without much difficulty. But the course of this river has shifted from time to time, and so we are not sure of Videha's eastern limit. The Kośī probably emptied its water into the Brahmaputra in the seventh century A.D. and therefore may have taken a much more easterly course in earlier times.[5] But it does not seem reasonable to suggest that the Videhas spread as far as the northern districts of Bengal. We think the boundary of Videha was a western branch of the main river Kośī.

1. P. H. A. I. p. 55.
2. II. 30. 4.
3. Supra p.
4. S. A. II, pp. 437. 439; D. A. III. 363.
5. Supra pp. 99-100.

It is even more difficult to trace the southern limit of the Videhan territory. In the sixth century B.C., there were two main states on the northern side of the Gaṅgā-Videha and Vaiśālī. As the city of Vaiśālī has been located at Basāṛh, just to the north of the Gaṅgā, the Videhan territory must have been to the north of this.

There should be no doubt about the western boundary. The Sadānīrā[1] as we have shown, is the modern Gandak. The people inhabiting the western bank of the Gandak are quite different in speech and culture from the people on its eastern side. They must have originally belonged to a separate tribe and a different state. Pargiter,[2] taking Sadānīrā as the modern Rāptī, states that "Videha comprised the country from Gorakhpur on the Rāptī to Darbhanga, with Kosala on the west and Aṅga on the east. On the north it approached the hills and on the south it was bounded by the small kingdom of Vaiśālī." As the boundary given by Pargiter is too far to the west, we cannot agree that Videha comprised such a large area. The *Suruchi Jātaka*[3] states that the whole kingdom of Videha was three hundred leagues in extent. This is typical of the exaggerations often to be found in the geographical data of Buddhist sources. That the kingdom was of this size does not seem to be plausible. The kingdom of Videha even including the Vaiśālī territory, could not have extended over 1500 to 1800 miles. In the *Rāmāyaṇa*,[4] the territory is generally referred to as Mithilā, but this epic does not throw any light upon its extent. It seems to have been an important kingdom as it has not been included among the states[5] under the influence of king Daśaratha. Varāhamihira[6] locates Videha to the west of the Soṇa and the Narmadā. We are really surprised to see that a scholar of his status could make such a mistake. It is possible that a group of the Videhans might have settled in Central India and gave the region the name of Videha as we find in the case

1. Supra p. 89.
2. J. A. S. B. 1897, p. 89.
3. J. 489 IV pp. 314-325.
4. Bāl. 13,21 etc.
5. Ayo.-10. 37.
6. *Bṛhatsaṁhitā*-11. 11.

of the Ikshvākus and the Kosalas. Otherwise it is impossible to account for Varāhamihira's statement.

In the sixth century B.C., before the rise of Buddhism the Videhan kingdom had sunk to a low position. The monarchy had been replaced by a republic and the territory itself formed a component part of the Vajjian confederacy. This is probably the reason why Videha has not been enumerated as one of the sixteen great Janapadas in the *Aṅguttara Nikāya.*[1]

The territory ceased to be a separate state in the sixth century B.C., but its glories and memories persisted for a long time in literature. Inscriptions, which generally refer to states actually in existence, do not mention Videha. Its glory had dwindled long before it became the custom to engrave inscriptions recording the regions conquered by successful kings.

From the sixth century B. C. onward, Videha was almost merged into the Vajji confederacy, whose chief metropolis was Vaiśālī. Since then, the fate of both these regions was joined together and their history is almost the same.

Before dealing with the joint history of these regions, let us discuss the position of the Vajji territory.

VAJJI

The people known as Vajji or Vṛijji are referred to by Pāṇini[2] and Kauṭilya.[3] They appear to have almost merged with the tribe of the Lichchhavis who are more widely referred to. In Indian literature we find the word written in varying forms—Lichchhavi, Lichchhivi, Lechchhavi, Lechchhai and so on. In the Pāli scriptures and the *Arthaśāstra.*[4] they are designated Lichchhavis. The *Mānava Dharmaśāstra* calls them Nichchhavī.[5]

We do not find any reference to the Lichchhavis in Vedic literature. They had probably a late origin in comparison with Videha and Magadha. They championed the causes

1. I. p. 213.
2. IV. 2.131—Madravṛijyoḥ kan
3. *Arthaśāstra* p. 378.
4. Ibid.
5. *Manusaṁhitā* X. 22.

of Buddhism and Jainism and so we find them often referred to and praised in the Buddhist and Jain literature.

The territory of the Lichchhavis was called Vaiśālī, which was also the name of their capital, and lay on the north bank of the Gaṅgā. We have not found any detailed account of its boundary, but from various casual references in Pāli, Prākrit and Sanskrit literature, we can determine it roughly.

The *Rāmāyaṇa*[1] says that Viśvāmitra showed the city of Viśālā, which is probably no other than Vaiśālī, to Rāma and Lakshmaṇa just after crossing the Gaṅgā. The *Udāna*[2] explicitly mentions that the Vaggumuddi river flowed to the east of the Vajji territory. This is the Bāgmatī of modern times, which flows through the Darbhanga district. This river thus seems to have been the eastern limit of the Vaiśālī territory. The kingdom of Videha was on the northern border of the Lichchhavi territory, but no line of demarcation can be traced to distinguish the two territories. As modern Basārh, the site of ancient Vaiśālī, is to the east of the Gaṇḍak we may assume that this river formed a natural boundary on the west. It should be noted that then the Gandak flowed a little to the west of its present course.[3] Rāhula Sānkṛtyāyana believes that modern Dighawara, wherefrom the Gandak flowed in those days, was the western limit of the Vajji territory.[4]

Thus the territory was bounded on the west, south and east respectively by three rivers—the Gandak, the Gaṅgā and the Bāgmatī—while on the north was the kingdom of Videha.

The modern districts of Champaran, Muzaffarpur and a part of Darbhanga may have been comprised in the Lichchhavi territory[5] at the beginning of the sixth century B. C., when the Lichchavis were at the zenith of their power.

The Vajji confederacy consisted of eight members of which the Lichchhavis were by far the most important.[6] Videha

1. Bāl. 45. 10.
2. Udāna III. 3. Vajjisu anupubbena carikañ caramānā yena Vaggumudā nadī.
3. See above. p. 92.
4. *Buddhacharyā*, p. 407.
5. Ibid.
6. P. H. A. I. p. 118.

was also one of them, but it had virtually lost its independent existence and the residents of Vaiśālī or Lichchhavi territory were known as Vaidehī[1] or residents of Videha, while sometimes the whole tract was known as Videha.[2] This suggests that Videha, although no longer an independent and powerful territory, had prevailed over Vaiśālī by the superiority of its culture.

The joint territory of the Videhas and the Lichchhavis was bounded by the Nepalese Terai on the north, the Kośī on the east, the Gaṅgā on the south and the Gandak on the west.

Kauṭilya[3] draws a distinction between the Lichchivikas and the Vṛjjis. Hsüan-Tsang[4] distinguishes Fu-li-chih (Vrijjis) from Fei-she-li (Vaiśālī). The Vṛjjis were probably a separate clan of some power, but Vaiśālī was the common capital of the confederacy. Of the remaining tribes of the Vajjian confederacy, only one name is known that of the Jñātṛikas, famous in Jain legend; they appear to have been largely merged with the Lichchhavis and to have resided in the neighbourhood of Vaiśālī, the Lichchhavi capital.[5] The remaining four tribes must have been quite insignificant.

In the early medieval period, this region was known as Mithilā We have many inscriptions from different sites which designate the tract by this name. But the common people may already have known it by the more modern name of Tirhut. This word is probably a corruption of Tīrabhukti which has been explained in different ways in medieval Sanskrit works. According to the *Mithilā Kāṇḍa*[6] of the *Bṛhadviṣṇu Purāṇa* Tīrabhukti means the land along the banks of the fifteen rivers which flow from the Himālayas to the

1. *Āchārāṅga Sūtra* II. 15, 17; see introduction to S. B. E. XXII p. 12.
2. Ibid.
3. *Arthaśāstra* p. 378.
4. *On Yuan Chwang* p. 81.
5. P. H. A. I. p. 118.
6. Gaṅgāhimavatormadhye nadipañchadaśāntare
Tairabhuktiritikhyāto deśaḥ paramapāvanaḥ
Kauśikīm tu samārabhya gaṇḍakīmadhigamya vai
Yojanaṁ chaturviṁśat vyāyāmaḥ Parikirtitaih.
quoted in History of *Tirhut* by S. N. Singh, p. 2.

Ganges between the Kośī and the Gandak. Some scholars[1] explain Tirhut as connected with Trihutam which means the land of three sacrifices. The second explanation seems to be merely based on an eulogy of this region by its local paṇḍitas and we do not think that it carries any weight. The first explanation may be correct in the sense that the land was encircled by three rivers—the Gaṇḍakī, the Gaṅgā and the Kauśikī.

However we may offer a third explanation. Some seals[2] of the Gupta period have been discovered from the Vaiśālī region with inscriptions addressed to the officers incharge of Tīrabhukti. This seems to suggest that Tīra may have been the proper name of a *bhukti*, which was definitely an administrative unit during the Gupta period. This '*Bhukti*' of Tīra may have been situated in the adjoining tract of the Gandak and Gaṅgā whence the whole region derived its name. The Sanskrit grammarian Vāmana,[3] whose probable date was eighth century A.D., has mentioned Tīrabhukti as the name of a country.

Al-Beruni,[4] who came to India in the train of Mahmud of Ghazni, seems to have referred to this region. He states that opposite to Tilwat,[5] the country to the left is called Nepal. This Tilwat can be no other than the modern Tirhut, which seems to have extended in those days to the extremity of the Nepalese Terai. The Terai people even at present use a dialect which is more akin to the Maithilī language than to Nepali.

As quoted above, the *Mithilā Khaṇḍa* of the *Bṛhad-viṣṇu Purāṇa*, defines the boundary of Tīrabhukti as the Himavat on the north, the Gaṅgā on the south, the Kośī on the east and the Gandak on the west. The *Śaktisaṅgamatantra*, which seems to be a work of the 16th or 17th century[6] A. D., attempts to give a estimate of the limits of the fifty-six countries in and outside India. Sometimes the size of these countries

1. *History of Tirhut* p. 6.
2. A. S. I. (1903) pp. 8-122.
3. *Liṅgānuśāṣana*, p. 18. Vārendrah Tīrabhuktirnāma deśaḥ.
4. *Al-Beruni's India* p. 201.
5. Ibid.
6. I. C. Vol. VIII, pp. 33-34.

is given narrower and sometimes wider than they actually were. The text[1] describes Tīrabhukti as extending from the Gaṇḍakī to the end of the Champakāraṇya, Here the Gaṇḍakī may mean its confluence with the Gaṅgā; Champakāraṇya is definitely the Champaran of modern times. The text is silent about the borders in the other three directions. We may accept the boundary of early Tirhut as given in the *Mithilā Khaṇḍa* of the *Bṛhadviṣṇu Purāṇa*, Even at present this is the boundary of Tirhut excluding the Nepalese Terai.

The inclusion of the Terai in Tirhut or Videha is supported by the Buddhist literature also. The *Saṁyutta Nikāya Aṭṭhakaṭhā*[2] says that there was a 'Pabbataraṭṭha' in Videha. There is no hill in north Bihar excepting a few ranges in the district of Champaran. We may therefore suggest that the 'Pabbataraṭṭha' of the *Saṁyutta Nikāya Aṭṭhakathā* should be identified with the Nepalese Terai.

The Buddhist literature throws a flood of light upon the geography of the Terai. There were many cities and civilized tribes settled in the Terai region. But in modern times the case is quite reverse. At present it is full of jungle and is thinly populated. There seem to have been changes in the climate of the Terai. However we have not got data to tell explicitly when these changes took place and the Terai became depopulated, but from the account of Fa-hsien, who found Kapilavastu deserted, it would appear probable that the process was completed by about A.D. 400.[3]

MALLA

The modern district of Saran, which lies to the west of the Gandak, should have fallen in the Kosala *janapada* according to the evidence of the *Śatapatha Brāhmaṇa*.[4] Owing to the scarcity of facts with a firm chronological basis, we cannot say how long the Kosalan monarchs ruled over this region. From the *Aṅguttara Nikāya*,[5] we learn that the tribal or re-

1. Ch. VII, 48, p. 67.
2. S. N. A. 1, p. 26.
   Videharaṭṭha majjhe pabbataraṭṭhanāma nagaram
3. Fa-hsien,—*The Record of the Buddhistic Kingdoms*, *Ch.* XXII p. 49.
4. I. IV. I.
5. I. p. 213.

publican states such as the Mallas and Moriyas held sway in this region. The Mallas were divided into two branches—the Mallas of Pāvā and the Mallas of Kuśīnārā.[1] Both places have been identified in the district of Gorakhpur.[2] We are not sure of the region where the Moriyas ruled. The Buddhist literature associates them with Pipphalivana which is generally identified with Nyagrodhavana[3] of Hsüan-Tsang, a village in the Gorakhpur district of Uttar Pradesh and therefore they are outside our province. Having all these considerations in view, we can assume that the modern Saran district was a part of the Malla territory. The people living in this region differ in dialect and culture from those who inhabit the area to the east of the Gandak. The Mallas were the close allies[4] of the Lichchhavis and they formed a confederation to oppose the Magadhan ruler. We do not certainly know what became of the Mallas, but it is possible that they were subjugated by Ajātaśatru with their neighbours, the Lichchhavis.[5]

AṄGA

The ancient state of Aṅga has been variously mentioned in Sanskrit, Pāli and Prākrit literature, but altogether the references are hardly sufficient to give any detailed knowledge of this state as they do in the cases of Magadha and the Vajji territories.

We find the Aṅgas mentioned for the first time in the *Atharvaveda*,[6] where they are held in contempt with the Gāndhārīs, Mujavants and Magadhas. The *Gopatha Brāhmana*[7] alludes to the Aṅgas with the Magadhas. From this it appears that the Aṅgas were a people of the east and hence it can be assumed that they had settled in the region to the east of the Magadhas which later came to be known as Aṅga after the name of the tribe.

1. Kuśā Jātaka No. 531, pp. 278-312; D. II. p. 165.
2. A. G. I—Map XI, opposite p. 445.
3. D. A. II. p. 609; *On Yuan Chwang* II pp. 23-24; A. G. I. p. 491.
4. *Kalpa Sūtra* p. 266 (S. B. E. XXII).
5. Bhandarkar—Charmichael Lectures (1918) p. 79.
6. V. 22. 14.
7. II. 9.

The *Rāmāyaṇa*[1] mentions the Aṅga country between the river Gaṅgā and the Sarayū. We know certainly that the Aṅgas were not found in this region in the historical period. However N. L. Dey[2] derives the conclusion from this that "the northern portion of the country of Magadha along the southern bank of the Ganges was then included in the country of Aṅga." But this is hardly credible when we see the Aṅgas occupying only a small territory in the beginning of the sixth century B.C. It seems probable that the *Rāmāyaṇa* contains an ancient tradition of the migration of the Aṅgas from west to east in the remote past, when they may have settled between the Gaṅgā and the Sarayū in the course of their eastward march.

According to the *Rāmāyaṇa*,[3] the country was named Aṅga, because Madana (the Hindu Cupid), being burnt by the anger of Śiva, had cast off his body in this region. The *Mahābhārata* and the Purāṇas do not admit this story and ascribe the origin of Aṅga to a son of Bali who bore the name Aṅga. But all these derivations seem to be mere legends. It is probable that the territory got its name from the tribe inhabiting the area.

Aṅga is identified with the present districts of Bhagalpur, Monghyr and a portion of Santhal Paraganas. However its limits have varied from time to time. The natural boundary on the north was the Gaṅgā and according to the *Champeya Jātaka*,[4] the river Champā flowed between the states of Magadha and Aṅga and thus formed the latter's western boundary. Taking the Champā as the western limit of Aṅga, we shall have to assume on the basis of its present course, that a major portion of the district of Bhagalpur was not under the Aṅgas as scholars erroneously think, but under the Magadhas. The Aṅga territory seems to have comprised the portions of Santhal Parganas and Bhagalpur districts. We have no authoritative evidence to determine its limit on the south and east. In the south-east of the Bhagalpur district, there is a place on the border of Bihar and West Bengal, called

1. Bāl. Ch. 23.
2. J. A. S. B. (1914), p. 318.
3. Bal. 23. 14.
4. J-IV. o. 506 pp. 454-468. Aṅga Magadha raṭṭhānam antare.

Teliagarhi, which was very important from the strategical point of view. In former days, armies would march from west to east through this pass of the Rajamahal hills.[1] This pass might have been the eastern limit of Aṅga, while on the south this state comprised the northern portion of Santhal Parganas. But, according to Sir George Birdwood, the districts of Birbhum and Murshidabad also formed a part of Aṅga.[2] We have no evidence that at any time Aṅga expanded over such a large tract. If it is true, the Aṅgas must have risen to such an eminent position before the rise of Magadha. It seems that the kings of Aṅga in those days expanded their territory in all directions. The *Vidhura Pandita Jātaka*[3] describes Rājagṛha as a city of Aṅga. The *Mahābhārata*[4] refers to a king of Aṅga who sacrificed on the mount Vishṇupada, which is probably the sacred hill at Gayā. This shows that Magadha was at sometime or other under the suzerainty of Aṅga. We find Aṅga and Vaṅga forming one Vishaya in the *Sabhāparva* of the *Mahābhārata*.[5] The *Kathā-saritsāgara*[6] says that Vithāṅkapura was a city of Aṅga on the sea.

We have grave doubts in accepting Vaṅga as a part of Aṅga. In later times Vaṅga was a territory in the south-east corner of the united Bengal. The area now falls in Eastern Pakistan. As far as we know there was no territory called Vaṅga when the power of Aṅga was in the ascendancey. If the resources of such a vast dominion were at the disposal of the rulers of Aṅga, we do not find sufficient reasons for their defeat at the hands of Bimbisāra, who was the chieftain of the then petty state of Magadha.

From the *Rāmāyaṇa*[7] we may gather that at some time the Aṅga kings either ruled the Kośī area (*Kauśikī Kshetra*) or had overwhelming influence in this region. The courtesans of Aṅga are said to have beguiled Rishya Śṛṅga from his hermitage in this area and brought him to the Aṅga capital.

1. *History of Bengal* Vol. II pp. 5-6.
2. G. D. A. M. I. p. 7. The author does not give a reference to the work of Birdwood, much less to Birdwood's original source.
3. J. Vol. VI. No. 545 pp. 225-329.
4. Śānti Parva, 29. 35.
5. II. 44. 9.
6. pp. 25, 26, 35, 115 etc.
7. Bāl, Ch. 10.

It would be hardly possible to perpetrate such an act in a foreign territory.

AṄGUTTARĀPA

The *Kauśikikṣetra*, which lies to the north of Aṅga across the river Gaṅgā, was probably known as Aṅguttarāpa[1] to Buddhist scholars. The *Saṁyutta Nikāya Commentary*[2] explains it as a kingdom of Aṅga, near the water, across the Gaṅgā. This makes it quite clear that the region to the north of the Gaṅgā was sometimes looked upon as a part of the Aṅgadeśa. This Aṅguttarāpa should thus be identified with the modern Purnea and Saharsa districts. A large part of these districts in our days remains submerged under water for the major part of the year. It is not improbable that the present condition prevailed in this area in the remote past and is indicated in the *Saṁyutta Nikāya* by the term *Aṅguttarāpa*, "the waters to the north of Aṅga."

This is probably the land which has been referred to as 'Jalodbhava' (reclaimed from the swamp) in the *Mahābhārata*[3] Raychaudhuri[4] is inclined to identify this land with that of Videha but the Videhan king defeated by Bhīma has been referred to separately in the same chapter.[5] Nor was Videha ever so much under water as the area to the east of it.

The only doubt which can be raised is the location of the river Mahī[6] to the north of which Aṅguttarāpa is said to have been situated. The Mahī has been identified with a small rivulet of the same name in the district of Saran.[7] All the rivers of this region flow from the north to south, therefore Aṅguttarāpa cannot be to the north of any river other than the Gaṅgā. Here *Mahī* seems to be used as an adjective of the mighty Gaṅgā which flows from west to east.

1. Vol. II. pp. 437, 439; Dh. A. III p. 363.
2. Ibid. Aṅga eva so janapado, Gaṅgāyā (Mahāmahī Gaṅgāyā) pana ya uttarena āpo, tāsm avidure.
3. II. 30. 4.
4. P. H. A. I. p. 55 (footnote).
5. II. 30. 13.
6. S. N. A. II. pp. 437, 439.
7. See above p. 59.

Thus it would not be surprising if the Aṅga territory extended on both banks of the Gaṅgā. The modern Saharsa district was formerly the northern part of the Bhagalpur district, from which it was separated only a few years back.

Magadha, which seems originally to have been a vassal of Aṅga, apparently threw off the yoke of servitude from its neck, sometime in the first half of the sixth century B.C. and later on Bimbisāra invaded Aṅga itself.[1] The Aṅgas could not stand before the rising power of Magadha and their territory was permanently annexed, and a prince from Magadha ruled over Aṅga with its capital at Champā.[2]

Although Aṅga had no separate existence after the sixth century B. C., the later literary works very often refer to the kings of Aṅga. This is probably because the early rulers of Aṅga[3] had once wielded a great deal of influence, which found expression in the works of scholars of later centuries. The *Śaktisaṅgama Tantra*[4] gives a fanciful boundary of the Aṅga territory. It says that Aṅga extended from Vaidyanātha to Bhuvaneśa. Vaidyanātha is a well-known place in the district of Santhal Parganas and Bhuvaneśa is probably no other than Bhuvaneśvara, the new capital o Orissa. It seems quite an exaggeration to suggest that Aṅga ever extended to such a distance as to comprise modern Bhuvaneśvara. It may be that the divisions of the countries in the *Saktisaṅgama Tantra* are based on some special geographical terminology of Śāktism. On the other hand this passage may simply represent the echo of the ancient glory of the king of Aṅga.

Although the kingdom of Aṅga had become an integral part of the Magadhan empire, the region long retained its separate identity and we find it often mentioned in the inscriptions of the tenth and eleventh centuries. In the early 12th century it was under the sway of Mahana, the maternal grandfather of Kumāra Devī, the wife of Govindachandra of Kanauj (1174—84 A.D.), who was king Rāmapāla's viceroy in Aṅga.[5]

1. S. B. E. XVII. p. 1; Pariśiṣṭaparva VII. 22.
2. *Niryāvalī Sūtra*, p. 3; J. A. S. B. (1914) p. 321.
3. Ait. Bra. VIII. 2. Samantāṁ Sarvataḥ pṛthivīṁ Jayan.
4. Ch. VII. 16.
5. *History of Bengal*, Vol. I. pp. 165-166.

With the fall of Magadha in the beginning of the 13th century A.D. this region too passed into the hands of the Muslims.

MODĀGIRI

From the *Mahābhārata*,[1] we gather that the *Kauśikī-Kshetra* and Modāgiri had their own kings, who were defeated by the Pāṇḍava prince. The word Modāgiri seems to have been derived from Mudgagiri. These references may in fact represent petty chiefs reigning in post-Mauryan times, when the legend of the *Mahābhārata* was brought up-to-date and almost every region of the then known India was incorporated into the story. The former kingdom, which was to the north of the Gaṅgā, might have cut off its conneetion with Aṅga and formed a principality of its own. But we have no material available to ascertain the limit of Modāgiri. The territory of Modāgiri or Mudgagiri (Monghyr) may have comprised the region adjoining the present Patna and Gayā districts.

Hsüan-Tsang[2] mentions the capital of a kingdom under the name of I—lan-na-po-fa-to which has been generally identified with the Hiraṇya Parvata. This is probably the hill in the neighbourhood of Monghyr, the Modāgiri of the *Mahābhārata*. The pilgrim estimated the circuit of this kingdom as 3000 li, equivalent to 500 miles. Cunningham,[3] therefore, observes that "the kingdom was bounded by the Ganges on the north and by the great forest-clad mountains on the south and as its circle has been estimated as 3000 li or 500 miles, it must have extended to the south as far as the famous mountain of Pārasanātha." He, therefore, fixes its limit as extending from Lakhiserai to Sultangunj on the Gaṅgā in the north and from the western end of the Pārasanātha hill to the junction of the Barakar and the Damuda river in the south.[4]

But we have every reason to doubt the statement of Hsüan Tsang when he mentions Hiraṇya Parvata as an independent kingdom. We have no authoritative source to show when an independent kingdom was founded in that

1. II. 30. 21.
2. *On Yuan Chwang* II p. 178.
3. A. G. I. p. 546.
4. Ibid.

region to last until the reign of Harsha. The only possibility is that there may have been local chieftains who told the pilgrim that their territory covered such a wide area. In the early part of the seventh century A.D., the kingdom must have been under Harsha and the inscription from the Mandāra[1] hill shows that the whole tract had passed under Ādityasena of Magadha in the latter half of the seventh century A.D.

We have no independent historical evidence other than Hsüan-Tsang to throw any light upon the independent principality of Modāgiri. Hence the existence of this kingdom is not above suspicion.

MAGADHA

We do not know how the word 'Magadha' originated or what it signifies. *The Ṛg-veda* does not mention this word. In the *Yajur-veda*, we often find minstrels called 'Māgadhas' singing on the occasion of sacrifices.[2] It is possible that the region from which the minstrels went to attend the sacrifices, was called Magadha. But we are not sure whether the land 'Magadha' was named after the 'Māgadha' or minstrel or vice-versa. Martin[3] thinks that Magadha was named after the Maga caste of Brāhmaṇa who are said to have come from Śākadvīpa, but we now know that the region was known by the name of Magadha long before the Śakas had penetrated into India.

There are some scholars such as Zimmer[4] and Weber,[5] who identify Magadha with the region known as Kīkaṭa in the Ṛg-veda. From a hymn of the Ṛg-vedə.[6] it appears that Kīkaṭa was famous for its cows which were not milked, The Aryans must have looked towards those cows with greedy eyes. At present however Magadha is definitely not famous for her cows, nor do we find any reference to the abundance of cows in Magadha at any later period of history. This

2. A. S. I. A. R. (1902-3) p. 203.
1. *Vājasaneyī Saṁhitā* xxx. 5. 22; *Taittirīya Brāhmaṇa* III. 5, 1.1.
2. *Eastern India* Vol. I. p. 406.
3. Altindisches Leben 31. 118.
4. Indisches Studien 1, 186.
5. III. 53, 14.
Kim te kriṇvanti Kīkaṭeṣu gavo nāśiraṁ duhe natapanti dhanaṁ.
Ānu śai Pramagandasya vedo naichaśākhaṁ Maghavanra ndhyāmaḥ

would suggest that Kīkaṭa was a land other than Magadha. The Hidiyana region of the Punjab is more famous for its cows and abundance of milk. It might have been outside the Aryan zone in the days of the *Ṛg-veda*, but near enough for the Aryans to be well-acquainted with its cattle. Secondly Pramagaṇḍa, the king of the Kīkaṭas, was well-known to the Aryans[1] who fought against them. This battle must have taken place somewhere in the western part of U.P. We do not see any possibility of Pramagaṇḍa coming from such a distant place as Magadha to oppose the Aryan horde. However Yaska[2] has identified Kīkaṭa with Magadha and following him later writers usually did so without considering the point. The author of the *Vāyu Purāṇa*[3] identified Kīkaṭa with Magadha, while its commentator identified with Gayā district only. The *Śaktisaṅgama Tantra*[4] also follows the *Vāyu Purāṇa* and explains Kīkaṭa as a region extending from Charṇādri to Gṛdhrakūṭa to the south of Magadha. Martin[5] identifies Charṇādri with Chunar in the district of Mirzapur and the latter with Gidhaur in the Jamui sub-division of the Monghyr district. He further says that "It is by many alleged that the whole Kīkaṭa in more modern times took the name of Magadha from the Magas who settled in its eastern part; but this is here denied and all the country west from the Sona retains the name of Kīkaṭa, which it anciently held, while the Magas from the Śākadvīpa communicated their name to the eastern part alone."[6]

We do not know on what basis the author of the *Śaktisangama Tantra* extended Kīkaṭa from Chunar to Gidhaur. The area round about Chunar must have been in ancient times either under Kosala or Vatsa. It cannot have been a part of the original Kīkaṭa. The *Abhidhānachintāmaṇi*[7] also identifies Kīkaṭa with Magadha. But the identification is uncertain and doubted by Oldenburg[8] and Hillebrandt.[9] It would

1. Ṛg—III. 53, 14.
2. *Nirukta* VI. 32.
3. Ch. 108- 74.
4. Ch. VIII.
5. *Eastern India* Vol. I. p. 406.
6. *Eastern India* Vol. I. p. 406.
7. Ch. 4. 26.
8. *Buddh* pp. 400, 402, 403; *Ṛg-veda-Noten* 1, 253.
9. *Vedische Mythologies* 1, 14-18.

seem that while Kīkaṭa was originally the name of a Punjab tribe in Vedic times, it was later sometimes used for parts of Magadha.

The word Magadha actually occurs in the *Atharva-Veda*[1] where its inhabitants are held in deep contempt together with the Aṅgas, Gāndhāris and the Mujavants. Even at a later date there was much uncertainty as to whether Magadha was to be included in the sacred land of the Madhyadeśa, where Brahmin orthodoxy was supposed to prevail. According to Varāhamihira,[2] Magadha was situated in the eastern division of India. However a Brāhmanical work, the *Vāyu-Purāṇa*[3] included Magadha—in earlier texts often considered a non-Aryan land—in the Madhyadeśa.

Though Magadha was not actually the Kīkaṭa of the *Ṛgveda*, the name was occasionally given to this region on the basis of Yāska's erroneous statement. The later Vedic literature almost ignores Kīkaṭa, but we find that the word Magadha[4] is in general vogue. The Jain and Buddhist literature also full of references to this region. Mahāvīra and Buddha spent the major part of their ascetic lives in Magadha.

The *Rāmāyaṇa* and the *Mahābhārata* often refer to Magadha. Aśoka used the word Magadha in one of his inscriptions[5] referring to himself as king of that land. The Hāthīgumphā inscription[6] of Khāravela also refers to it. We find it frequently mentioned in the inscriptions of the Chandelas, Rāshṭrakūṭas, and the Pālas etc.

Sir George Grierson[7] states that the inhabitants of the Gayā district still call it Maga, a name doubtless derived from Magadha. But in our personal experience, no word such as Mag is now-a-days in use. The people of this locality and its adjoining tract call it Magah, which is definitely a Prākṛitised form of Magadha.

1. V. 22. 14.
2. *Bṛhatsaṁhitā* Ch. XVI—6.
3. Ch. 45. 111.
4. *Baudhyāyana Dharma Sūtra* 62. 13; *Śrauta Sūtra* XX, 13 etc.
5. C. I. I. Vol. I. pp. 172-73.
6. *Select Inscriptions* p. 209.
7. E. R. E. V. 18 ff.

In literature and inscriptions, we often find a word Pīṭhīpati.[1] The *Rāmacharita*[2] explicitly mentions Pīṭhī, a state which helped Rāmapāla in overcoming his enemies. The Janibigha inscription[3] recorded in the 83rd expired year of the Lakshmana Sena era (Nov. 1202 A.D.) also refers to the state of Pīṭhī. As the inscription has been discovered in a village only six miles to the east of Bodha Gayā, H. Pandey arrived at the conclusion that the name Piṭhī seems to have been given to the southern portion of Magadha at least about the 12th century A.D. Dr. R. D. Banerjee[4] is not definite about its location and simply state that Pīṭhī may have been a state between Kānyakubja and Gauḍa. K. P. Jayaswal[5] thinks that in the early Sena times Pīṭhī denoted the whole of Bihar except Mithilā. The commentator[6] of the *Rāmacharita* expounds Pīṭhīpati as Magadhādhipati. Dr. Jayaswəl's opinion is positively erroneous, as we find a few other states situated in Bihar which are also said in the *Rāmacharita* to have helped Rāmapāla. Secondly if the King of Pīṭhī had the whole of south Bihar under his suzerainty, as Jayaswal's identification would show, how could he accept Rāmapāla as his overlord, who was inferior to the Pīṭhīpat in resources and strength ? We do not understand how the whole of Magadha could have been included in the state of Pīṭhī. If Pīṭhī covered the whole of Magadha, there was no necessity of referring to Magadha as Pīṭhi. The name Magadha is better known and reputed than Pīṭhī, and any king would have been proud of ruling Magadha, whose ancient history is so glorious. Mr. Pandey[7] seems to be right in locating this state, and the name must have been derived from the Vajrāsana (Pīṭhī=throne or seat) of Buddha at Bodh Gayā. The Pīṭhīpati may have been a chief enjoying much power on account of the religious merits of the place. But S. S. Majumdar[8]

1. E. I. IX pp. 319—28; J. B. O. R. S. Vol. IV pp 273-80.
2. II. 5 (Commentary) p. 42.
3. J. B. O. R. S. Vol. IV opp. 273-280.
4. M. A. S. B. V. No. 3, pp. 86-89.
5. J. B. O. R. S. Vol. VI p. 267.
6. pp. 36, 38.
7. J. B. O. R. S. IV. p. 277.
8. I. C. V. pp. 379-85.

thinks that modern Pirpainti in the eastern part of Bhagalpur district may be identified with the name Piṭhī on philological grounds. His arguments do not seem very sound and we find little similarity in Pīṭhī and Pirpainti. He locates both Pīṭhīs at Pirpainti, and thus totally rejects the existence of any Pīṭhī in the neighbourhood of Bodh Gayā. It is possible that there may have been two Pīṭhīs, one in the district of Gayā and another in that of Bhagalpur, both of which are quite unknown to us at present. In the tenth and eleventh centuries, when the Pālas had a very loose hold on their feudatory chiefs, it was just a fashion to regard oneself as a king. Thus the Sarnath inscription of Kumāradevī and the Janibigha inscription probably refer to two different feudatory chiefs. The place cannot be certainly identified at present.

None of the sources present a clear picture of the exact extension of Magadha. In modern times Magah or Magadha is identified with the district of Patna and Gayā including the northern fringe of the Hazaribagh district. Hence Grierson[1] thinks that Magadha in the time of the Buddha corresponded to the modern district of Gayā only. But the ancient Magadha seems to have had a larger area than the modern word implies. The *Champeya Jātaka*[2] states that the river Champā flowed between Aṅga and Magadha, which shows that a fair portion of the modern Bhagalpur district was actually in Magadha. The Gaṅgā flowed between the Lichchhavi state and Magadha.[3] But we are not sure how far Magadha extended on the west and south. Malalasekara[4] says that "At the time of the Buddha, the kingdom of Magadha was bounded on the east by the river Champā, on the south by the Vindhyan mountains, on the west by the Soṇa and on the north by the Gaṅgā." He gives no reason for his specification of the southern and western boundaries, which are not definitely described in any source known to us.

From the *Mahābhārata*,[5] it appears that there was a state

1. E. R. E. V. p. 171.
2. J. IV. 506.
3. Dh. A. III, 439 ff; Dvy. p. 55.
4. D. P. P. N. Part II p. 403.
5. II. 30. 21; for details, see above p. 99.

called Modāgīri between Magadha and Aṅga. It is possible that this formed a small separate state during the epic period, although it is very doubtful, but this does not show that it was outside the zone of Magadhan culture and language. In a particular region there may be more than one state and so Modāgiri may have been a separate political entity for a time, though it was a part of the Magadhan rāshṭra, in periods when central government was weak, such as that between the fall of the Mauryas and the rise of the Guptas to which much of the geographical information in the epics may apply.

In a vast country like India, dialects change at a distance of a few miles but in spite of slight changes in the dialects of the Monghyr and Gayā and Patna districts, there is much similarity. The people up to Vaidyanatha[1] still use the Māgadhī dialect.

The extension of Magadha on the south has not been defined clearly , though Malālasekara[2] seems to be right when he says that Magadha was bounded on the south by the Vindhyan hills which would form a natural boundary. But the whole chhotanagpur area is full of the Vindhyan ranges. Cunningham[3] therefore extends the limit of Magadha upto the Damudā on the south and N. L. Dey[4] goes as far south as the Singhbhum district. The modern Chhotanagpur area in those days was full of dense forest and human intercourse may have been difficult and rare. It is, therefore possible that those wild areas were loosely under the influence of Magadha but were not actually a part of it. The people of the northern part of the Hazaribagh district still use the Magadhi language and therefore this area may have formed a part of Magadha in ancient days.

On the west N. L. Dey[5] thinks that Magadha extended up to Benaras or near it during the reign of Bimbisāra or Ajātaśatru, but this simply implies that the whole region up to Benaras was under the control of the Magadhan rulers and not that it was a part of Magadha. Cunningham[6] contracts

1. See map opposite p. 1—Linguistic survey of India Vol. 5, Part II.
2. D. P. P. N. II p. 403.
3. A. G. I. p. 518.
4. G. D. A. M. I.; p. 116.
5. Ibid.
6. A. G. I.; p. 518.

the western limit to the Karmanāśā, which is at present the western boundary of Bihar. He bases his arguments on the distances given by Hsüan-Tsang. But the rough measurements given by the pilgrim should not be taken too seriously.

The area to the west of the Soṇa in Bihar to-day falls under the jurisdiction of the Shahabad district. The local dialect is quite different from that of the Gayā and Patna districts and the people do not include themselves in Magadha. At present, they call themselves Bhojpuris, from a place Bhojpur, said to have been founded by king Bhoja of Mālava. The majority of the population is of the Rajput class and belongs to the Parmār clan. On the other hand the population of Magadha is much more mixed. History proves the untrustworthiness of the tradition. King Bhoja of Mālava never extended his power to this region. We can simply conjecture that some Parmār chief may have emigrated to the east after the fall of Mālava into the Muslim hands and named the place after his famous king. The local dialect is also known as Bhojpuri. The people of this region are more akin to the inhabitants of the Balia, Ghazipur and Azamagarh districts of eastern Uttar Pradesh than to those of the rest of southern Bihar.[1] This would point to the fact that the Shahabad district was not normally a part of Magadha.

From the *Rāmāyaṇa*[2] it appears that the hermitage of Viśvāmitra, which is tradionally located at Buxar in the district of Shahabad, was situated in the Kārusha and Maladadeśa. The *Brahmāṇḍa Purāṇa*[3] refers to Vedagarbhapurī, which is identified with modern Buxar, as situated in the Kāruṣa-deśa. Martin[4] says that according to the local tradition the land between the Soṇa and the Karmanāśā was called Kāruṣa-deśa after a daitya of the same name.

The Kāruṣa tribe is scarcely mentioned in the Vedic literature. But it is often alluded to in the epics and the Purāṇas. The Kāruṣa seem to have had several settlements The *Vishṇu-Purāṇa*[5] mentions them with the Matsyas, Chedīs

1. See map opposite p. 1; See p. 41; Linguistic Survey of India Vol. V. Part II.
2. Bāl. 24. 17.
3. Pūrva Khaṇḍa Ch. 5.
4. *Eastern India* Vol. I. p. 405.
5. Vol. II. pp. 158-190.

and Bhojas. Pargiter[1] locates their country to the south of Kāśī and Vatsa between Chedi on the west and Magadha on the east enclosing the Kaimur hills.

The *Vāyu*,[2] *Matsya*[3] and *Mārkaṇḍeya*[4] Purāṇas ascribe the Kāruṣas to the Vindhyan region (*Vindhyāprishṭhavāsinaḥ*). But it is evident that the Karuṣas were also settled in the region between Reva and Shahabad in early times at least.

We are quite at a loss about the Maladas, who, the *Rāmāyaṇa* would suggest, lived in the same region. We have no knoewledge of their origin. However their name may have some affinity with that of the Mallas of the Buddhist literature. Like the Kāruṣas, the Maladas also might have occupied a part of the region simultaneously or one after another. We do not know what happened to them. The Buddhist literature is quite silent about them. But the region became a part of Magadha when Prasenajit finally offered it to a Ajātaśatru.

Hence we can say that Magadha was bounded on the north by the Gaṅgā, on the west by the Soṇa, on the east by the Champā and on the south by the northern fringe of the Hazaribagh district; that is, the region through which the modern Grand Trunk Road passes in this district formed its southern border.

JHĀRAKHAṆḌA

The modern Chhotanagpur area is bounded on the north by the Patna and Bhagalpur divisions, on the east by the state of West Bengal, on the south by the state of Orissa and on the west by the state of Madhya Pradesh.

The tract was almost a complete wilderness in ancient times and human intercourse was very rare and difficult. We hardly find reference to this region in our ancient literature. We have no authoritative source available to tell us the nomenclature or the size of the tract. There were apparently certain isolated places, such as the Pārasnāth hill, where a few ascetics went to meditate in peace and solitude; these are the only places clearly referred to in our sources.

1. J. A. S. B. (1895) p. 255; J. R. A. S. (1914) p. 271.
2. Ch. 45.
3. Ch. 114. 52.
4. Ch. 57.

The Jain literature[1] mentions a region named Sambhuttara or Sumhottara. This region is probably that which was known in later times as Sumha. Rāhula Sānkṛtyāyana[2] understands that Sumha covered a portion of the Hazaribagh and Santhal Pargana districts. As the Jain literature was composed in later centuries we cannot hold the name to be very ancient. The *Mahābhārata*[3] mentions a further region Paśubhūmi in the east, conquered by Bhīma. This region has not been indentified, but one may be tempted to locate it somewhere in the region of Chhotanagpur. In modern Chhotanagpur, there are numerous place names which end in bhūmi, such as Manbhūm, Dhalbhūm, Singhbhūm, and the like. It is possible that Paśubhūmi was a district in this area which received its name from the abundance of its wild animals.

N.L. Dey[4] on the basis of the Greek historians conjectures that the region round the Parasnath hill was called Malladeśa. But the mount Maleus of the Greek writer cannot be definitely located in the region of Parasnath Hill and this information is not supported by any indigenous sources available to us.

Hsüan-Tsang[5] mentions a state Kie-lo-na-su-fa-la-na or Kiraṇa-suvarṇa, the capital of which was 700 li to the north west of Tāmralipti and the same distance from Odra. Cunningham[6] conjectures that the chief city of Kiraṇasuvarṇa must be looked for "along the course of the Suvaṇaṛksha river, somewhere about the districts of Singhbhum and Barabhum" As this territory was 4000 to 4500 li in circuit, Cunningham concludes that it must have comprised all the petty hill states lying between Midnapur on the east and Surguja on the west and between the sources of the Damuda and Vaitaraṇi on the north and south respectively. Cunningham's view is not generally held now-a-days, since it is now known that there was an important city Karṇasuvarṇa in north Bengal[7]

1. Hoernle—the *uvasagadasao* II Appendix.
2. Buddhacharyyā p. 293 (Foot note)
3. II. 30.
4. G. D. M. I., p. 123.
5. *On Yuan Chwang* II p. 191.
6. A. G. I. p. 578.
7. *History of Bengal* Vol. I pp. 13, 28, 31 etc.

and this seems to be refered to by the pilgrim, though his directions would rather take us to the wild regions of south Bihar.

In referring to Jhārakhaṇḍa, Mangovind Banerjee[1] tells us that "the ancient names by which this country was called were Muruṇḍa in the *Vāyu Purāṇa*, Muṇḍa in the *Viṣṇu Purāṇa*, Mindala by Ptolemy and Mondes by Pliny."

The conjecture of Mr. Banerjee is open to doubt. So far as the identification of the Muṇḍas with the Mindala and Mondes are concerned, the statement may be correct. Ptolemy places the Mandali to the south of the Gaṅgā[2] whose chief metropolis was Pāṭaliputra. The Mandalai may denote the Magadhas also, because Pāṭaliputra was their famous seat of Government. If the word Mandalai has been used for the Muṇḍas it shows that the whole tract of Chhotanagpur was regarded as a part of Magadha. They are probably the same people as the Mandeis of Pliny who with the Sauri or Saurabatis occupied the region to the south of Pāṭaliputra.[3]

But we cannot say that the Murundas and the Mundas are identical. Purāṇas such as the *Viṣṇu* and *Vāyu* use different terms for them as accepted by Banerjee himself. The Mauruṇḍas, in Sanskrit literature and inscriptions are generally referred to in association with the Śakas.[4] According to Konow[5] the word 'Muruṇḍa' means master in the language of the invaders. It suggests that they were connected with the royal families. On the basis of the Khoh Copper Plates[6] of the G.E. 193 and 197, Smith[7] arrived at the conclusion that "The Muruṇḍas may possibly have been settled in the hill country of Riwa along the Kaimur range or more probably further south in the Vindhya or north Dekkan or possibly in the Chhotanagpur." But there is nothing in the inscription which may suggest their home in the region located by Smith. If the occurrence of the name Muruṇḍa Devī or Muruṇḍa Svāminī, suggests that the queen so called

1. J. B. O. R. S. Vol. XXVI pp. 189-223.
2. *Ancient India* (Ptolemy) VII', I, 72-3.
3. Ibid. p. 135.
4. C. I. I. Vol. III. p. 8.
5. C. I. I. Vol. II. p. 20.
6. C. I. I. Vol. III. pp. 125-32
7. I. A. pp. 192. 257-60.

belonged to the Muruṇḍa race, we cannot suppose that they lived in the region, to the ruler of which she was wedded. Hemachandra[1] explicitly states that the Muruṇḍas belonged to Lampāka which is commonly identified in the north west. The Allahabad Pillar Inscription[2] of Samudra Gupta also suggests that the Muruṇḍas dwelt in the northwest with other foreign tribes. This evidence is strong enough to show that the Muruṇḍa had not spread so far to the east as to occupy the Chhotanagpur region. Their association with the Śakas suggests their elevated position in the society. Howsoever barbarous and pastoral the Muruṇḍas might have been before their immigration into India, when they held the sceptre in their hands they must have been endowed with the quality and capacity to rule over a people who were highly civilized. Such a race could hardly have sunk to a position so low as the Muṇḍas are at the present time. Moreover the Muṇḍas are a dominant division of the aboriginals of the Chhotanagpur region. Had they been the descendants of the Murṇḍas, we should have found them in other parts of Central India also because the Muruṇḍas might have been expected to have penetrated other parts of India as well as this small region so far from their place of origin.

As far as the evidence of the Purāṇas is concerned, we know that these texts were compiled in later times and many discrepancies have crept in owing to the mistakes of the copyists. We cannot rely much upon them. The *Vāyu* and *Viṣṇu Purāṇas* say that the Muruṇḍas will succeed the Tocharians a component tribe of the Yueh-chis[3]. Should we assume that the Yueh-chis or the Kushāṇas ruled over this region and that they were succeeded by the present Munda race ? The hypothesis of Mr. Banerjee is not tenable in the light of further research. Therefore we cannot identify the Muruṇḍas with the Muṇḍas of the region of modern Chhotanagpur.

The Jain sources throw a faint ray of light on the geography of this region. But they are so vague in their description that it is very difficult to identify the places they mention with any

1. *Abhidhānachintāmaṇi*, 4. 26.
2. C. I. I. Vol. III. p. 8.
3. *Studies in the Mahābhārata* p 141.

amount of certainty. However scholars have tried to locate a few places in the Jhārakhaṇḍa area.

Bhanga[1] or Bhaṅgī is included in the twenty-five Aryan countries with Pāvā as its capital. This kingdom is referred to in the *Mahābhārata*[2] also. It probably comprised the districts of Hazaribagh and Manbhum.[3] Its capital Pāvā is located in the region near Pārasnāth hill.[4]

Another region Daḍḍhabhūmi is said to have been inhabited by many Mlechchhas.[5] It may be identified with modern Dhalbhum in the Singhbhum district.

Lādāhadeśa of the Jains was divided into Vajjabhumi and Subhabhūmi.[6] The latter may be the Singhbhum[7] district of Bihar.

The word Jhārkhaṇḍa has been used for this region in later Sanskrit literature but we cannot actually ascertain when it was first named thus. The Muslims call this region Kokrah.[8] There were no kings of sigificance in this area. The petty chiefs who occupied small lands belonged generally to the aboriginal tribes. Local traditions declare that they were Nāgavaṁśī[9] chiefs, which is sufficient to indicate their descent from wild tribes.

About 1100 A.D. this region is said to have contained certain small kingdoms whose rulers helped Rāmapāla in recovering his ancestral throne. These are the Kujavatī, Tailakampa and Kayaṅgala Maṇḍala. The Kujavatī[10] kingdom is identified with a place of the same name, 14 miles to the north of Nayadumka in the Santhal Parganas. Tailakampa,[11] on the basis of similarity of names, has been identified with modern Talkupi in the Manbhum district. The Kayaṅgala[12] Maṇḍala is to the south of the Rajamahal hills. It is probably the same as Kajangala mentioned by

1. *Bṛhatkalpa Sūtra* I. 50.
2. II. 31. 11.
3. S. B. M. p. 379.
4. Ibid p. 375.
5. *Life in Ancient India as Depicted in the Jain Canons* p. 278.
6. *Āchārāṅga Sūtra* p. 281.
7. Imperial Gazeteer Vol. XII. p. 529.
8. Birt-*Chhotanagpur* p. 12, Ain-i-Akbarī.
9. Ibid p. 11.
10. *Rāmacharita*, II. 5. (Commentary) p. 42.
11. *Birbhumer Itihās* p. 59.
12. *History of Bengal* Vol. I. p. 157.

Hsüan-Tsang.[1] The small territory of Rāmapāla thus spread over the border of Western Bengal and eastern Bihar and it is very possible that all these states were under petty chieftains who helped their nominal overlord. All these states soon passed into the hands of the Muslims in the beginning of the the 13th century A.D.

ADMINISTRATIVE DISTRICTS OF BIHAR

In ancient India, states were divided into several types of administrative unit. All such administrative divisions depended upon the size of the state. The terms applied to these divisions differed from state to state and time to time. However from Gupta times onwards numerous inscriptions show that Bihar was divided into *Bhuktis* and that the latter were subdivided into the *Viṣayas*. It seems possible, from one inscription that we consider below, that the *Viṣayas* were also sometimes divided into smaller units which comprised several villages.

The names of only two *Bhuktis* of ancient Bihar have come to light through inscriptions. These are Tīrabhukti[2] and Śrīnagarabhukti[3] which was probably known as Magadhabhukti[4] also.

No literature or inscriptions throw any light upon the size and limits of these *Bhuktis*. However Tīrabhukti seems probably to have comprised the whole of the modern Tirhut division, excluding the Saran district[5] but including Purnea and Saharsa district of our own time. The Bangaon[6] Copper Plate (12th Century A.D.) refers to a Hardeya Viṣaya in Tīrabhukti. As Bangaon is situated in the Saharsa district, it is apparent that the eastern limit of Tīrabhukti extended up to that district. To the north of Gangā, this is the only *Bhukti* known to us. We have no evidence that the district of Saran was a part of Tīrabhukti, as it is of present Tirhit.

There may have been a large number of Viṣayas or districts in Tīrabhukti but we find only a few of them mentioned.

1. *On Yuan Chwang* II. pp. 182-83.
2. A. S. I. (190?-4) Vaiśālī seals pp. 107-20.
3. E. I. Vol. XVII. pp. 310-27; XVIII. pp. 304-7.
4. M. A. S. I. No. 66 (S. 1, 687) p. 33.
5. See above p. 191.
6. E. I. Vol. XXIX. pp. 48-56.

The Panchobha Copper Plate[1] (12th Century A. D.) records the Jambūbanī Viṣaya, while the above mentioned Bangaon Copper Plate refers to Hardeya Viṣaya. The Panchobha-Copper Plate does not mention the Bhukti in which Jambūbani Viṣaya was situated. This Viṣaya has been identified with Jamui[2] in the Monghyr district to the south of the Gaṅgā. But there is no valid proof of its identification except the similarity of sounds. The plate was found in a village, five or six miles to the south of Darbhanga. In it, the Māṇḍalīka Sangrāmagupta is described as the lord of Jayapura, which is identified with Jayanagar in the same district. One cannot imagine that the territory of a *Māṇḍalīka rājā* or local baron would have extended to such a distance as to cover the Jamui sub-division. We shall deal with its identification in the chapter on place-names.

An image inscription of the reign of Vigrahapāla III, from Nawalgaḍha[3] in the Begusarai sub-division, which is to the north of the Gaṅgā, mentions a Kṛmilā Viṣaya. The same Viṣaya has found mention as being in Śrīnagarabhukti[4] in inscriptions found to the south of the Gaṅgā. Taking these inscriptions at their face value it appeares that the viṣaya of Kṛmilā spread on both banks of the Gaṅgā, as does the Monghyr district in our times. But we have grave doubts whether the Kṛmilā Viṣaya occupied any portion of land to the north of the Gaṅgā. Though this Viṣaya is more than once mentioned in inscriptions from south Bihar, the Nawalgaḍha Image Inscription is the solitary example from which we may infer its extension to the north of the Gaṅgā. But the region to the north of the Gaṅgā formed a part of Tīrabhukti. There is no reason to believe that a single Viṣaya spread on both banks of the Gaṅgā and formed a part of two different *Bhuktis*. The image which has been found at Nawalgaḍh might have been taken there from south Bihar, which also formed a part of the Pāla territory.

The Hardeya Viṣaya of the Bangaon Copper Plate has not yet been properly identified. But this administrative

1. J. B. O. R. S. Vol. V. pp. 582-96.
2. Ibid.
3. G. D. College Bulletin No. I.
4. E. I. Vol. XVIII p. 306.

unit must have been somewhere in the district in which the plate was found, as we shall discuss in our chapter on topography.[1]

A seal[2] from Basaṛha records the Vaiśālī Viṣaya. Vaiśālī was definitely an important place during the Gupta kings. This Viṣaya should have occupied the area now in the jurisdiction of the Muzaffarpur district. But the Panchoba Copper Plate of Sangrāmagupta (12th century A.D.) records a village Baniyagrāma which is probably the village Bania[3] in the vicinity of Vaiśālī, which ought to fall within the limit of the Vaiśālī Viṣaya. From this record, we arrive at the conclusion that Vaiśālī had lost its importance in later centuries and there was probably a redistribution of administrative units under the Pālas, when Vaiśālī was not selected as the headquarters of any administrative division. The Bhagalpur Copper Plate of Narayanapāla mentions the Kakṣa Viṣaya. The location of this Viṣaya is still uncertain.

The only *Bhukti* to the south of the Gaṅgā which has been referred to is Śrīnagara Bhukti. Dr. Hirananda[4] identified Śrīnagara with modern Patna. Śrīnagara means "the celebrated city" and thus he seems to be right in his conjecture. Pāṭaliputra was the chief metropolis of the Pālas and had enjoyed its eminence for a very long time; hence people may have referred to it as Śrīanagara out of respect. But Hirananda further suggests that Śrīnagara might have been only a part of Pāṭaliputra. At present there is no part of Patna which has a name bearing the slightest similarity to Śrīnagara. This Bhukti may have contained several Viṣayas but we find only Gayā, Rājagṛha and Kṛmilā mentioned in our sources.[5] The Nālandā Plate[6] of Samudragupta mentions a Viṣaya Vaiva (y)........., the full reading of which is not clear. This record[7] is said to be a spurious one and of a later date. This does not however invalidate its geographical data, and the places referred to must have existed somewhere in the locality.

1. See below p. 265
2. A. S. I. A. R. 1903-4, Seal 27, p. 110.
3. See below p. 265
4. E. I. Vol. XVII, p. 311.
5. E. I. XVII p. 311 ff.; XVIII. p. 306 etc.
6. *Select Inscription* p. 263.
7. Ibid.

The existence of this Viṣaya, however, is not corroborated by any other evidence. The Rājagṛha and Gayā Viṣayas must have been adjacent to each other. We find the villages recorded in the Nālandā Copper Plate[1] of Devapāla as existing in the same locality. We must assume therefore that between the time of the spurious plate (perhaps 6th or 7th century A.D.) and the Pāla period, there was a redistribution of boundaries and changes in the official nomenclature. The Kṛmilā Viṣaya probably covered the area round modern Kiul, which is the western part of the Monghyr district. The Deovarnarak inscription mentions the Vālavī Viṣaya in the Śrinagar Bhukti. This Viṣaya should be in the Shahabad district, but exact location is not certain.

There are some other small administrative units referred to in inscriptions. The Nālandā Copper Plate describes a few *Nayas* and *Vīthis* which seem to have been sub-divisions of a Viṣaya. They may have been like the *Thanas* of modern times.

It is strange that terms *Naya* and *Vīthi* seems to be used for divisions of equal status but in different Viṣayas. Although the Gayā and Rājagṛha Vishayas were situated adjacently, the smaller units in Rājagṛha Viṣaya were called *Naya*, while those of the Gayā Viṣaya were called *Vīthis*. We are not in a position at present to tell why such different terms were used in two adjacent Viṣayas for the same units. The word *Vīthi* signifies a market place or street. Hence we can conjecture that the Vīthis might have been administrative units centred on important market places in the Gayā Viṣaya.

We do not know what the word *Naya* signifies in this context. This would seem to have some affinity with the root 'Ni' meaning 'to lead', and so the word may signify the leading place of a small area. The Gayā Viṣaya contained Kumuda-sūtra Vīthi and Jambūnadī Vīthi.[2] We have found no reference to other *Vīthis* in the district. The Kumuda-sūtra Vīthi[3] has not been identified. But a village in this Vīthi is mentioned along with the villages in the Rājagṛha Viṣaya, recorded in the Nālandā Copper Plate of Devapāla (9th century A.D.). The villages of Rājagṛha Viṣaya have

1. E. I. Vol. XVII, pp. 310-27.
2. E. I. Vol. XXIII. p. 261.
3. E. I. Vol. XVII. p. 310-27.

been located at a little distance from each other, therefore it is not unlikely that the village of the Kumuda-sūtra Vīthi was in the adjoining locality. Therefore the Kumuda-śūtra Vīthi must have been somewhere round about Rājagṛiha. Our conjecture is that this Vīthi may have been in the modern Nawada or Sadar sub-division of the Gayā district. The Jambūnadī Vīthi may have been in the Jehanabad sub-division of the Gayā district. A small river called Jamunā flows through that sub-division and therefore it is probable that this Vīthi was on the bank of that river, as the name indicates.

The Rājagṛha Viṣaya contained Ajapur, Pilipinka and Achalā Nayas. Hirananda[1] has identified the first two of these Nayas with the areas surrounding the modern villages of Ajapur and Pilikh or Pilichha, which are not very far from Nālandā. The Achalā Naya has not been identified. On the similarity of sounds, the first two identifications seem to be correct.

The Maner Copper Plate of Chandradeva[2] (12th century A.D.) alludes to a further administrative terms. The record refers to a Maniyāra Pattala. Maniyāra[3] has been identified with modern Maner in the Patna district. This is an important place in the Patna district even at present. But we have no knowledge as to what the term '*Pattala*' stands for. It may have been applied to a Vīthi or even to a Viṣaya.

We know the name of another Viṣaya from one of the Nālandā seals[4] which was issued by an officer of the same Viṣaya. It is called Soṇantrāla Viṣaya which means the region between the Soṇa. But the sense is not at all clear. Hirananda explains that the unit comprised the region between the Soṇa and the Gaṅgā, that is the district of Shahabad. But his conjecture cannot be finally accepted because these rivers do not flow at all parallel to one another and hence there is no real intermediate region between them. Secondly, if we take the region on the confluence of the two rivers, it can be applied for the district of Patna also. We think that *antarāla* indicates that land where the Sona fell into the Gaṅgā

1. E. I. Vol. XVII. pp. 310-27.
2. J. B. O. R. S. Vol. II. pp. 441-47.
3. Ibid.
4. M. A. S. I. No. 66 S. 1. 793 p. 33.

and which we call 'Diara' at present. The 'Diara' falls in both the districts—Shahabad and Patna. But the eastern Diara—that of the Patna district probably fell under the jurisdiction of Maniyāra Pattala, which we find mentioned in the Maner Copper Plate of Govindchandra[1] (12th century A. D.). Therefore, the western Diara may have been known as the Soṇāntarāla Viṣaya.

There must have been other Bhuktis and many more smaller administrative units. But owing to the scarcity of official records of that period and their destruction, only a very few are known to us.

1. J. B. O. R. S. Vol. II, pp. 441-47.

CHAPTER VI

PLACE NAMES

The state of Bihar has played a dominant role in the history of ancient India. For centuries, the history of Bihar was the history of India, not only in the arena of politics, but also in that of culture and religion as well. It was the cradle land of Buddhism and Jainism and it saw the rise and fall of many Vihāras such as Nālandā, Vikramaśila and Odantapura, which performed the function of modern universities. No doubt, during the course of centuries, changes crept into its society, but their speed has been so slow that we can still feel the sense and fragrance of antiquity in its villages. We can boldly say that there is hardly a village in Bihar which does not contain a relic of antiquity, or where we do not find any ancient image—Brahmanical or Buddhist. Archaeological excavations, conducted at certain sites, have laid bare something of the local history, but a vast number of places, concealing their history in their wombs, are still awaiting the spades of future archaeologists.

The courses of the rivers in north Bihar change very swiftly, therefore it is not improbable that a large number of old places have been washed away and hence we cannot identify them. But nature has helped south Bihar in this respect at least. Most of the places referred to in Pāli, Prākṛit and Sanskrit literature can still be traced, but their archaeological excavation requires a large number of men and much money, and thus can only be sponsored by an enthusiastic government. Besides archaeology, philology also helps us in tracing the location of ancient places, whose names have changed owing to the gradual changes of language.

There are many sites in the Chhotanagpur area whose antiquity may be traced back to the pre-historic period. We do not find any reference to such places in any literature.

They are generally known as Asura sites,[1] because it is supposed that they are the remains of the settlements of aboriginal races whom the Aryans referred to as Asuras. In north Bihar also there are many sites about which literature is quite silent and we cannot estimate their history accurately. Some places which have not been described in Indian literature, have been alluded to by the Chinese pilgrims. Besides these places, there is a multitude of sites which abound in ancient ruins, but we find nothing in black and white about them, although we cannot doubt their antiquity and historical significance.

From the "Buddhist period" to the Muslim invasion, Buddhism had a strong hold upon the minds of the people of this state. To express their zeal and sentiments and to obtain the bliss of the other world, many Vihārās and ārāmas were built in the bigger villages. Some of these still contain the ruins of such vihāras. The modern names of such villages generally end with the syllable 'Wān' which may be a shortened form of *ārāma*. We find a large number of such villages round about Nālandā in the Bihar-sharif sub-division of the Patna district.

We should here say something about the terms applied to town and villages in early times. The big towns were generally called *Nagara* or *Pura*, while the small towns were known as *Nigama*. The coins from Taxila used the word *Nigama* for that city,[2] but we know that Taxila was a big city about the beginning of the Christian era. This suggests that the term *Nigama* was specially used for those towns which had local managing committees, municipal corporations and the like. However, in eastern India, we do not find any large cities termed *Nigama*.

The villages were called *Grāma* which in Pali or Prākṛit literature are turned into *Gāma*. These literatures refer to certain village as *Bambhanagāma* or villages of the Brāhmaṇas. This word does not appear to be a proper name, but probably shows the nature of the population of a village. Such villages may have been mostly occupied by the Brahmins. We are

1. District Gazetteer of Ranchi p. 20.
2. *Catalogue of the Coins of Ancient India*, p. CXXVI

not however in a position to tell whether those villages were of the nature of the *Agrahāras* of later days, or were so designated simply from the majority of the population. The latter explanation seems to be more plausible.

We often find reference to places which are called *Sanniveśa*. This term is usually translated into English as "settlement", but we cannot definitely say how far this explains the original word *Sanniveśa*. The latter seems to have been a kind of small village such as were situated on the outskirts of big cities or towns. Nearly all the places referred to by this term were in the neighbourhood of Rājagṛiha or Vaiśālī. Hence it seems that the Sanniveśas were a kind of suburban villages. The Jain works use different terms for particular types of settlement. Muni Ratnaprabha Vijaya[1] explains the term *Madambas* as small towns with villages within a distance of about four to six miles, *Karbatas* as ill-managed disorderly villages and *Khetas* as villages with mud walls.

The Buddhist scriptures generally mention the region in which a particular town or village existed, but the Jain authors were not very careful about the localities. Hence it is very difficult to locate most places mentioned in the Jain literature. As the Jain works were compiled and written in the western part of India, it can be surmised that their authors had a very hazy idea of the geography of the eastern India. Jainism and Buddhism flourished in India simultaneously and therefore it can be naturally concluded that their works would depict the geography of a region quite similarly. But the student finds himself in a dilemma when the Jain scriptures present the geography of a region about which the Buddhist scriptures are quite silent. For instance, the Jain scriptures mention territories such as Bhanga and Malaya to the south of Magadha, apparently in the district of Hazaribagh.[2] Their accounts are not corroborated by any other source. It is probable that such territories were not states or kingdoms but were regions under local chiefs who owed their allegiance to the kings of Magadha.

The Sanskrit works also mention places in Bihar, but

1. S.B.M. Vol. II, Part I. p. 289.
2. *Life in Ancient India As Depicted in the Jain Canons* p. 255.

they are generally big and famous towns or cities and places of pilgrimage. Moreover, they belong to later centuries.

In spite of all these difficulties, we have tried to identify a number of villages hitherto unidentified. All the places mentioned in literature and inscriptions have been dealt with district-wise. They have been arranged in three sections under sub-headings A, B and C. Section A consists of those places which have been mentioned in ancient literature and inscriptions and are identified; section B deals with those places which are referred to in different works and inscriptions, but are not identifiable; section C deals with modern places which abound in ruins but the names of which we do not find referred to in any form in original works. We conclude this chapter with a consideration of those ancient place-names which cannot be located, but which appear to have been in Bihar. Within each section place-names are considered in order of their apparent importance.

GAYĀ DISTRICT

(A)

GAYĀ

Gayā is at present the headquarters of this district, at a distance of about 60 miles due south of Patna. This city played no major role in politics at any period of history as far as we know. But it was certainly a centre of religious movements. As Bodha Gayā is sacred to the Buddhists, so is Gayā to the Brāhmaṇical Hindus.

We have no information as to how the city derived its name. It was certainly known by this name even before the Buddha. The *Vāyu Purāṇa*[1] tells us that this city was named Gayā after an Asura, Gayā by name. Viṣṇu killed this demon, but granted him a boon that his city would be held highly sacred. Since then, the city became a place of pilgrimage for the Hindus. But these are mere legends. If there is any grain of truth in this story, Dr. R. L. Mitra[2] seems to

1. Ch. 112, 4—5.
2. *Buddha Gayā* p. 117.

be right in assuming that the narrative reflects the expulsion of Buddhism from the city.

From the religious point of view, Gayā is something different from Magadha Kshetra, although it was an integral part of the same kingdom. According to the *Gayā Mahātmya*[1] Gayā extends to the Pretaśilā on the north and to the Bodhi druma at Bodh Gayā, on the south. The city was deemed so sacred in the eyes of the Brāhmaṇas that they specified Gayā and its surrounding country side as a separate tract, as if to make it something different from Magadha, a stronghold of Buddhism, for which they had accumulated deep hatred in their hearts.

Gayā was a stronghold of Brāhmanism even before Buddha. It was the seat of the famous Kaśyapa[2] brothers and it was at Gayā on the Phalgu that they held festival in the month of Phālguna.

Gayā may have been a centre of Buddhism in its early stages, but it never showed any favour to Buddhism as Rājagṛha or Śrāvastī had done. This is perhaps the reason why the Buddhist and Jain literature do not attach so much importance to this city.

Fa-hsien and Hsüan-Tsang visited the town. Fahsien[3] found that all within the city was desert. We do not know how or why a religious stronghold such as Gayā became desolate during the classical age of Hinduism. It seems possible that Buddhism had recently been expelled from the town and Hinduism had not got a proper opportunity to establish itself there. Later Hsüan-Tsang[4] found the city Kia-Ye (Gayā) to be a thriving Hindu town well defended, difficult of access and occupied by a thousand families of Brahmins, all descendants of a single ṛshi. Hsüan-Tsang probably had in mind the ancestors of the modern Gayāwālas.

We find a large number of fragmentary inscriptions in Gayā, mostly belonging to the Pāla period.[5] But they do not throw any light upon the history of the town excepting this,

1. *Vāyu Purāṇa* Ch. 108.
2. *Udāna* p. 6.
3. *Record of the Buddhistic Kingdoms* Ch. XXXI, p. 74.
4. *On Yuan Chwang* Vol. II, p. 110.
5. *Dynastic History of Northern India* Vol. I, Ch. VI.

that till the end of the twelfth century A.D. it was under the Pālas.

URUVELĀ

This place is often mentioned in Pāli literature.[1] It was probably a forest tract which covered a large area to the south of the Gayāśirsha[2] (Brahmayonī) in the time of the Buddha, and may have spread on both banks of the Phalgu or Nerañjanā. The Buddha came to Uruvelā to practise penance in its sylvan solitude, its landscape gladdened his heart[3] and he stayed there for six years.

The name has been interpreted in different ways. According to the *Mahāvaṁsá Tīkā*,[4] the word means 'heaps of sand'. Dr. R. L. Mitra[5] states that the name indicates a tract full of trees, bearing big Bel fruits. As it was a wild tract when the Buddha attained enlightenment, there may have been *Bel trees* in the area, but at present, this place is definitely not famous for Bel fruits. However one can still find huge mounds of sand in this locality, deposited by the current of the Lilajan. The explanation of the *Mahāvaṁsa Tīkā* seems thus to be more plausible. Uruvelā is a compound of two words (Uru+Velā) which together suggests big or wide shore. The river at Bodh Gayā is very wide even at present and so it is possible that the whole tract may have derived its name from this source.

At Uruvelā, there appears to have been a large number of ascetics busy in the practice of conquering their souls. Uruvelā Kaśyapa,[6] the foremost of the Kaśyapa brothers, lived at this place with his five hundred disciples. This tract has been identified with the place where the modern village of Urel[7] stands. We do not know whether there was actually any village then known by the name of Uruvelā. Hence the identification is not above suspicion. However, the modern

1. S. Vol. I, pp. 103, 136; V. pp. 167, 185, 232.
2. *Gayā and Buddha Gayā* p. 105.
3. *Lalitavistara* p. 311.
4. *Mahāvaṁsa Tīkā* 1,12. p. 84.
5. *Buddha Gayā* p. 8.
6. *Manoratha Pūraṇī* I, p. 297.
7. A.S.I.A.R. (1908-09) p. 144, *Mahābodhi* p 2.

village of Urel shows close similarity of name and its location also seems to indicate its relation with the ancient site of Uruvelā.

Gautama, on realizing the futility of penance, gave it up, and meditated for weeks under a pipal tree in this very tract. The spot is traditionally located at the place where a Pipal tree stands in the compound of the Bodhi temple. While we have no definite proof of the tradition, we have no good reason to disbelieve it, for it is definitely very ancient.

After the enlightenment of the Buddha, the place became associated with his name. We can conjecture that a name purporting to show the relation of the Buddha with Uruvelā became prevalent first among the disciples of the Buddha, who used the new name to attach greater importance to this insignificant place. The people of distant provinces were not so familiar with it and knew of Gayā rather than of Uruvelā. As Gayā was a stronghold of Brāhmanism, the site of Uruvelā was given the name of Buddha Gayā or Bodhi Gayā to distinguish it from the Brāhmanical Gayā. We cannot ascertain the exact date when the site became known as Buddha Gayā. Aśoka[1] in one of his inscriptions refers to this place as Saṁbodhī. Though some earlier scholars suggested that the phrase *ayāya Saṁbodhiṁ* implied Aśoka's progress towards enlightenment, there seems no doubt that a pilgrimage to the Bodhi tree[2] is referred to.

The place was probably indicated by the situation of the Bodhi tree only. Even Hsüan-Tsang[3] does not mention the name of the place. He simply says that a journey of 14 or 15 li south-west from the Prāgbodhī mountain brought him to the Bodhi tree. We do not find the name Bodh Gayā or any equivalent of this name mentioned in Pāli literature. The name may have been applied to this place quite late in the medieval period.

Hsüan-Tsang[4] mentions that the Buddha took the rice-gruel offered to him by Sujātā on the Prāgbodhī mountain

1. C.I.I. Vol. I, p. 59 etc.

2. For the most recent study of the subject, see *The Chronology of the Reign of Asoka Moriya*, p. 77 ff.

3. *On Yuan Chwang* Vol. II, p. 112.

4. *On Yuan Chwang* Vol. II. p. 112.

which is to the east of the Lilajan river. If we take his statement to be correct, we must presume that Buddha performed his austerities on the eastern bank of the river and Senānīgāma, the village where Sūjātā dwelt, was also in the neighbourhood of the Prāgbodhī mountain. Hence it is natural to conclude that the Buddha had to walk 14 or 15 *li* (2½ miles) to reach the Pipal tree for meditation. But this account is not supported by the testimony of the Pāli scriptures. None of them mentions that Buddha had to cross the river to come to the tree for meditation. The pilgrim had no clear conception of these places when he was writing his itinerary.

Bodh Gayā is at present famous for its great temple. The scholars differ in opinion as to when the present temple was erected. There must have been a temple here since early times. As the erection of a large number of stūpas is ascribed to Aśoka we can reasonably conclude that he must have built a stūpa at this place, which is one of the four great shrines of the Buddhists. The famous railings, which are among the master-pieces of early Indian sculptures prove with certainty that Bodh Gayā was the site of an important Buddhist shrine before the Christian era.[1] Fergusson[2] states that "a temple was erected according to an inscription found on the spot, about the year 500 by a certain Amaradeva, and was seen and described by Hsüan-Thsang in the seventh century, but having become ruinous was rebuilt by the Burmese in or about the year 1306."

As the erection of temples had become the fashion of the day and a matter of glory during the Gupta period, we should not think that there was no temple before 500 A.D. It is true that we have no written document to throw light in this direction, but we learn from the *Mahāvaṁsa*[3] that Kittisirimegha, the king of Ceylon, sought permission from Samudragupta to erect a Sangharama here for the use of the Ceylonese monks. It shows that there must have been a temple even before that, which was visited by pilgrims from foreign lands.

1. *Mahābodhī* pp. 11—14.
2. *A History of Indian and Eastern Architecture* p. 474.
3. D.P.P.N. p. 321.

There may have been other buildings also but the remains of these structures are buried under ground and await further excavation.

SENĀNĪGĀMA.

This was a village situated in the neighbourhood of Uruvelā on the bank of the Nerañjanā.[1] It evidently formed a part of the Uruvelā tract, which covered a large area. The name of the village is spelt Senānīgāma.[2] The *Lalitavistara*[3] calls it Senāpatika Nagara. It was in this village that the famous Sujātā and her father Senānī lived. The name[4] of the village shows that it may have been inhabited by soldiers at some early period. We do not know its actual position. The Pāli scriptures inform us that the name of Sujātā's father was Senānī. But they are not explicit as to whether it was his personal name, an official designation or a hereditary title. As the village was situated almost on the southern border of Magadha, beyond which lay a wild tract, we can hazard a conjecture that there may have been a military outpost in the neighbourhood to check the sudden advance of the wild tribes. Thus it is also possible that the village may have been a fief given to the commander, to whom was assigned the duty of protecting the border, and hence the village was named thus. The father of Sujātā may have thus held that hereditary title of Senānī.

In some Pāli texts,[5] the village is described as a *Nigama* or market town, which shows that it had grown fairly important. We do not find any remains of this village at present. Its site is no doubt now included in the modern Bodh Gayā.

BUDDHAVANA.

Hsüan-Tsang[6] visited this place. He locates this village 100 li (about 17 miles) to the north-east of Kukkuṭapāda hill. The identification of this hill is doubtful, but we

1. J.I. p. 68.
2. S. I. p. 106; *Vinaya* I. 21; M. I, pp. 106, 240.
3. P. 311.
4. S. A. 1, p. 135.
5. S. A. 1. p. 135; Sujātāyā vā pitu senānī nāma nigamo.
6. *On Yuan Chwang* II, p. 146.

have tentatively identified it with Gurpa hills.[1] As the pilgrim was visiting the places in the locality of Rājagṛha, Cunningham[2] is right in identifying this place with modern Buddhain on the basis of similarity of names.

YASHTIVANA

Hsüan-Tsang[3] visited this place which he says, was situated at a distance of five miles to the east of Buddhavana. This is probably the Latthivana[4] of the Pāli literature. Cunningham[5] correctly identified it with Jakhtivan, which is modern Jethian[6] or Jethin.

UMANGA NAGARĪ

The modern name of this place is Umaga. It is situated in the Aurangabad sub-division of the Gayā district. There is a temple of Mūngā Deva on the hill, which is a spur of the Kaimur range. The name 'Mūngā Deva' may be a short form of Umaṅga Deva, the God of Umaṅga Nagarī[7] which we find in an inscription in the temple. Kittoe[8] published the inscription for the first time. The inscription is dated in the year 1496 of Vikramāditya (A. D. 1439). Although this inscription belongs to later centuries, it deals with the early history of the town. It records that Umaṅga Nagarī was once a flourishing town on the top of the hill, under the rule of the Somavaṁśī rājās. The founder of this dynasty is said to be Durdama. The name of twelve kings of this dynasty are listed therein. But we know very little about these rulers from any other independent source. They seem to be merely local chiefs.

The name Umaṅga Nagarī is, no doubt, written in an inscription of the first half of the fifteenth century A.D., but we think that the place may have had the same name in the Hindu period also.

1. See above, p. 76.
2. A.G.I. p. 528.
3. *On Yuan Chwang* II. p. 146.
4. J. 1. 68.
5. A.G.I. p. 461.
6. *Bengal village Directory* Vol. XXVII. p. 84.
7. A.S.I. Vol. XI. p. 141.
8. J.A.S.B. Vol. XVI, p. 657.

Although, at present, Umaga is a village, it might have been a flourishing town in its early period, which is evident from the large number of ruins. As we find an Arabic inscription in the temple, it seems that the town was destroyed by the Muslims.

NAVAKO

The name of this village[1] is engraved on one of the Nālandā seals. Hiranand suggests that the letter 'KO' may be deciphered as 'DA'. Hence he is inclined to identify the place with Nawada, the headquarters of a sub-division of the Gayā district. This is a few miles to the south-east of Rājagṛha.

GHANĀÑJANA.

The name of this village occurs on one of the Nālandā seals.[2] Hirananda suggests that its correct form may be Ghṛitāñjana. The village abounds in Buddhist remains. He indentifies the village with Ghenjan, which seems to be correct.

PAḌAPĀGA.

The name of this village is engraved on one of the Nālandā seals.[3] It has been identified with Paḍapa, a village six miles to the south of Rājagṛha in the Gayā district.

NANDANA

This village is mentioned on one of the Nālandā seals.[4] It may be identified with the modern village of Nānan, in the Silao Police area of the Patna district, which was the ancient Nālaka, the birth place of Sāriputta. But we prefer to identify it with Nandana, a village in the Ghosi police area of the Gayā district, which bears exactly the same name. The name of this village is not included in the *Bengal Village Directory*.

VASANTAPURA

This was a village in Magadha.[5] J.C. Jain[6] identifies

1. M.A.S.I. No. 66 (S. 9, R. 92) pp. 32-33.
2. Ibid. (S.o, R. 19 and R. 1A) p. 33.
3. Ibid. (S. 1, 348) p. 41.
4. Ibid. (S. 1, 831) p. 42.
5. *Suyagadaṅga Niryukti* II. 6. p. 190 ff.
6. *Life in Ancient India As Depicted in Jain Canons* p 353.

it with a village called Basantapur in the Purnea district, which is quite wrong, because Purnea was never a part of Magadha. It may have been in the Patna or Gayā district. There are many villages of this name in the Gayā district[1] and at least one in the Patna district.[2] It is difficult to say which is the ancient Vasantapura.

MALAYISHṬHIKĀ

The name of this village occurs in the Amauna Plate[3] of Mahārāja Nandana (501-02 A.D.) We identify the village with Malathi[4] in the Jehanabad Police area of the Gayā district.

UDRADVĀRASTHĀNA

The name of this village is engraved on one of the Nālandā seals.[5] Hirananda is inclined to read it as Udumbarakasthāna. We identify this village with Uderathana, a small village at the foot of the Barabar hills in the Makhadumpur Police area of the Gayā district. The village is not listed in the *Bengal village Directory*, but we can make the identification from personal knowledge.

JAMBŪNADĪ VĪTHĪ

The Nālandā Plate of Dharamapaladeva mentions Jambūnadī[6] as a *Vīthi* in the Gayā Vishaya. The place may be identified with a village Jamuawan[7] in the Jehanabad Police area of the Gayā district.

REVATIKĀ

This village is recorded in the so-called spurious Gayā Copper Plate Inscription[8] of Samudragupta, which seems to have been forged about the beginning of the eighth century

1. *Bengal Village Directory* Vol. XXVII. p. 15.
2. Ibid. Vol. XXVI. p. 13.
3. E. I. Vol. X. p. 50.
4. *Bengal Village Directory* Vol. XXVII p. 120.
5. M.A.S.I. No. 66 (S. 9. R. 92) p. 32.
6. E.I. Vol. XXIII, pp. 290—92.
7. *Bengal village Directory*, Vol. XXVII. p. 83.
8. C. I. I. Vol. III. pp. 254-57.

A.D. Whatever may be said for and against the validity of the plate, the place mentioned in the grant must be correct, because it was the main purpose of the donee to obtain the control of the village. On a philological basis this village may be identified with Reworu[1] in the Tikari Police area of the Gayā district.

UTTARĀMA

This village occurs in the Nālandā Plate[2] of Dharmapāladeva. It was situated in the Jambūnadī Vīthi[3] of Nagara Bhukti. As Jambūnadī Vīthi must have occupied the area round about the small Jamuna river in the Jehanabad subdivision of the Gayā district, this village may be identified with Utrawan[4] in the Kurtha Police area of the same district.

(B)

SAPTAGHAṬṬA

This place is mentioned in the Janibigha Inscription[5] (1202 A.D.). It was probably some sort of administrative unit, but the inscription is not quite distinct. The place is not identifiable.

KOṬATHALA

This is a village recorded in the Janibigha Inscription[6] of the year 1202 (A.D.). It was given to the Bodh-Gayā temple for the maintenance of the Diamond throne. The village is not identified, but it must have been somewhere in the locality of Bodh-Gayā.

PUDGALA

The Amauna Plate[7] of Maharaja Nandana was issued from this place. It is not identifiable.

1. *Bengal Village Directory*, Vol. XXVII, p. 166
2. E. I. Vol. XXIII pp. 310-27.
3. See above, p 181.
4. *Bengal Village Directory*, Vol. XXVII. p. 198.
5. J.B.O.R.S. Vol. IV. p. 279.
6. Ibid.
7. E.I. Vol. X pp· 49-54.

PALĀMAKA

This village[1] was situated in the Kumudasūtra vīthi of the Gayā Vishaya. It may have been situated in the Nawada or Sadar sub-division of the Gaya district, because we see that all the villages of this grant are situated in the locality of Nālandā. Hence this village could not have been far from that place. The village is not identifiable.

NIGUHA

This village[2] is mentioned in the Nālandā Plate of Dharmapāladeva. No village of a similar name exists at the present time.

DATTAGOLĀ, MĀSAVĀGRA

There is an inscription[3] on the throne at Bodh Gayā which records the dedication of the image by Bodhikshana of the village of Dattagolā, and it was engraved by Upavyayapurva, an inhabitant of Māsavāgra.

From the record, it is not clear where these villages were situated. Had the dedicator been an inhabitant of a distant place, he would have mentioned the name of the territory also. The name of the village shows that it was somewhere in the locality of Bodh Gayā.

As far as the village Māsavāgra is concerned, it must be a neighbouring village because the dedicator would not be expected to bring an engraver from a distant place. These villages are not identifiable.

MAHATĪTTHA.

This was a Brāhmaṇa[4] village in Magadha. It may have been in the Gayā or Patna district. It is not identifiable.

PRĪTIKŪṬA

This was the native village of Bāṇa[5] where his ancestors

1. E.I. Vol. XVII. pp. 310-27.
2. E.I. Vol. XXIII, pp. 290-92.
3. J.A.S.B. (1864) p. 177.
4. *Therīgāthā* 294.
5. *Haṛshacharita*, p. 38.

lived. The village was situated on the eastern bank of the Śoṇa. It is not identifiable.

NĀLA

The Therīgāthā Commentary[1] says that Nāla was a small village in the vicinity of the Bo-tree. It is supported by *Cūlavaṁsa*[2] also, which says that it was the birth place of Buddhaghoṣa, the famous Pāli commentator. There is no village in the locality bearing any similarity to this name at present.

SĀLISISA.

Mahāvīra came to this place from Gamayā and proceeded to Bhaddiyā.[3] The place is not identifiable, but it seems to be in south Bihar.

MANINAYIKA.

This is mentioned on one of the Nālandā seals.[4] The place is not identifiable but it should be either in Gayā or Patna district, because these two districts are adjacent in the neighbourhood of Nālandā.

KĀLIGRĀMA.

The name of this village is engraved on one of the Nālandā seals.[5] Although it is not identifiable it should be located in the Gayā or Patna district because most of the places engraved on the Nālandā seals have been located in these two districts.

SUVANNA KHALAYA

The Sanskṛit name of this place seems to be Survarṇa Khalaya. Mahāvīra is said to have journeyed[6] here from Kollaka, which was in the vicinity of Nālandā. The village may thus have been in the Gayā or Patna district. But there

1. p. 225.
2. Ch. 37. 224.
3. *Life in Ancient India As Depicted in the Jain Canons*. p. 259.
4. M.A.S.I. No. 66 (S. 9, R. 16) p. 33.
5. M.A.S.I. No. 66 (S. 9, R. 55) p. 33.
6. *Bhagavati Sūtra* 15.

was another Kollaka which was a suburb of Vaiśālī. Thus Suvarnakhalaya may have been in North Bihar.

KUMUDASŪTRA

This was a small administrative unit[1] in the Gayā Vishaya. It seems to have adjoined the Rājagṛha Vishaya, because the village of Palāmaka in this unit was evidently in the locality round about Nālandā. It is not identifiable.

(C)

KURKIHAR

This village is in the Gayā district. "The remains at Kurkihar consists of several ruined mounds, in which numerous statues and small votive topes of dark blue stones have been found."[2] Cunningham found there some short inscriptions whose age ranges between A.D. 800 and 1000. The correct name of the place seems to be Kurkavihāra or Kukkuṭavihāra which Cunningham confused with the Kukkuṭapādagiri described by Fa-Hsien and Hsüan-Tsang.[3] But, as the Kukkuṭapādagiri is a hill and not a Vihāra, it seems to be the Gurupa hills.[4] The name of this village is not found in any Indian literature.

DHARAWAT

This village is situated near the Barabar hills in the district of Gayā. A large number of relics have been unearthed there by spades of the local farmers, but no proper excavations have been conducted[5] at this place. The Gunamati monastery described by Hsüan-Tsang was located[4] at this place. As it abounds in the Buddhist relics, it can be inferred that it was an important centre of Buddhism. But we do not know the name by which it was known in ancient days. Beglar[6] thinks that

1. E.I. Vol. XVII pp. 310-27.
2. A.S.I. Vol. I, p. 14.
3. *On Yuan Chwang* p. 143.
4. See above, pp. 75-76.
5. A.S.I. Vol. VIII p. 39.
6. Ibid.

the ancient name of the place was Dharmapura, but we do not know how he arrived at this conclusion.

GUNARIA

This is situated in the Gayā district. Kittoe[1] reconstructed its name as Guṇacharita but he gave no reason for his assumption. It was the site of a large Vihāra and town. There are remains of many temples. We do not know the name by which it was known in early days.

APSANḌA

This village is commonly known as Afasara and falls in the jurisdiction of the Gayā district. It contains several ancient remains. A famous inscription[2] of the later Guptas was discovered in this village.

BAKROR

This is situated on the eastern bank of the Lilajan opposite Bodh Gayā. There is a ruined mound here which is called Katani. Several seals impressed with the figure of the Buddha were discovered[3] here. It seems quite likely that the village had some direct relation with the Bodhi temple at Bodh Gayā. Some pieces of a broken pillar have been found here. Cunningham[4] states that the ancient name of the place was Ajayapura. But we do not know the source through which he arrived at this conclusion.

PATNA DISTRICT

(A)

PĀṬALIPUTRA

Pāṭaliputra, the modern Patna is situated on the south bank of the Gaṅgā. Its site was undiscovered for a long time and it was located at various places such as Allahabad[5] and

1. J.A.S.B. (1847) Vol. I. p. 278.
2. C. I. I. III pp. 200-08.
3. A.S.I. I. p. 12.
4. Ibid.
5. *Compendium of Ancient Geography* (Trans. 1791) Part II, p. 543.

Bhagalpur.[1] It was Rennel[2] who for the first time identified the place correctly, and he was followed by other early scholars like Wilford[3] and Cunningham.[4] Archaeological excavations have left no doubt of its identification and now the question has been finally settled.

As legends gather round the origin of any city of India, so was the case with Pāṭaliputra. Various tales[5] were fabricated in later centuries to justify the name of the city, but those stories contain no historical truth. The city was given several names in the past such as Pāṭaliputra, Kusumapura[6] and Pushpapura[7]—all having connection with flowers. Vātsyāyana[8] calls it simply "The Town" (*Nagara*). The *Mañjuśrīmūlakalpa*[9] calls it Nandanagara and we find a place Nandapura[10] mentioned in a 4th century Buddhistic inscription of Mysore, which may be Pāṭaliputra. But we are not sure whether this Nandapura is the same as Nandanagara of the *Mañjuśrīmūlakalpa*. The city was called Palibothra[11] by the Greeks. The Pala inscriptions call it by the name of Śrīnagara.[12]

The Piṭakas[13] give some information on the early history of Pāṭaliputra. There was a village named Pāṭaligāma on the site where Pāṭaliputra was founded in later years. The Lichchhavis often attacked this village and harassed the inhabitants. Ajātaśatru in order to repel the Lichchhavis entrusted his two ministers Sunīdha and Vassakāra with the responsibility of constructing a fortress[14] at this place. The text uses the term *Nagaram* which means both a city and fortress. As Pāṭaligāma was a border village and was frequented

1. *Inquiry concerning the site of Ancient Pataliputra* Part II, preface p. III.
2. *Memoir of A Map of Hindoostan*. p. 50.
3. Asiatic Researches Vol. XIV p. 380.
4. A.G.I. p. 520.
5. *Pariśishṭa Parva* VI. 22-180. *Āvaśyaka Niryukti* XVII. II. 2. *Abhidhāna Rājendra* Vol. 5. p. 823; *Kathāsaritasāgara* I. pp. 18-24.
6. *On Yuan Chwang* Vol. II p. 87.
7. *Gārgāsaṁhitā* (J.B.O.R.S. 1928 p. 401).
8. *Kāmasūtra* Ch. IX.
9. Verse. 782.
10. E.I. Vol. II p. 329.
11. *Indika* Fragm. XXV, Strabo XV.
12. E.I. XVII. p. 321.
13. *Vinaya* I, 226-30.
14. D. II. 86 ff. (*Mahāparinibhāna Sutta*)

by the Lichchhavis, it would not have been possible from the military point of view to build an unfortified town at that place, because the Lichchhavi menace was not yet averted. We would therefore suggest that *Nagaram* should here be interpreted as a fortress or citadel with a wall encircling the village of Pāṭaligāma. This inference is corroborated by the fact that the *Mahāparinibbānasutta*[1] says that the gate through which Gautama passed was called the Gautamadvāra and the ferry was known as the Gautamaghāṭa. The Buddha passed through this village on his last journey. He stayed in the village for the night and is said to have prophesied its future prominence. He also warned against the danger of its destruction by fire, water or internal dissension which turned out to be true, as the history tells us.

We do not know why the village was called Pāṭaligāma. There may have been an abundance of Pāṭala flowers in the vicinity or it may have been named after some person called Pāṭalī. However the association of all its names with flowers has some mystery behind it which has not been satisfactorily explained as yet. Even at present a part of Patna is known as Phulwari.

What was the position of this village during the reign of Bimbisāra and Ajātaśatru, is not known to us, but it must have been an important place on the southern bank of the Gaṅgā as it was the site of a ferry. After the construction of the fortress, a battalion of the soldiers must have been stationed there and a bazaar would have come into existence to meet their daily necessities. On the destruction of the Lichchhavis, there was no fear of any sudden attack and then the village would have grown into a town. As the town was situated on the confluence[2] of the Gaṅgā and the Śoṇa, it may have soon become a flourishing trading centre.

Udāyībhadra, the son and successor of Ajātaśatru transferred his capital to the newly built town, which then became known as Pāṭaliputra. This is supported both by the *Vāyu Purāṇa*[3] and the *Gārgīsaṁhitā*.[4] No other city of ancient India

1. D. II. 86 ff.
2. *Indika* Frag XXV, Strabo XV.
3. Ch. 99. 319.
4. Lines 9-12, J.B.O.R.S. (1928) p. 401.

known to us had a name ending in *Putra*. The explanation of this strange termination has yet to be given. Aśoka used the name Pāṭaliputra in his edicts.[1]

During the time of the Mauryas and the Śuṅgas, the city seems to have expanded along the banks of the Śoṇa and the Gaṅgā. Megasthenes informs us that 'this city stretched in the inhabited quarters to an extreme length on each side of eighty stadia, and that its breadth was fifteen stadia and that a ditch encompassed it all round, which was six hundred feet in breadth and thirty cubits in depth, and that the wall was crowned with 570 towers and had four and sixty gates.[2] The city on the bank of the Śoṇa was perhaps the more thickly pupulated part. Patañjali,[3] illustrating the use of a certain preposition says '*Anuśoṇaṁ Pāṭaliputraṁ*' which means Pāṭaliputra on the Śoṇa. The grammarian seems to have attached more importance to this part of the city, than to that along the bank of the Gaṅgā. In the following ages the city was probably divided into two parts[4]—Eastern Pāṭaliputra and Western Pāṭaliputra. Western Pāṭaliputra may have been the same as that referred to by Patañjali, while Eastern Pāṭaliputra was mostly along the Gaṅgā.

It is really surprising that the *Rāmāyaṇā* and the *Mahābhārata*, which are said to have been composed in their present form during the Post-Mauryan and Pre-Gupta period, do not mention this metropolis. What can be the reason of the total omission of this city ? Should we think that this metropolis always remained a stronghold of faiths such as Buddhism and Jainism ? If it is so, we can say that it was natural for these epics, being the representative works of Hinduism, to omit this city. We may certainly assume also that the material used by the editors who brought the epics to something like their final form was pre-Mauryan and contained no reference to Pāṭaliputra. Though evidence of additions from the later period is very clear, it may be that no interpolator was suffi-

1. Girnar, R.E. 5—Line 7 (Hultzsch) p. 9. Pataliputc cha, Vahiresu cha.
2. *Indika* Fragm. XXVI, Arrian X.
3. *Mahābhāṣya*. I. 1. 2.
4. *Kāśikā* VII. 3.14. Purvesmin Pāṭaliputre bhavaḥ, Purvapāṭaliputrakāḥ, Apara Pāṭaliputrakāḥ.

ciently ignorant to include a reference to a city which was known to be comparatively recent and the capital of an unpopular dynasty. However the reasons are still obscure.

During the Brāhmaṇic rule of the Śuṅgas and the Kāṇvas, this city probably lost its former position and glory. The seat of culture was shifted to central India in the region of Vidiśā. The regicide dynasties of the Śuṅgas and the Kāṇvas could not find popularity in Pāṭaliputra and so they had no interest in its prosperity. In this period the city may have fallen a prey to the ferocity of foreign[1] invasion. During the Gupta period, Pāṭaliputra again enjoyed the privilege of being their capital and its lot must have improved much. But Fa-hsien says nothing in detail about the city except to mention a few Buddhist sites in and outside it. By this time the Gāṅga may have shifted its course farther to the north, for Fa-hsien[2] mentions that he had to walk for a yojana to reach the city after crossing the Gaṅgā. The distance seems to have been mixed with a little exaggeration. From this time onwards, the city was probably better known by the name of Pushpapura or Kusumapura[3] than by that of Pāṭaliputra. Hsüan-Tsang[4] states that the older name of the city was Kusumapura and later on it was known as Pāṭaliputra. He says that the city had long been a wilderness. It seems that it fell into the hands of the rival parties when Magadha became a bone of contention between the Maukharīs and the later Guptas and thus was partly destroyed. During excavations,[5] ashes have been found which show that this city was burnt at some period of its history. In the absence of any certain evidence, we may conjecture that it fell a victim to the vandalism of the Hūṇas. According to Hsüan-Tsang,[6] the Hūṇa Mihirakula carried his arms far into Eastern India.

Harsha established his capital at Kanauj and so people were naturally attracted towards it. It became a centre of

1. Gārgisaṁhitā, Line 23-24 (J.B.O.R.S. 1928) p. 402. *The Indo-Greeks* pp. 81 ff.
2. *Record of the Western Kingdoms*, Ch. XXVII p. 61.
3. *Vāyu Purāṇa* 99. 319; *Raghuvamsa* Ch. 6-24 etc.
4. *On Yuan Chwang* Vol. II. p. 87.
5. Annual Archaeological Report (1912-13) pp. 53-81.
6. *On Yuan Chwang* Vol. I pp. 288-89.

trade also and took the place of Pāṭaliputra as the chief city of northern India. Thus the position lost by Pāṭaliputra during the reign of Harsha could not be regained.

The capital of the Pāla Kings has not yet been identified and we cannot say whether Pāṭaliputra was their regular capital. But from their inscriptions, it is evident that it was their chief metropolis.[1] As we have said, the city was also called Śrīnagara which means the city of wealth. The city must have been flourishing during the Pāla regime. The name Śrīnagara seems to have been in official use only. The common people called it by the old name. Al-Beruni[2] knew this city by the name of Pāṭaliputra. With the decline of the Pālas, Pāṭaliputra sank into oblivion and did not rise again until Sher Shah came into power.

Some architectural remains of ancient Pāṭaliputra have come to light after excavations at Bulandibagh and Kumharar which are in the vicinity of the city on its south. Dr Spooner[3] found there a structure which had almost eighty pillars. It was probably a hundred pillared hall for some official use. During recent excavation in 1952-53, an inscription was found from a ruined structure engraved '*Ārogya Vihāra*' in Mauryan Brahmī. The place is at a little distance from the hundred pillared hall on its south. The '*Arogya Vihāra*' may have been some kind of hospital or sanitorium. But as the structure seems to have been in the neighbourhood of the hall, we have grave doubts about its exact purpose.[4]

The city on the bank of the Śoṇa may have been washed away and we do not get materials enough to present a picture of Pāṭaliputra as described by Megasthenes.

ODANTAPURA.

The Mahāvihāra of Odantapura is famous in the Buddhist literature of Tibet[5] and Nepal.[6] The place was also known

1. E.I. Vol. IV, pp. 243-254.
2. *Al-Beruni's India* p. 200.
3. Annual Archaeological Report, (1912-13) pp. 53-81.
4. Information obtained at the actual excavation in which the author took part.
5. Taranathas Edelstermine pp. 92, 93, 105.
6. Sanskrit-Buddhist Literature of Nepal, p. 88.

as Dandapura, Odaṇtapurī or Udantapura. N. L. Dey[1] understands that the Tibetan Odantapurī is a corruption of Uḍaṇḍapurī. All these names are simply variations of one name. However we cannot derive any sense from these names nor do we know anything of their antiquity. Beglar,[2] relying upon the local traditions, suggests that the place was called Daṇḍapura because the Daṇḍī ascetics had made it their headquarters. But he forgets that the Daṇḍis are a Brāhmanical sect and the people of the time must have recognised the distinction between a shaven headed Hindu ascetic and a Buddhist monk. As it contained a very important Mahāvihāra, the place was associated more with the Buddhists than with any other sect. Hence, it is hardly likely that the name originated from that of a Hindu ascetic sect. This place is identified with the town of Bihar-Sharif in the Patna district at a distance of 40 miles to the north-east of it. A few images with inscriptions dedicated by Nayapāla[3] and Surapāla[4] have been found here which leave no doubt in its identification since they mention the place as Uḍaṇḍapura.

The Ghosharawa Buddhist inscription[5] mentions a few places in this region, and one of them is Yaśovarmapura. Cunningham identifies the place with the town of Bihar-Sharif, since the inscription was found only a few miles away. Yaśovarman of Kanauj had started on a *digvijaya* and it is possible that, after his conquests, he tried to give this place a name after his own, which probably disappeared soon after his fall.

We do not know when and how this place came into prominence. The most ancient relic that we find here is a pillar inscription[6] of Kumāragupta and Skanda-Gupta. But the inscription is so damaged that it does not throw any light upon the history of the place. Hence we do not know the name by which it was known in Gupta days. As the pillar

1. G.D.A.M.I. p. 208.
2. A.S.I. Vol. VIII, p. 25.
3. I.A. (1918) p. 110.
4. J.A.S.B. Vol. IV, p.
5. A. S. I. Vol. III, pp. 38-39.
6. *Select Inscriptions.* p. 316.

is in Situ, it is clear beyond any doubt that the place must have been an important one in the Gupta period, if not earlier. The Chinese pilgrims may have visited this place but they say nothing significant about it. Their silence shows that this place was not very important from the Buddhist point of view until the seventh century A. D.

It may have been an important place during the Pāla period and may have served as their early capital,[1] but has no important record here of Gopāla or his successors like Dharmapāla and Devapāla. The Mahāvihāra of Odantapura was definitely very famous from the ninth century A.D. onwards. As the place is in the vicinity of Nālandā, we do not think that it could have ever been a famous seat of learning. There may have been a big monastery, accomodating a large number of monks and a few scholars who may have continued to impart religious education in that monastery. From Hsüan-Tsang's statement about the very strict entrance requirements at Nālandā, which resulted in the turning away of many students, it may be suggested that this monastery was established in order to meet the growing demand for Buddhist education, and perhaps accepted less able students. It is probable that only those local students studied there who were refused admission to the Nalanda University. In any case Udantapurī could not have been a Mahāvihāra of the same status as Nālandā or Vikramaśīla.

Bakhtiyar Khilji[2] destroyed this place at the end of the twelfth century A.D. As he had found a large monastery (Mahāvihāra) there, he named this place Bihar-Sharif which has almost the same meaning.

NĀLANDĀ.

Although Nālandā was not originally closely associated with Buddhist life, it has got as much importance in later Buddhism as any other sacred site. In the Jain literature too, we have various references to Nālandā in connection with the sojourns of Mahāvīra there. Nālandā was situated at a distance of one Yojana[3] only from Rājagṛha, and as it was

1. A.S.I. Vol. VIII. p. 75.
2. *Tabqat-i-Nasiri* p. 551.
3. D.A., I. p. 35.

on the high road running from Rājagṛha to Pāṭaligāma, it had become an important halting centre. From the Kevaṭṭa Sutta[1] we learn that it was already a prosperous and thickly populated town in the time of the Buddha. This fact makes it quite clear that the place had become important even before the Buddha.

The Origin of the word Nālandā has been variously explained, but no explanation seems to be plausible. Hsüan Tsang records a tradition that the place was so called because a serpent of this name 'Nālandā' lived in a tank at this place.[2] But he does not believe in this story. The pilgrim is of the opinion that the place was named Nālandā because the Buddha in one of his previous births gave ample charity at this place. All these explanations are not at all convincing and seem to be later fabrications to justify the meaning of the name.

On the site of the ancient Nālandā, stands the modern village of Baḍagaon. T. Bloch[3] thinks that the modern name is derived from the so called Bar tree (Nyagrodha) which grows in its ruins. N. L. Dey[4] is of the opinion that the older name of the village was Vihāragrāma. None of these assumptions seem to carry any weight. As there are remains of huge structures and the village itself is situated on mounds, the people call it Badagaon meaning simply 'big village.'

Nālandā was long associated with holy men such as the Buddha and Mahāvīra. But it became more famous after the fourth century A.D., when the great university of Nālandā came into existence. From the description of Fa-hsien, we can gather that Nālandā was not so famous in his time as it later became. He simply mentions Nāla[5] as the birth place of Sāriputta and passes on. It is just possible that the pilgrim did not visit Nālandā at all and the Nāla of Fa-hsien has been erroneously identified with Nālandā. However it is apparant that there was no monastic establishment famous enough to attract the pilgrim. On the other hand Hsüan-Tsang[6] describes

1. D. I. p. 211 ff.
2. *On Yuan Chwang*, Vol. II, p. 166.
3. J.R.A..S., (1909). p. 440.
4. G.D.A.M.I. p. 136.
5. *Record of the Buddhistic Kingdoms* Ch. XXVIII, p. 68.
6. *On Yuan Chwang* Vol. II. pp. 170-71.

the university in great detail. So it is easy to arrive at the conclusion that the university was founded between the fourth and the sixth centuries A.D., and zealous donations of successive kings made the University famous throughout the length and breadth of the Asian continent. Dr. R. K. Mookerji[1] understands that "Nālandā even in the fifth century was still the seat of Brāhmanical learning and the chosen home of the Tīrthakas." The long association of this place with the so called heretical sects leaves no ground for such inferences. Buddhist and the Jain studies may have been carried on in the monasteries at Nālandā even before the University was founded and scholars of great repute visited this place from time to time. Both the Brāhmanical and Buddhist types of education were imparted in this University. In due course it became a famous centre of Mahāyāna Buddhism. The missionary propogation of Buddhism started by Aśoka and continued by Kaniṣka, was taken to its apex by the scholars of this University who went to the land beyond the snowy Himalayas to preach the gospel of Tathāgata. In those days, Nālandā was probably one of the most important cultural links connecting the Indian subcontinent with other countries of Asia.[2]

In the beginning of the 13th century A.D. this famous seat of learning and culture fell a prey to the wanton ferocity of the Muslim hordes. Their leader Bakhtiyar Khilji took the buildings of this university as a fortress of some local chief. He broke down its walls, slaughtered all the monks and students whom he could find, and burnt the whole university to ashes. Nālandā never revived and small villages are still situated in its remains.

After a few centuries, people forgot even the place where once this famous university stood. In the first half of the nineteenth century, Cunningham located the site and excavation supported his conjecture. The seals and inscriptions excavated from the ruins of Nālandā leave no doubt of its identification.

RĀJAGṚHA.

Rājagṛha, locally known as Rajgir, is one of the oldest cities of India and has a glorious history in the domains both

1. *Ancient Indian Education*, p. 558.
2. E.I. Vol. XVII, pp. 310-27.

of politics and religion. Its soil has been sanctified by its long and cordial association with famous preachers such as the Buddha and Mahāvīra and this is perhaps the reason why we find this city mentioned in the Buddhist and Jain literature in greater detail than in any Brahmanical works.

This city of yore, now a village only, is situated at a distance of 60 miles to the south-east of Patna in the same district. We do not know certainly who was its founder or when it was founded. The Vedic literature is totally silent about it, but Pāli and Prākrit literature speak of its power, prosperity and magnificence in the life time of the Buddha and Mahāvīra.[1] They also inform us that Magadha had a long rivalry with Aṅga and Vaiśālī and consequently her capital Rājagṛha had been formerly subjugated by the Aṅgas.[2]

All these traditions are sure proofs of its existence long before the sixth or seventh century B. C. The *Rāmāyaṇa*[3] and *Mahābhārata*[4] often refer to this city. The antiquity of Rājagṛha is corroborated by the archaeological sources also. The N.B.P. wares[5] which are now referred to the seventh century B.C. have been found in the deepest layer at Rajagṛha. But A. Ghosh[6] is of the opinion that "occupation in Rajagir must have been earlier as is indicated by the presence of pottery in the layers earlier than those producing the wares." It is doubtful whether the archaeologists have reached the virgin soil.

The city had several names at different periods of its history and it may have been known by different names simultaneously. Some of these referred to its ancient kings while the rest indicate its situation.

The *Rāmāyaṇa*[7] calls it Vasumatī, probably after Vasu, whose race was traditionally the first to rule over Magadha.[8] The *Mahābhārata* calls it by the name of Bārhadrathapura[9] and

1. Divy. p. 307.
2. *Manual of Buddhism* p. 166.
3. Bāl. 32.8.
4. I. 2. 135; II. 21.12; 30. 17.
5. Ancient India (1951-52) p. 66.
6. Ibid.
7. Bāl. 32.8.
8. I. 63. 29-39.
9. II. 24.44.

Māgadhapura.[1] The legendary King Bṛhadratha was the first to establish his capital in Rājgṛha. One of its earliest names was Girivraja[2] which means hill enclosure that is a hill girt city. As the old city was encircled by five hills, we can say with some certainty that Girivraja was the earliest name given after its location.

Later on several names such as Rājagṛha, Kuśāgrapura[3] and Bimbisārapurī were given to it, and are connected with the names of the Kings and their royal residence. The Jain sources[4] give us another name to it, Chanakapura. This name seems to be given to the new town which was built by Bimbisāra or Ajātaśatru, for the simple reason that it was built in the fields where gram (Chaṇaka) grew in abundance.

In the ancient world, the defence of a capital played a great role in the expansion and prosperity of a Kingdom. As far as the defences are concerned, Rājagṛha was a unique capital in ancient India. Perhaps, there was no city in India which was so well-guarded by nature herself. This city was situated in a valley encircled by five hills. "At a very early stage in the life of the city the natural defences were substantially re-enforced by a fortification consisting of a high rubble wall running at the top of the hills, with a circuit of about 25 miles and the natural gaps between the hills were utilized as gates in fortification."[5] "Inside the valley were other defensive walls generally built of heaped up earth with a rough rubble core and enclosing a pentagonal area with a perimeter of five miles."[6]

The Sāmaññaphala Sutta[7] speaks of the thirty two large gates and sixty four small ones in Rājagṛha. It seems that one cannot rely upon this statement. When the city was so jealously guarded, so many gates would have proved loop-holes in the defence of the capital. If so many gates

1. II. 20. 30.
2. *Sārattha pakāsinī* II p. 159—Magadha raṭṭhasa giribajje, giri—pārikkhe pethitoti attho.
3. M.M.K. LXVIII; *On Yuan Chwang* II. p. 148.
4. *Life in Ancient India as depicted in the Jain Canons* p. 276.
5. Ancient India (1951-52), pp. 66-78.
6. Ibid.
7. D.A.I.P. 150.

existed, they must have been either in new Rājagṛha or in the inner defensive walls of the old Rājagṛha rather than in the defences which survive to this day. There cannot have been such a large number of gates in the outer wall which crosses the hills. The gaps in the hills suitable for entry are much smaller in number at present.

Excavations show that the city of Rajagṛha had probably no planning before its foundation. It was situated in a valley for the sake of necessity and safety. It had no space for more expansion, so the city cannot have been very large, such as Vaiśālī or Taxila.

With the expansion of power and of the city, it became a necessity for Bimbisāra to found a new capital outside the valley. As the king was the first to take his residence in the newly built city, it was known as Rājagṛha. The remains[1] of this city within a circuit of 3 miles are still visible outside the northern gate of the hill.

Majumdar,[2] on the basis of Hsüan-Tsang, thinks that the old city had two separate divisions, the Palace city and the Mountain city. He thinks that the Palace city was the residence of the king and his courtiers while the mountain city was meant for the general population. The ruins of the defences, which are taken to be inner defensive walls, he thinks are actually the eastern enclosure of the city. The Palace city may have been just like Westminister of our days, without any sharp line of demarcation from the neighbouring city. The ruins may have been actually the inner defensive walls round the city inside the valley. There may have been some caravan-serais or a market place between the inner defensive walls and the hills, where people could stay at night if the city gates were closed, If we assume that the gaps in the hills were closed we should also assume that the city had expanded beyond the hills and had small suburbs beyond the outer walls.

Rājagṛha was an important centre[3] of trade, where merchants flocked from different quarters. Routes to the

1. Ancient India (1951-52) p. 69.
2. J.A.S.B. (1949) pp. 165-80.
3. Divy, p. 307.

different *Janapadas* passed through this city. It was one of the six great cities[1] during the life time of the Buddha—the others being Sāketa, Śrāvastī, Kauśāmbī, Champā and Kāśī.

The Buddha and Mahāvīra passed several rainy seasons here. There are various sites associated with their sacred memories. Udāyī, the son and successor of Ajātaśatru, shifted his capital to Pāṭaliputra.[2] From then onward Rājagṛha began to loose its glory and at present is only an old village.

MANIVĀṬAKA.

This was situated in the Ajapura Naya[3] of the Rājagṛha Viṣaya. Hirananda[4] has identified it with Maniawan in the Bihar Police area.

HASTIGRĀMA.

This was a village in the Achalā Naya.[5] Hirananda[6] offers a suggestion that it might be the Hatheo Bigha of the Bihar Police area, if not the Hathi tola of the Maner police area. The former identification is more probable because it is in the vicinity of Nālandā to which the village was donated for maintenance.

NĀLIKĀ

This was a village in the Pilipiṅka Naya.[7] It has been identified with Naipokhar[8] of our day in the Silao police area.

PILIPIṄKA

This was a small administrative unit[9] in the Rājagṛha Viṣaya. It has been identified with Pilikh[10] or Pilichchha, a village of the Silao Police area in the Patna district.

1. D. II, p. 147.
2. *Pariśishṭhaparva* VI. 34, pp. 175-80.
3. E.I. Vol. XVII pp. 310-27.
4. Ibid. p. 317.
5. Ibid. pp. 310-27.
6. Ibid. p. 317.
7. E.I. Vol. XVII, pp. 310-27.
8. ibid.
9. Ibid.
10. Ibid. p. 318.

MORĀNIVĀPA.

The *Dīgha Nikāya*[1] mentions this as a village, on the bank of the Sumāgadhā, which was probably a tank, according to Buddhaghosa,[2] in Rājagṛha. There is no village at present near Rājagṛha which may be identified with this place, but at a little distance in the Silao police area there is a village called Mora[3] which we believe may be an abbreviation of the ancient name Morānivāpa.

DHANĀÑJANA.

This village is referred to on one of the Nālandā seals.[4] We identify it either with Dhanchuhi[5] in the Silao police area, which is in the neighbourhood of Nālandā, or with Dhangaon[6] in the Nawada Police area of the Gayā district. As the former is nearer to the site, it seems therefore more probable.

JAKKURIKA.

One of the Nalanda seals[7] refers to this village. We identify it with Jakia[8] in the Bihar Sharif police are of the Patna district.

VARAKIYĀ

The name of this village is engraved on one of the Nālandā seals.[9] We identify it with Barkar,[10] a village in the Silao police area of the Patna district.

ANGĀMI.

The name of this village is engraved on one of the Nālandā seals.[11] We identify it with Aungari[12] in the Islampur police

1. D. III, p. 39.
2. D.A. p. 835.
3. *Bengal Village Directory* Vol. XXVI, p. 84.
4. M.A.S.I. No. 66 (S. p. R. 1A) p. 48.
5. *Bengal Village Directory* XXVI, p. 32.
6. *Bengal Village Directory* Vol. XXVII, p. 52.
7. M.A.S.I. No. 66 (S.I. 780) p. 48.
8. *Bengal Village Directory* Vol. XXVI, p. 52.
9. M.A.S.I. No. 66 (S9, R91) p. 33.
10. *Bengal Village Directory* Vol. XXVI, p. 11.
11. M.A.S.I. No. 66 (S9, R 144) p. 33.
12. *Bengal Village Directory* Vol. XXVI. p. 6.

area of the Patna district. Hiranand is inclined to decipher it as 'Bhutika'. We are really surprised that two so dissimilar words can be confused even in an indistinct epigraph. As the seal is not reproduced we cannot give our own conclusions.

KARA (JÑA)

The name of this village is engraved on one of the Nālandā seals.[1] We identify it with Karajara[2] in the Silao police are of the Patna district.

NANDIVANĀKA

This village is referred to in the Nālandā Copper Plate[3] of Devapāla. It was situated in the Ajapura *Naya* of the Rājagṛha Viṣaya. Hirananda[4] identified this village with Nadiune or Naunvan in the Bihar Police area which seems to be correct.

KOLITAGĀMA

This was a village[5] in Magadha where Mahamoggalānā was born. We identify it with Kolia,[6] a village in the vicinity of Rājagṛha. It is locally known as Kol.

NĀLA

This was a village[7] in Magadha in the neighbourhood of Rājagṛha. It is written as Nāla, Nālaka and Nālikā. It is also called Upatissagāma. This village was the birth place of Sāriputta. Fa-hsien probably visited this place. On the assumption that he had visited Nālandā, which he calls Nāla, this village is identified with Nālandā. But from the study of the Buddhist literature it will be quite clear that Nālaṅdā was a different place from Nāla since both are referred to in the same text. The former is identified with Nanan. The *Mahāvastu* wrongly calls it Nālandā. The name of the village Nanan is not recorded in the *Bengal Village Directory*.

1. M.A.S.I. No. 66 (S. 1A, 455) p. 37.
2. *Bengal Village Directory* Vol. XXVI, p. 58.
3. E.I. XVII pp. 310-27.
4. Ibid p. 317.
5. S.A. I, 326; D.A. I, 73; MTU. III. 56.
6. *Bengal Village Directory* Vol. XXVI, p. 65.
7. S.A. II. 172; Thag. A.I. 108 etc.

TILAKĀṆḌA VIKĀYA

This place is mentioned on one of the Nālandā seals.[1] There is no village bearing any similarity to this name in the locality except Teladha, which was visited by Hsüan-Tsang[2] in the seventh century A.D. He calls it Ti-lo-shi-ka that is, Tailadhaka. It is very surprising that this village which was known as Tailāḍhaka in his time came to be known by a much longer name a few centuries afterwards. It is possible that this place may have been elsewhere.

PURIKĀ.

The name of this village occurs on one of the Nālandā seals.[3] We believe that it is the modern Puri[4] a part of Pāvā, seven miles to the south-east of Bihar Sharif in the Patna district. This village is recorded as Pava Bu-urg in the Directory.

PĀPĀ

This village is often mentioned in Jain literature.[5] It is also called Majjhima[6] Pāvā. From the study of the Buddhist and the Jain literature, we arrive at the conclusion that there were three famous places which bore the name of Pāvā; the Pāvā of the Mallas in the Gorakhpur district, the Majjhima Pāvā in the Patna district, and Pāvā the capital of the Bhaṅga[7] kingdom somewhere near the Pārasanāth hill in the Hazaribagh district. As the modern Pāva in the Patna district lay between the two Pāvās, it was known as middle Pāvā. It was also known as Apāpāpurī.[8] The place came to be regarded as sacred because Mahāvīra is said to have breathed his last there. If we study the Jain scriptures minutely, it will appear that the place where Mahāvira died was not the modern Pāvā in the Patna district, but it may have been the capital of the Bhaṅga country in the Hazaribagh district. This conjecture

1. M.A.S.I. No. 66 (S. I, 1006) p. 37.
2. *On Yuan Chwang* Vol. II, p. 105.
3. M.A.S.I. No. 66 (S. I. 374) p. 32.
4. *Bengal Village Directory* Vol. XXVI, p. 98.
5. *Kalpa Sūtra* p. 269.
6. *Life in Ancient India as Depicted in the Jain Canons*, p. 310.
7. Ibid.
8. *Religion of the Hindus* Vol. I, p. 302.

seems to be more sound when we learn that Mahāvira had died in the house of Hastipāla, who was king. It is not possible that there could have been a king in the neighbourhood of Rajagṛha, when Ajātaśatru was reigning there. A large number of Jain monks died on the Pārasnāth hill and therefore the place was deemed highly sacred. So it is possible that Mahāvira in his last days was wandering in that region when he suddenly died at Pāvā. As this place cannot be located in that region, people associated this event with Majjhima Pāvā which is identified by Jain tradition with the modern village of Pāvā,[1] seven miles to the south-east of Bihar Sharif in the district of Patna.

JAGGHERĪ.

This was a *nigama*[2] in the neighbourhood of Rājagṛha. It seems that the word *nigama* indicated a small town with a market place. Many *nigamas* are mentioned in the Buddhist and Jain literature in the neighbourhood of Rājagṛha, but we do not find any remains of such places. Jaggherī was also known as Sakhara.[3] This place may be the modern village Jagae[4] in the Bihar police area of the Patna district.

KHĀNUMATA

This was a Brāhmaṇa[5] village in Magadha. A garden called Ambalaṭṭhika seems to have been situated there. Buddha often visited this village and probably stayed in this garden.

In the Silao police[6] area of the Patna district, there is a village called Khanpur. This village is in the vicinity of Rājagṛha. On the basis of its name, the village may be identified with ancient Khānumata.

TAPODĀ

This place is mentioned in various contexts in the Buddhist literature.[7] It was probably a lake or spring in the neighbour-

1. G.D. A.M.I. p. 9.
2. J. I. 347.
3. Ibid 348
4. *Bengal Village Directory* Vol. XXVI, p. 51.
5. D. I. 127.
6. *Bengal Village Directory* Vol. XXVI. p. 63.
7. *Vinaya* III, 108; IV. 116; Udāna. A. 110.

hood of Rājagṛha. The place has been identified with the modern village of Tappo, also called Tapovana, at a distance of seven miles from Rājagṛha. We do not find any lake there in our own day, but there is certainly a spring of hot water. This corresponds to the name Tapodā "the heat giver". There are some springs of hot water at Rājagṛha also. As both places are connected by a range of hills, it may be surmised that both are affected from sulphur which may be found at the bottom of these hills. The nearness of the place of Rājagṛha and the etymology of its name leaves no doubt in the correctness of its identification.

KALLAVĀLA

This village is several times mentioned in the Buddhist literature.[1] It was also known as Kallavālamutta. It was situated in the neighbourhood of Rājagṛha and Moggalānā seems to have often visited this place.

At present, there is a village, called Kadam Tal[2] in the Silao police area. This is the only village in the locality which bears some similarity to the old name, although its identification is not free from doubt.

(B)

BRĀHMAṆĪ

This name is engraved on one of the Nālandā seals[3] and may be deciphered as Brāhmaśrī also. The village is not identifiable.

DAṆṬHA

This village is referred to on one of the Nālandā seals.[4] Hiranand gives the alternative reading Danda. This village is not identifiable.

CHANDEKAYA

This village name is engraved on one of the Nālandā seals.[5] It is not identifiable.

1. A. IV. 85; *Therīgāthā* 341, 382 etc.
2. *Bengal Village Directory*. Vol. XXVI. p. 56.
3. M.A.S.I. No. 66 (S. 9, R. 92.) p. 32.
4. Ibid. (S. 9, R. 56) p. 33.
5. Ibid. (S. 9, R. 1A) p. 33.

ALIKAPṚISHṬHA

This name is engraved on one of the Nālandā seals.[1] This is not identifiable.

MALLIRASĀLA

The name of the village is engraved on one of the Nālandā seals.[2] It may also be deciphered as Malligrāmina. The place is not identifiable.

ANIKOṬHASATTĀ.

This place name is engraved on one of the Nālandā seals.[3] Its decipherment is still doubtful. It is not identifiable.

SE (VATTHA) LIKA

The decipherment of the name of this village is not yet final. It occurs on one of the Nālandā seals.[4] It is not identifiable.

DVITRA

This village is mentioned on one of the Nālandā seals.[5] No village bearing any similarity to this name exists in the locality. It is not identifiable.

PAṬIYALOKA

The *Vinaya Piṭaka*[6] mentions a village called Paṭiyaloka in the neighbourhood of Rājagṛha. The name of Rājagṛha is always associated with this place. It is possible that it was a part of Rājagṛha. If it is a place quite separate, it is not identifiable.

PAḌALĪ

This is a village recorded in the Maner Copper Plate[7] of Govindachandra (1126 A.D.). The village should be some-

1. Ibid. p. 48.
2. Ibid. (S. 1, 645 and 811) p. 41.
3. Ibid. (S. 1, 836, 807) p. 42.
4. M.A.S.I. No. 66 (S. I, 787) p. 42.
5. Ibid (S. I, 547) p. 42.
6. *Vinaya* IV 79, 131.
7. J.B.O.R.S. Vol. II, pp.441-47.

where in the western part of the Patna district, but it is not identifiable.

ACHALĀ

This was a small administrative unit.[1] It is not identifiable.

SĀLINDIYA

This village[2] stood to the east or north east of Rājagṛha, near a hill. But there is no hill to the north east of Rājagṛha, so it must be to the east of Rājagṛha where hills are found. The village is not identifiable.

PAŚUKALPA

The name of this village is engraved on one of the Nālandā seals.[3] It is not identifiable.

SUCHAṆḌĀDAKĪYA

The name of this village occurs on one of the Nālandā seals.[4] This place is not identifiable.

VARASHAKA

We find the name of this place on one of the Nālandā Seals.[5] It is not identifiable.

BHALLĀṬAVĀṬAKA

The name of this place is engraved on one of the Nālandā seals.[6] It is not identifiable.

ANDHAKAVINDA

It was a settlement[7] near Rājagṛha. The place is not identifiable.

1. E.I. Vol. XVII pp. 310-27.
2. J. IV. 276, II.. 293.
3. M.A.S.I. No. 66 (S. 1. 666) p. 48.
4. Ibid. (S. 9, R. 79) p. 51.
5. Ibid. (S.I., 673) p. 55.
6. Ibid. (S. I., 350) p. 56.
7. Vinaya I, 109.

VAṬAKA

This is engraved on one of the Nālandā seals.[1] The village is not yet identified.

VALLADIHIYA

This village occurs on one of the Nālandā seals.[2] It is not identifiable.

MU(KKYA).

The decipherment of this name is not beyond doubt. This place is referred to one of the Nālandā seals.[3] It is not identifiable.

TATAKA

The village is mentioned on one of the Nālandā seals.[4] It is not identifiable.

VAITALA.

The name of this place is engraved on one of the Nālandā seals.[5] It is not identifiable.

KĀLAPINĀKA

The name of this village occurs on one of the Nālandā Seals.[6] It is not identifiable.

ŚIVAPURA

This village is engraved on one of the Nālandā seals.[7] It is not identifiable.

PAÑCHAMUTIKĀ

The name of this village we find recorded, on one of the Nālandā seals.[8] The village is not identifiable.

1. M.A.S.I. Nc. 66 (S.I, 806) p. 34.
2. M.A.S.I. No. 66 (S.1, 159) p. 46.
3. Ibid. (S.I. 813) p. 42.
4. Ibid. (S. I. 668) p. 42.
5. Ibid. (S. I, A, 401) p. 43.
6. Ibid. (S. Ia, 442) p. 43.
7. Ibid. (S. I, 1006) p. 44.
8. Ibid. (S. 9, R. 92) p. 47.

(C)

GHOSHRAWAN

This village[1] is at a distance of seven miles to the south-east of Bihar Sharif in the Patna district. The ruins at Ghoshrawan are few and not very important. But an inscription of probably the eighth century A.D. was found there by Kittoe. Several place names are mentioned in that inscription but it tells nothing about Ghoshrawan. The village seems to have been deeply under the influence of Buddhism. Its ancient name may have been Ghoshitārāma.

TITRAWAN

This village is situated two miles to the north of Ghoshrawan in the Patna district. There are some remains which seem to be of a monastery. It may have been the Kapotika Sanghārāma or 'Pigeons' monastery' of Hsüan-Tsang,[2] since the pilgrim's directions and locality are consistent with its location. But the first syllable of the modern name is a Hindi word which means partridge. It seems that people forgot its actual name in course of time, and only remembered its association with a bird, and hence named it Titrawan.

PARABATI

This village is eleven miles to the south-east of Bihar Sharif in the Patna district. There is a small hill in the neighbourhood which Cunningham thinks, has been referred to by Hsüan-Tsang. Near the foot of the hill, the whole surface is covered with ruins—the remains of a multitude of Vihāras and temples. A short inscription was found which shows that a sanghārāma must have existed there.[3] Cunningham[4] thinks that this place is the site of the pigeon's monastery of Hsüan-Tsang, as the name Parabati may be a form of Pārāvata meaning a pigeon. But the village may have derived its name from the hill which stands in its neighbourhood.

1. A.S.I. Vol. I, pp. 38-39.
2. *On Yuan Chwang* Vol. II, p. 175.
3. A.S.I. Vol. XV. p. 10.
4. Ibid. p. 7.

ŚAHPUR

This village is in the Patna district. It is situated on a mound. Many images of Viṣṇu and Sūrya, mostly of the Pāla period, have been found together with an inscription of Ādityasena.[1] We do not know the ancient name of the place.

THE SHAHABAD DISTRICT

(A)

VEDAGARBHAPURI

The *Brāhmānda Purāna*[2] mentions this town. It is identified with modern Buxar,[3] which is the headquarter of a sub-division of the same name. Cunningham[4] and Dey[5] suggest that its earlier name was Vyāghrasara which was probably derived from a tank in the vicinity. We do not know the reason why the tank was named thus, but it is possible that the area, being dense jungle, was infested with tigers which visited the tank to quench their thirst.

MAHĀSĀRA

This is a village in the district of Shahabad only six miles to the west of Arrah. At present the village is known as Masar, but from several inscriptions of the 13th and 14th centuries which have been discovered at this place we learn that the place was named thus. Cunningham[6] thinks that the place is the same as the Mo-ho-solo of Hsüan-Tsang[7] which was occupied mainly by the Brahmins in his time.

VĀRUNIKĀ

This place is situated 27 miles to the south-west of Arrah. There is a temple of considerable antiquity which was probably a sun—temple but at the present it contains an image of Viṣṇu.

1. Ibid. p. 12.
2. Pūrva khaṇḍa. Ch. 1—5.
3. G.D.A.M.I. p. 28.
4. A.S.I. Vol. III. p. 66.
5. G.D.A.M.I. p. 28.
6. A.S.I. Vol. III, p. 65.
7. *On Yuan Chwang* Vol. II. p. 60.

The famous inscription[1] of Jīvitagupta II was found at this place. The place is now known as Deo-Barnark.

(B)

MALLAKŪṬA

This was the village[2] where Bāṇa stopped for the first night after he left his home. The village should be somewhere in the Shahabad district, which lay across the Sona.

(C)

ARRAH

This is the headquarters of the Shahabad district. Cunningham[3] thinks that this is the place where Hsüan-Tsang[4] saw an Aśokan pillar, built in commemoration of the Buddha's subduing of a demon. He compares the story narrated by the pilgrim with many similar Hindu legends and at last comes to conclusion that it was ancient Ārāmanagara. No doubt, Arrah seems to be a contracted form of the name, but the pilgrim seems to refer to an Aśokan pillar on the northern side of the Gaṅgā. Whatever the myth behind the subduing of the demon, the place was definitely not on the south of the river as we find Arrah at the present time. So, we cannot say how the place came to be know as Arrah.

SAHASRAM

This is the headquarter of a sub-division in the Shahabad district. Several inscriptions including one of Aśoka have been found here. The local traditions[5] tell that the place is called thus because Sahasrarjuna had been killed by Paraśurāma at this place. But this is a mere myth upon which no one can rely. As the Aśokan inscription is still there, none can doubt its antiquity. However we cannot give the name by which it was known in ancient times.

1. C.I.I. Vol. III pp. 213-18.
2. *Harshacharita* p. 45.
3. A.S.J. Vol. III, pp. 72-79.
4. *On Yuan Chwang* Vol. II, p. 60,
5. A.S.I. Vol. XI. p. 135. ff

THE MONGHYR DISTRICT

(A)

KṚMILĀ

Kṛmilā was the name of a Viṣaya[1] and a city as the headquarters of the same Viṣaya. This place is not referred to in early Pāli literature, but a city named Kṛmilā is mentioned in the *Aṅguttara Nikāya Commentary*.[2] The Purāṇas[3] often allude to this city and call it a city of Kṛmi, a legendary king.

The city finds mention in various inscriptions[4] of the early medieval period. One inscription explicitly calls it an *Adhiṣṭhāna*[5] or local headquarters.

As some inscriptions referring to this city have been found in the village of Balgudar in the Monghyr district, Dr. Sircar[6] thinks that the area round the present village of Balgudar may be the Kṛmilā Viṣaya. He is inclined to identify the city of Kṛmilā with Balgudar. But we have no materials available to identify the city of Kṛmilā with Balgudar. According to the *Aṅguttara Nikāya Commentary*, this city stood on the bank of the Gaṅgā. But in our days the Gaṅgā flows at a distance from this region, which may be due to a change in its course during so many centuries.

However the city does not seem to have been very important and we do not know how and when it disappeared. It may be just by chance that some slabs and images bearing the name Kṛmilā, which have been found at Balgudar, may have been taken to that village from other places. The name of this village does not bear any rseemblances to the name Kṛmilā. At present we cannot trace even the ruins of the city; therefore it seems possible that it was washed away by the Gaṅgā. The modern village of Kiul bears some similarity to the name of medieval Kṛmilā and so the city may have been somewhere in that locality.

1. E.I. Vol. XVIII, p. 306.
2. Vol. II, p. 642.
3. *Brahmāṇḍa* III, 74; *Vāyu* Ch. 99.22.
4. E.I. Vol. XVIII, p. 306; XXVIII pp. 137-145.
5. E.I. Vol. XXVIII, p. 145.
6. Ibid. pp. 140-41.

MUDGAGIRI

This place is identified with the modern Monghyr and there is no doubt about its identification as inscriptions[1] recording this name have been found here. We do not know much about the ancient history of this place. The *Mahābhārata*[2] mentions it as a separate state, although we have grave doubts in the trustworthiness of the statement. It is said that Mudgalaputra, a disciple of the Buddha, converted a rich merchant of the place to Buddhism. Hence the place was known after him.[3] The correct name may be Mudgalyagīri.[4] The *Hiraṇya-Parvata* of Hsüan-Tsang is identified with the Mudgala-giri,[5] a hill in the vicinity of the town. During the Pāla period, the place became more famous and often served as their Skandhāvāra or military headquarters.[6] It is known as Mudgagiri in the Pāla records. Al-Berūnī[7] calls it Mungiri.

KĀKANDĪ

It was variously known as Kāgandī or Kaindī. It is said to be the birth place of the ninth Tīrthaṅkara[8] and Mahāvīra[9] is said to have visited this place. It is identified by Rāhula Sāṅkṛtyāyana with Kakan[10] in the Monghyr district. The identification seems to be correct.

ROHINĀLĀ

Hsüan-Tsang[11] visited a place which he calls Lo-pan-ni-lo. Jullien[12] restored this name as Rohinīla and Cunningham[13] identified it with Rohinālā on the Gaṅgā, but at another

1. E. I. Vol. XVII' pp. 310-27; XVIII pp. 304-07.
2. II. 30. 21.
3. G.D.M.I. P. 132.
4. G.D.A.M.I., p. 132.
5. A.G.I., p. 545.
6. E.I. Vol. XVII' pp. 310-27.
7. *Al-Berūnī's India* Vol. I, p. 200.
8. *Āvasyaka Niryukti*, 382.
9. *Anuttara*, p. 61.
10. Bhāratīya Vidyā (July 1944) p. 8.
11. *On Yuan Chwang* Vol. II, pp. 176-177.
12. *Hiouen Thsang* (Jullien) Vol. III, p. 385.
13. A.G.I. p. 545.

place he says that there is no place such as this and the village is Rajaona[1] in the same locality, which abounds in extensive ruins of mounds both Buddhistic and Brāhmaṇical. Watters interprets the Chinese Syllables as Lavaṇanīla.[2] This place must be somewhere in the Monghyr district, but its identification by Cunningham is by no means certain because its very name is not above doubts.

(B)

KĀVĀLA

A Nālandā seal[3] mentions a village Kāvā (or Cha) la in the Kṛimila Vishaya. This village may have stood somewhere in the locality round Kiul in the Monghyr district. This village is also referred to in the Nālandā Plate[4] of Samudragupta. The place is not identifiable.

MESHIKĀ

The village is mentioned in the Monghyr[5] Plate of Devapāla. It was situated in the Kṛimila Vishaya. The place is not identifiable.

NAGALADĀMAKA

This place is referred to in an inscription[6] which Dr. Sircar found in the Teghara police area of the Monghyr district. The inscription probably belongs to the 13th or 14th century A.D. and so it is to be expected that the name of this place was the same even in earlier centuries. The place is not identifiable.

BHADRAPUSHKARAKA & PURNANAGA

These places[7] are mentioned in the Nālandā Plate of Samudragupta. We cannot identify them in the present state of our knowledge.

1. A.S.I. III. p. 152.
2. *On Yuan Chwang*, pp. 175-77.
3. M.A.S.I. No. 66 (S. I. 824) p. 34.
4. E.I. Vol. XXV, pp. 50-53.
5. Ibid. Vol. XVIII, p. 306.
6. Ibid. Vol. XXX, p. 86.
7. Ibid. Vol. XXV, pp. 50-53.

(C)

INDAPE

This is situated near Jamui in the Monghyr district.[1] There are huge ruins of an ancient structure which was probably a fort. The place has not been closely studied from the archaeological point of view. The site may belong to the Pāla period.

NONGARH

This is a village in the Monghyr district.[2] There are many ancient remains in this village. Some subterranean chambers have also been discovered there. The place seems to be an old one, but in the absence of any evidence, we cannot find out its actual name or history.

NAWALAGADH

This village is situated in the Begusarai sub-division of the Monghyr district.[3] Several archaeological finds have been discovered here, and there are the remains of an old fort. The place seems to be an ancient one, but we cannot identify it with any known ancient place name. Its antiquity goes back to the Buddhist period.

JAIMANGALAGADH

This place is in the Begusarai sub-division of the Monghyr district. Some figures of Hindu and Buddhist divinities[4] of the Pāla period have been found here. There are large ruins which bear testimony to its antiquity. The local people state that it was connected with Nawalagadh, and there may have been some link between both these places as they are in the same locality. These places seem to be ancient Buddhist sites of which we have no detailed account.

1. A.S.I. Vol. VIII, p. 120.
2. Ibid.
3. G. D. College Bulletin No. I.
4. G.D. College Bulletin No. I.

THE MUZAFFARPUR DISTRICT

(A)

VAIŚĀLĪ

In the history of ancient India, there is probably no city which is so closely associated with democratic principles and strange customs as the city of Vaiśālī in Bihar. With its wonderful background of curious legends and history of democratic administration, its site remained unidentified for a long time and scholars tried to identify it variously. According to Rhys Davids[1], the site of Vaiśālī was quite uncertain; W. Hoey[2] identified it with the village of Cherand in the Saran district; W. Vost[3] identified the site in the same district, but at a different place called Manjhi on the left bank of the Ghaghara. The conejecture of Cunningham[4] was more accurate and V. Smith[5] also came to the same conclusion. The Archaeological excavations in 1903-4 at Bania Basarh, which is 27 miles to the north of Patna in the Muzaffarpur district brought to light many antiquities and seals which leave no doubt about its identification.[6]

The city of Vaiśālī was hallowed many a time by the visits of the Buddha and it was virtually the birth-place of Mahāvīra. In this way, it was closely associated with both creeds—Jainism and Buddhism. Unlike Pāṭaliputra it has found mention in the *Rāmāyaṇa*[7] and the Purāṇas also, but their store of information is very meagre. However, we should bear in mind that the Hindu scriptures only refer to Vaiśālī because they trace the origin of its rulers to the Ikshvāku dynasty which plays a dominant role in their narratives. From the point of view of Hindu tradition, no important kings ruled in Vaiśālī and no great events took place there.

We do not know the date when Vaiśālī was founded. This city is not referred to in the Upanishads, a fact which

1. *Buddhist India* p. 41.
2. J.R.A.S. (1901) p. 41.
3. Ibid. (1903) p. 583.
4. A.S.I. Vol. XVI p. 6.
5. J.R.L.S. (1902), pp. 267-288.
6. A.S.I. (1903), pp. 81-123.
7. Bāl. Chs. 45, 46, 47.

apparently shows its later origin. But in the time of the Buddha, it was an opulent, prosperous and populous town, and this would strongly suggest that it had been founded long before in the early seventh or eighth century B.C.

The *Rāmāyaṇa*[1] and the *Vishṇu*[2] and *Bhāgavata*[3] *Purāṇas* state that the city was founded by an Ikshvāku prince, Viśāla by name. It is by no means unusual for these works to ascribe the origin of the name of a city to a noble prince of the same name. This was a common practice in ancient and mediaeval times and the tradition may be correct; in support it can be argued that even at present the ruins at Basarh are known as *Rājā Viśāla Kā Gadh*[4] or 'the fortress of king Viśāla.' Butit should not be forgotten that after the disappearance of Buddhism from the land, the life of the general people was deeply coloured by Hindu mythology and they became so blind to the past th at they put their trust in nothing but their own scriptures. Hence the traditional name of the site may have been taken from Purāṇic tradition as passed on by local Brāhmaṇas and may not be an authentic survival.

Buddhaghosha[5] says that the city was named thus because owing to its large population, it had to be extended again and again. The reference to its three walls each one Yojana apart in the Jātaka[6] and the Tibetan Dulva[7] probably indicate the fact that the city had to be extended three times to cover its growing population which was encircled each time with a wall. The explanation offered by Buddhaghosha must apply to a later phase of the city and the question remains still unanswered as to why it was called Vaiśālī or Viśāla in the beginning. We can merely conjecture that even at the time of its foundation the city may have been larger in area than other neighbouring cities of its time and consequently it was called Viśālā or Vaiśālī.

The compiler of the *Mahābhārata* seems to have had so

1. Bāl. 47. 12.
2. *Vishṇu Purāṇa* (Wilson), Vol. III, p. 246.
3. IX. 2. 33.
4. A.S.I. Vol. XVI, p. 6.
5. D.A. Vol. I, p. 309.
6. J. I, p. 504.
7. Quoted in the *Homage to Vaiśālī* p. 30.

much antipathy to the places under the influence of non-Hindu creeds that he omitted to mention Vaiśālī.

From the literary references to this city one can easily arrive at the conclusion that the city must have been very large in its own day. Fa-hsien[1] calls this city Pi-she-li, while Hsúan-Tsang[2] names the chief city of the region Chan-shu-na which Cunningham[3] identifies with modern Janakapura on the northern border of the Darbhanga district, which is generally identified with ancient Mithilā. But the detailed description of the ruined and the deserted city which the pilgrim refers to tallies better with the walled city of Vaiśālī, since archaeology gives no evidence that such ruins existed on the site of Janakapura. Watters[4] reads the name as Fei-she-li and thus there remains little difference between the names given by the Chines pilgrims. It would appear that Cunningham relied on Juliens' translation of Hsüan-Tsang, which has been improved on by later scholars, the characters which Julien read as Chan-shu-na are read by Watters as Fei-she-li which is clearly Vaiśālī. The Jātakas and Buddhist works tell us that the city was encompassed by three walls each a league distant from the next. As these measurements may well be exaggerated, we cannot say the exact length and breadth of the city, but from the detailed description of the ruined city by Hsüan-Tsang, we can infer that it was definitely large.

In the time of the Buddha Vaiśālī was a very beautiful city, full of tanks, parks, temples and chaityas. The whole city[5] was divided into three parts : Vaiśālī, Kuṇḍagrāma or Kuṇḍapura, and Vaniyagrāma. The three encompassing walls of the city had three gates with watch towers.[6] The *Mahāvastu*[7] says that the people of Vaiśālī were called Abhyantara Vaiśālikas and Bahiravaiśālikas or inner and outer Vaiśālians. It appears that the original inhabitants who were within the three walls were called inner Vaiśālikas while those

1. *Record of the Buddhistic Kingdoms*, Ch. XXV, p. 56.
2. *On Yuan Chwang* Vol. II, o p. 63.
3. A.G.I. p. 510.
4. *On Yuan Chwang*, Vol. II, o. 63.
5. J. I. 504.
6. Ibid.
7. Vol. I, p. 263.

who occupied the places outside that wall after the growth of the population were designated outer Vaiśālikas.

From the Buddhist and the Jain literature, it appears that the inhabitants of Vaiśālī led a very disciplined and cultured life. Their judiciary process shows that they had faith in the goodness of human kind. These things can be expected only from those societies which have a sound economic background. The land of north Bihar is more fertile in our days than that of the south, and it would seem that even in the time of the Buddha it was more prosperous.

After the defeat of the Lichchhavis at the hands of Ajātaśatru, the city lost its position, but its ancient fame and glory continued to attract pilgrims from time to time. It may be because it had long association with Buddhism and the second Buddhist council had assembled here. We do not know its position during the Mauryan period, but the Aśokan pillar in the neighbourhood of Baniya-Basarh shows that Vaiśāli was an important place even then. From various seals found at Vaiśālī, we can infer that it was the headquarters of the Tīrabhukti Vishaya under the Guptas. But we do not find it mentioned in contemporary literature such as the works of Kālidāsa. The rise of Pāṭaliputra may have been one of the causes of its decline.

The abundance of wood in the vicinity of the city suggests that wood was used as the chief building material at Vaiśālī.[1] The remains of brick buildings which were found there belonged mainly to the Gupta period. Rāhula[2] Sānkṛityāyana is of the opinion that the chief cause of the ultimate disappearance of the city was the Hūṇa invasion. But the advance of the Hūṇas in this part of the country is still doubtful and it is possible that Wang-Hsüan Tse conquered a large part of north Bihar during the confusion which prevailed after the death of Harsha. It is therefore not improbable that it was he who totally destroyed the city in the middle of the seventh century A.D. Since then it has been no more than a big village.

1. *Buddhacharyyā* p. 25.
2. Ibid.

VANIGAMĀ

This village was situated in the Jambubani Vishaya[1] The Jain literature often refers to this village as Vanīyagāma.[2] It has been identified with modern Baniya[3] near Basarh (Vaiśālī) in the district of Muzaffarpur.

KOLLĀGA

This was a suburb of Vaiśālī.[4] We often find it mentioned in Jain literature. This place is identified with Kolhua,[5] a village near Basarh.

KUMĀRAGĀMA

Mahāvīra came here from Kuṇḍapura and proceeded to Kollāka.[6] Since Kollāka has been identified in the Muzaffarpur district, the place may be in north Bihar. There is a village Kumār[7] in the Sitamarhee Police area of the same district which may be the ancient site of Kumāragāma.

MORĀGA

Mahāvīra often visited this place. He is said to have arrived here from Aṭṭhiyagāma and once from Kollāka.[8] The place was definitely in North Bihar because the places connected with it are all in the same region. The village Morang[9] in the Sitamarhi Police area of the Muzaffarpur district may be identified with ancient Morāga.

MAHĀKUṆḌAGĀMA, KHATTIYAGĀMA, KUṆḌAPURA

These were the villages in the suburbs of Vaiśālī.[10] Kuṇḍapura was a village[11] where Mahāvīra was born. It was divided into two parts—southern and northern. The southern part was mostly populated by the Brāhmaṇas and the northern

1. J.B.O.R.S. Vol. V, pp. 582-96.
2. *Āvaśyaka Niryukti* p. 496.
3. M.A.S.I. (1903-4) p. 87.
4. *Uvāsagadasāo* II, p. 4. note 8.
5. M.A.S.I. (1903-4) p. 88.
6. S.B.M. Vol. II Part I, p. 282.
7. *Bengal Village Directory*, Vol. XXX, p. 68.
8. S.B.-M., Vol. II, Part I, p. 288.
9. *Bengal Village Directory*, Vol. XXX, p. 88.
10. G.D.A.M.I., p. 107.
11. *Ācārāṅga Sūtra*, pp. 190-191.

by the Kshatriyas. The village is also known as Kuṇḍagrāma.[1] Some Jain traditions locate Kuṇḍapura at modern Bargaon in the district of Patna which is the site of ancient Nālandā. But it was evidently a suburb of Vaiśālī. It is identified with modern Basukunda.[2]

(B)

KĀLAYA

This was a settlement near Vaniyagāma to its north-east.[3] It is not exactly identified, but must have been in the Muzaffarpur district where Vaniyagāma was situated.

BELUVĀ

This was a village in the neighbourhood of Vaiśālī.[4] Buddha visited this place many times. The place is not identifiable.

NĀLIKĀ

This was a village also known as Nādikā.[5] Hsüan-Tsang seems to refer to this village as Na-te[6] or Nataka between Vaisālī and Magadha. It is not identifiable.

PUBBAJIRA

This was a village in the Vajji[7] territory. It is not identifiable.

GAGGALIGĀMA

This was a village somewhere on the bank of the Gaṅgā.[8] This is not identifiable.

KOṬIGĀMA

This village is often referred to in the Buddhist literature.

1. *Kalpa Sutra*, p. 219.
2. *G. D. A. M. I.*, p. 107.
3. *Āvaśyaka Ṭīkā*, p. 456.
4. S. Vol., V, 159. S.A., III, 201.
5. M.A., II, p. 235.
6. *On Yuan Chuang*, Vol. II, p. 86.
7. M. III, 266; S. IV, 59.
8. J. VI, 431.

The *Saṁyutta Nikāya*[1] expilcitely mentions that it was situated in the Vajji country. The *Vinaya Piṭaka*[2] states that the Buddha stayed at Koṭigāma after passing through Pāṭaliputra. Hsüan-Tsang[3] seems to refer to this village as situated to the south of Nādikā. He calls it Kou-li or Koti. The village was probably on the bank of the Gaṅgā and served as a port, opposite Pāṭaliputra. It is not identifiable.

UKKĀCHELĀ

This place was situated on the bank of the Gaṅgā in the Vajji territory.[4] It is stated to be a *nagara*.[5] Buddhaghosha[6] tells that once the people caught fish at this place with the help of lights, made of burning clothes dipped into oil, so the place was named Ukkāchelā. But this is simply a justification of the name. It is probable that the majority of the people were fishermen who used to fish at night with the help of light as is usually done at present. The place is not identifiable.

AṬṬHIKANAGRA

This was probably a village.[7] It was also known as Aṭṭhiyagama. It is said that a temple was built there on heaps of bones[8] and therefore it was named Aṭṭhigāma. From a certain Jain scripture.[9] it appears that the village was situated on the bank of the Gaṅgā. But as the village lay in route to Pāvā from Vaiśālī, it could not have been on the Gangā. There is a village called Hathagaon[10] on the Bāgmatī river which according to some scholars seems to represent the ancient Atthinagara. But there is no strong proof of its identification with Hathagaon, because the Bāgmatī river never flowed through this area.

1. S., V. 431.
2. *Vinaya*, I, p. 230.
3. *On Yuan Chwang*, Vol. II, p. 86.
4. *Udana*, A., 322.
5. M.A., I, p. 447.
6. Ibid.
7. M. I. 349; V. 342.
8. *Mahāvīra—His Life and Teachings* p. 33.
9. S.B.M. Vol. II, Part I. pp. 298-300.
10. *Vīra-Vihāra Mtmāṁsā* p. 23.

THE DARBHANGA DISTRICT

(A)

MITHILĀ

Mithilā was the name both of the country and its capital, which was formerly known as Videha.[1] The city occupies a prominent place in the Brāhmaṇical literature. It was the seat of the philosopher-king Janaka to whose court flocked teachers from different parts of the country. The Buddhist literature throws more light upon the city of Mithilā, but the city was never a stronghold of Buddhism and therefore the Buddhist works mainly narrate its past history, or it is possible that the city had ceased to be an important place before the Buddha. The *Mahāgovinda Sutta*[2] says that the city was founded by Mahāgovinda. The latter's name was originally Jotipāla.[3] After the death of his father, he was made the priest of the king Disampati and then he was known as Mahāgovinda. A man of the same name is said to have planned the city of Rājagṛiha[4] also. From the *Mahāgovinda Sutta* it is apparent that Mahāgovinda was not a personal name, but a designation which was conferred upon a priest. It is possible that the priests may sometimes have been trained as architects.

The city is said to have been seven leagues in extent.[5] According to the *Mahāummagga Jātaka*, there were four markets at the four gates of the city. The circumference of Mithilā described in the Jātakas should not be taken too literally. It is simply an echo of its ancient glories and prosperity.

The *Rāmāyaṇa*[6] and the *Mahābhārata*[7] refer to this city and its King, although it was a confederate ally of the Lichchhavi republic when these works were composed. As Mithilā is associated with the story of Rāma and Sītā the city is referred to in the Purāṇas and many other Brāhmaṇical works. But none of them presents any vivid account of the city.

1. See above, p. 88.
2. D. II. p. 235.
3. Ibid.
4. S. A. II. 413; D.A. I. p. 13 etc.
5. J. VI. 46. ff.
6. Bal. Ch. 13. 21 etc.
7. I. 113. 28; II. 20.28 etc.

On the basis of the name, Mithilā is identified with the modern town of Janakapura (city of Janaka) to the north of the Darbhanga district.[1] No archaeological remains have been found there. In the absence of any huge mounds, it can be suggested that this ancient city may be lying at another site still awaiting the spade of an archaeologist, and that the identification is not correct.

(B)

JAMBUBANĪ

This is a Vishaya recorded in the Panchobh Copper Plate[2] of Sangrāmagupta. The place has been identified with modern Jamui in the Monghyr district[3], but the identification is not convincing. It should be somewhere in the locality of Darbhanga, since Sangramagupta was a mere *māṇdalīka* whose territory centered in that region. The place is, however, not identifiable.

YAVANAMAJJHIKĀ

This was a village in the kingdom of Mithilā.[4] The place is not identifiable.

MITHILĀYYĀNA

The place seems from its name to have been in Videha. But the stanza[5] mentioning it throws no light upon its situation.

JAVAKACCHAKA

This village was situated in the neighbourhood of Mithilā.[6] The place is not identifiable but it should have been in modern Darbhanga district.

1. A.G.I. pp. 509-10.
2. J.B.O.R.S. Vol. V. pp. 582-96.
3. Ibid.
4. J. VI. 335.
5. B. U. XI. 23.
6. *Mahāvastu*, Vol. II, o p. 83.

THE SAHARSA DISTRICT

(A)

HARDEYA

This was a village recorded in the Bangaon Copper Plate[1] (12th. Century A.D.). We identify it with Hardi[2] in the Supaul police area of the Saharsa district which was formerly a part of the Bhagalpur district.

VASUKĀVARTA

This was a village in the jurisdiction of the Hardeya Vishaya, recorded in the Bangāon Copper Plate.[3] We identify it with Basauna in the Bangaon[4] police area of the Saharsa district.

IṬṬAHAKĀ

This was a village recorded in the Bangaon Copper Plate. It is also deciphered as Itrihoka. We identify this village with Itahari[5] in the Supaul police area of the Saharsa district.

(B)

KAÑCHANAPURA

This place is recorded in the Bangaon Copper Plate, It seems that the place was important as it served the purpose of a Jayaskandhāvāra[6] or military headquarters. It has not been found mentioned in any other grant. The place is not identifiable.

ĀPANA

This place is much talked about in the Buddhist literature. The *Saṁyutta Nikāya*[7] tells us that Āpana was a city of Aṅga and the *Majjhima Nikāya*[8] more precisely states that it was in Aṅguttarāpa, which was probably an integral part of Aṅga.

1. E. I. Vol. XXIX, pp. 48-56.
2. *Bengal Village Directory*. XXXIV. p. 49.
3. E. I. Vol. XXIX, pp. 48-56.
4. *Bengal Village Directory*, XXXIV. p. 13.
5. Ibid. p. 53.
6. E. I. XXIX. pp. 48-56.
7. S. V. p. 225.
8. M. I. 359; 447; II. 146.

The *Theragāthā*[1] says that it was a village in Aṅguttarāpa. Hence we can infer that Āpana was situated to the north of the Gangā in the modern Purnea or Saharsa district.

Buddhaghosha[2] says that the place was so called because there were twenty thousand bazars there. This seems to be an exaggeration. It may have been a market place connecting north and south Bihar. This place is not identifiable.

(C)

BARĀTAPUR

This village countains a ruined fort[3] which is ascribed to king Virāṭa of the *Mahābhārata*. But from the study of the epic, it is quite clear that the capital of Virāṭa should be somewhere in the vicinity of Hastināpura, where the Kauravas could attack easily and could take away king Virāṭa's cattle. So we cannot say any thing definitely about this tradition and hence its identification with the capital of king Virāṭa is doubt- ful.

THE BHAGALPUR DISTRICT

(A)

CHAMPĀ

This is one of the oldest cities of India, and is frequently mentioned in Pāli, Prākṛit and Sanskṛit literature. The *Aṅguttara Nikāya*[4] describes it as the capital of Aṅga. This city[5] was situated on the confluence of the Gaṅgā and the Champā, a river of the same name. This is corroborated by the itinerary of Hsüan-Tsang.[6] Its more ancient name was probably Mālinī[7]. It was also known by the name of Kālachampā.[8]

The name of the city seems to have been derived, according to Buddhaghosha,[9] from the Champaka trees which grew

1. p. 310.
2. M. A. II. 586.
3. *District Gazetteer—Bhagalpur* (1911) p. 162.
4. A. I., p. 213.
5. J. IV 506; *Mahābhārata* III. 84. 163; 307. 26.
6. *On Yuan Chwang*, II. p. 181.
7. *Vāyu Purāṇa* 99. 105, 106; *Matsya Purāṇa* 48. 97; *Mahābhārata* XII. 5. 6, 7, etc.
8. J. VI, 32.
9. M. A. II. 565.

in abundance on its site. Champā was a very flourishing and prosperous city in the sixth century B.C. It was considered one of the six great cities[1] of India in the time of Buddha. The *Mahājanaka Jātaka*[2] refers to its gates and watch towers. It apparently became a great trading centre, whose traders carried on business between India on one hand and the South East Asia and Ceylon on the other.[3] The traders of Champā were perhaps among the first Indians to establish their settlements in those countries some of which were named after their native city.

When the Aṅga territory was annexed to Magadha, Champā[4] remained the capital of viceroys coming from Magadha. But the city must later on have sunk into comparative oblivion after the establishment of Tāmralipti and Pāṭaliputra.

Although the city was not very important in later times, it was still deemed famous in literature,[5] which records the ancient fame of the city handed down by traditions.

We do not know the cause of the decline of the city nor can we say whether it faced any foreign invasions before the advent of the Muslims. As Tāmralipti was situated on sea-shore, it was easy and more advantageous to carry on foreign trade in later centuries. Its political significance was soon lost by the establishment of Pāṭaliputra as the capital not only of Magadha, but of whole India during the time of the Mauryas. At present, the site of this city is identified with two small villages-Champapur and Champanagar[6] in the neighbourhood of Bhagalpur. The identification is supported by Hsüan-Tsang[7] also, who says that the city was 140 or 150 li (about 23-25 miles) to the west of a hill crowned with a temple. Cunningham[8] identifies this hill with the Patharaghat which is exactly 24 miles to the east of Bhagalpur. Beside this, both villages bear similarity to the name of the ancient city.

1. D. II. p. 147.
2. J. VI. No. 539.
3. Ibid; See *Hinduism and Buddhism* (Eliot), Vol. III. p. 137 ff.
4. *Pariśishṭaparva*, VII. 22.
5. *Daśakumāracharita*, II. 2; *Harshacharita*, p. 199.
6. A.G.I.p. 547.
7. *On Yuan Chwang* p. 181.
8. A.G.I. p. 546.

VIKRAMAŚĪLA

The site where the Vikramaśīla Mahāvihāra was situated has not been finally identified. We learn from the Tibetan lama Tāranātha[1] that the Vihāra was situated on a high cliff on the right bank of the Gaṅgā. Cunningham[2] locates it at Silao, six miles to the north of Rājagṛiha. Dr. S. C Vidyābhushaṇa[3] locates it at the Jhangira hill, Sultangunj, in the Bhagalpur district. A. Banerjee Sastri[4] identified it with Keur, near Hulasgunj in the district of Gayā. The majority of sholars[5] are in favour of its identification with the Patharghat hill, 24 miles to the south-east of Bhagalpur. Cunningham's theory cannot be tenable in the light of the fact that the mounds which he found at Silao are not big enough to be the site of a university. The local tradition about the association of mounds with king Vikramāditya, which, according to him, suggests that it was Vikramaśīla, is not an unusal one in North India. Vikramāditya has been a symbol of ideal kingship and hence his memories are associated with any mound in the country. We cannot put much reliance upon such traditions. The same argument can be adduced in case of Keur also. Banerjee Sastri[6] thinks that as the same persons were in charge of the Nālandā and Vikramaśīla universities, both of them should have been in one locality. But he forgets that such a proximity becomes necessary only in circumstance, dictated by the daily routine work, but this does not apply to those concerned with the broad lines of principles only. It is hard to run two parallel universities in one locality in our days also, so how can we expect such things in ancient time, especially in connection with institutions of such high standard where only higher education was imparted. The hill at Sultanganj is in the river Gaṅgā bifurcating its water and its small space does not permit us to suppose it to have been the site of a big Mahāvihāra.

In the German Translation of Tāranātha's work[7], we

1. *Tāranātha's Geschichte des Buddhismusm in Indien*. p. 217.
2. A.S.I. III. p. 83.
3. Bhārati (Vaiśākha, 1315) 1909.
4. J.B.O.R.S. XV. pp. 263-76.
5. J.A.S.B. (1909) pp. 1—13.
6. J.B.O.R.S. Vol. XXV
7. *Tāranāth's Geschichte Des Buddhismus in Indien* p. 242.

are told that Gayā was almost one day's journey from Vikramaśīla. This may lead one to think erroneously that Vikramaśīla was in the neighbourhood of Gayā. But the original text[1] describes one of the masters of Vikramaśīla saying to a student "now go quickly and reach the city of Gayā at midday on the day after to-morrow."[2] It is not difficult to reach Gayā from Patharghat in two days or a little more on horse-back or any fast vehicle. But in any case Tāranātha wrote about India after the destruction of Vikramaśīla monastery and hence the source of his information was a tradition which may not be necessarily correct. The geographical data are generally more correct and reliable than traditions and hence his description of the site is more trustworthy than the distance of places which he probably never visited.

The Patharghat hill is situated on the right bank of the Gaṅgā. On its top there is a large number of ancient remains. This may be the hill referred to by Hsüan-Tsang[3] as there were Brāhmaṇical gods on this hill according to the pilgrim. N. L. Dey[4] concludes that the place was formerly in the hands of the Brāhmaṇas and was later taken over by the Buddhists.

The university is said to have been founded some time in the later part of the eighth century A.D. by king Dharmapāla.[5] We do not know by what name the place was known in earlier times. Franklin cites a line from the *Chaurapañchāśikā* which states that it was known as Śilāsaṅgama.[6] N. L. Dey[7] understands that Śilāsaṅgama is merely a corruption of Vikramaśīla Saṅghārāma. We went through the whole book of *Chaurapañchāśikā*, but we did not find the word Śilāsaṅgama, nor do we think that there is any necessity of its referring to this place. It seems that Franklin consulted a manuscript version of the poem with a corrupt reading. The meaning of Vikramaśīla seems to be in the sense of good conduct or morality and to have no reference to a *Śilā*,

1. *Tāranāthae de Doctrinae Buddhicae in India Propogationae*, p. 183, line 20.
2. We are indebted to Dr. D. S. Snellgrove for this translation.
3. *On Yuan Chwang*, II, p. 161.
4. J.A.S.B. (1909) pp. 1—13.
5. *Tāranātha's Geschichte des Buddhismus in Indien*, p. 242.
6. *Site of Ancient Pātaliputra* (1815) p. 55; Appendix XIII.
7. G.D.A.M.I. pp. 26-27.

"a stone". In other words, Vikramaśīla was a place where good conduct or high morality was the strength of the people.

The university was patronised by the Pāla kings. They helped the Nālandā university also, but the impression given by Tāranātha is that they probably paid more attention ro Vikramaśīla.[1] The latter was founded on the pattern of its elder sister Nālandā. Some scholars are of the opinion that the rise of Vikramaśīla Mahāvihāra was also a cause of Nālandā's decline. But there is actually no appparent sign of any decline of Nālandā Mahāvihāra until it was destroyed. During the reign of Devapāla,[2] the latter was definitely more respected in the south-eastern Asia than Vikramaśīla. If there were any decline in Nālandā the reason may have been financial rather than academic. The Pāla kings may have been reluctant to help Nālandā on the same scale as they did in the case of Vikramaśīla. The chief reason of this partiality seems to have originated from the fact that the rise of Nālandā could not be attributed to the Pāla kings, while Vikramaśīla was their own creation and they alone were credited for its rise. As the students must have been attractedt owards the newly founded university, the strength of students at Nālandā must have been smaller than it had been during Hsüan-Tsang's sojourn.

We have no early account of Vikramaśīla. It is not mentioned in Pali or Sanskrit literature. We do not know the reason why this site was selected for a university. However in due course Vikramaśīla became a famous centre of Tāntrism and some of its great scholars[3] went to Tibet to reform the deteriorated Buddhism of that land. Their works are still found in Tibetan literature. The university continued to flourish until it was destroyed by the Musalmans at the end of 12th. Century A.D.

KAYALISAMAGĀMA OR KAYALIGĀMA

Mahāvīra arrived here from Bhaddiya and left for Jambusaṇḍa.[4]

The place seems to be Kahalgaon[5] in the Bhagalpur district.

1. Tāranātha's Geschichte des Buddhismus in Indien, p. 242.
2. E.I. Vol. XVII, p. 322.
3. J.A.S.B. (1891) Vol. II, p. 51.
4. *Life in Ancient India As Depicted in the Jain Canons*, p. 258.
5. *Bengal Village Directory*, Vol. XXXIV. p. 70.

MANDIRA

It is said that this was the place where the sixteenth Tīrthaṅkara received his first alms.[1] According to Jains it may be identified with Mandāragiri[3] in the Bhagalpur district.

BHADDIYA

It was a *nagara* in the Aṅga kingdom. Buddha and Mahāvīra often visited this place which shows its importance. N.L. Dey[3] identifies it with Bhadaria, eight miles to the south of Bhagalpur. On the similarity of name. the identification seems convincing. Rāhula Sankṛityāyana[4] identifies it with Monghyr. But the place seems to be nearer to Champa, hence his conjecture is no more tenable.

(B)

ARAKKHURI

This village is stated to be on the border of Champā in the Āvaśyaka Niryukti.[5] Its exact situation is not known but it should be in the Bhagalpur district.

PĪṬHĪCHAMPĀ

Mahāvīra arrived here from Chorāga and proceeded to Kayaṅgala. The place was near Champā.[6] Its situation is not exactly known. but it should be in the Bhagalpur district.

ASSAPURA

This is mentioned as a *nigama* of Aṅga in the Pāli literature.[7] It is said to have been founded by the second son of king Uparichara[8] of Chedi. This may or may not be true since that most of the towns or states of Eastern India are ascribed to the Chedi dynasty. The *Chedi Jātaka*[9] states that Assapura was to the south of Sovatthī, the Chedi capital. The direction

1. *Āvaśyaka Niryukti*. p. 324.
2. *Life in ancient India As Depicted in the Jain Canons*, p. 311.
3. G.D.A.M.I., p. 30.
4. *Vinaya Piṭaka*, p. 248 (note).
5. p. 1297.
6. *Āvaśyaka Ṭikā*, 383a.
7. M. I. pp. 271, 281.
8. J. III. 460.
9. Ibid.

as recorded in the Jataka is wrong, if Assapura was in the kingdom of Aṅga which was to the east of the Chedi kingdom or it is possible that Assapura to the south of Sovatthī was another place. It is not identifiable.

(C)

SULTANGANJ

This is a famous place in the Bhagalpur district. The Gaṅgā takes its north-bound turn at this place and hence it has been deemed very sacred. There is a hill in the river which is called Jahangiri. It seems to be a corrupt form of Jahnugiri, the hill of Jahnu, the famous Hindu sage. There are many figures, mostly Brāhmaṇical. The famous bronze statue of the Buddha was found at this place. It is possible that Buddhism was soon replaced by Brāhmaṇism, because at present we scarcely find any Buddhist image at Sultangunj. A few short[1] inscriptions in Gupta characters prove the antiquity of the place. We do not know by what name it was known in early ages.

THE CHAMPARAN DISTRICT

(C)

LAURIYA NANDANGADH

Lauriya Nandangadh is situated in the Champaran district. The name of the village is Nandangadh, but it is commonly referred to with the prefix Lauriya because of the Aśokan pillar in its vicinity. A pillar in the local dialect is known as *Laur* or large rod.

This spot has attracted the attention of archaeologists for a long time, although no excavation has ever been carried on a large scale. There are two pillars of Aśoka in this locality one at Nandangadh and another at Araraj. Besides these, there are mounds "in three lines, two running north-south and one east-west. Exacavations revealed a composition of hard yellow clay unlike the surface soil and interlayed with regular strata of leaves and straw. In the centre of the exca-

1. A.S.I. Vol. XV. pp. 20—30.

vated mound a decayed wooden post was found, composed of Sal wood timbers bolted end to end with iron bolts."[1]

Scholars have not arrived at any definite conclusion about these mounds. T. Bloch excavated one of these mounds in the early part of this century. He found there the remains of a pole and a gold leaf with a female figure, probably that of the goddess of Pṛithvī. Taking all these into consideration, he came to the conclusion that the mounds were "the remains of some royal tombs, similar perhaps to those of the Vajjis, Mallas and other Rajput clans"[2] He dates them back to the Vedic period and quotes some verses from the *Ṛig-Veda* in his support. Codrington has nothing himself to say on the question and he seems to endorse the opinion of T. Bloch.

N. G. Majumdar throws more light upon the issue. He excavated some of these mounds in 1935-37. He found there a punch-marked coin and a number of ex-voto tablets bearing either the figure of the Buddha and the creed in the north Indian character or the device of a stūpa.

These finds convinced him that the mounds were Buddhist Stūpas[3] and their construction generally followed the plans of the early stūpas discovered elsewhere.

As we find there both Vedic and Buddhistic remains, it can be surmised that the place was used for burial even in the Vedic period, and was taken over by the Buddhists for the same purpose in the following ages, after the orthodox Brāhmaṇism had given up interring the ashes of the dead.

As these mounds run from east to west and north to south in order, it seems there was some plan before the place was brought into actual use. We may infer that the place was reserved for important personages. The importance of the site can easily be inferred from the erection of the Aśokan pillars in the vicinity. Either the place was chosen for the burials because it was the site of festive gatherings or because it stood on the junction of high roads-one leading to Nepal and another to Kuśīnagara. The place seems to have declined in importance after Aśoka, for which we cannot suggest any obvious reason. We do not find it mentioned in the Buddhist

1. *Ancient India* (Codrington), p. 17.
2. A.S.I. (1909), pp. 11—126.
3. A.S.I. (1935-37), p. 56.

literature. Hsüan-Tsang[1] may have visited this place, because he mentions many Aśokan pillars at different places in this part of the country. But we cannot exactly identify it from his account. In our present state of knowledge we are unable to go into further detail about these mounds, which are still archaeological mysteries.

LAURIYA ARARAJ

This place lies in the Champaran district at a distance of 20 miles from Kesariya. An Aśokan pillar with several edicts stands near this village. The place is off the main routes and no foreign traveller seems to have visited it. We have no source from which we may know its older name. No archaeological investigation of the site has taken place and thus we can say nothing about its ancient character. But as the Aśokan pillars must have been set up at important centres it would appear that despite the silence of the pilgrims, a town of some size existed here in early times.

KESARIYĀ

Hsüan-Tsang[2] mentions a place 200 li (33½ miles) to the north-west of Vaiśālī. He does not mention the name of the place and simply says that it had long been wasted with a very few inhabitants. On the basis of the distance,g iven by the pilgrim, Cunningham[3] identifies the place with modern Kesariya in the Champaran district.

CHANDAKIGADH

This village is situated eleven miles to the north of Lauriya Nandangadh. In the vicinity of this village, there is a large mound of "solid brick work"[4] about 90 feet high. No excavation has been conducted there and hence we can say nothing about it. This mound may be similar to those of Lauriya Nandangadh.

SAGAR-DIH

This is situated 13 miles to the south of Motihari in

1. *On Yuan Chwang*, Vol. II, pp. 5—20.
2. *On Yuan Chwang*, Vol. II. p. 72.
3. A.G.I. p. 511.
4. A.SS.I. XVI, p. 109.

Champaran district. Cunningham[1] mentions a large mound of ruins at this place. There is a stūpa also which stands on an older stūpa.

The local people associate the name of this place with Sagara, the hero of the Solar race. We know nothing of its history or even its ancient name.

THE SANTHAL PARGANA DISTRICT

(A)

KAJAṄGALA

This seems to be an important place as it has been often referred to in Pāli literature. From its mention in early Pāli exts, Kajaṅgala seems to be an old place. The *Vinaya Piṭaka*[2] describes it as a town situated in the east. In the time of the Buddha, it was a prosperous town where food could easily be obtained.[3] The *Milindapañho*[4] describes it as a Brāhmaṇa village and says that it was the birth place of Nāgasena. It seems that the place had deteriorated in comparison with its early condition. In the time of the *Milindapañho* (probably 1st century A.D.), it was a village only, while earlier it was a town.

Kajaṅgala has been determined as the eastern limit of the Majjhima deśa.[5] The Hindu works fix Benaras as the eastern limit of the Madhyadeśa. It may be suggested that after the spread of Buddhism in the whole country, scholars from the eastern region dominated the field and as there were many sacred sites of Buddhism in those parts, therefore they extended the eastern limit of the Madhyadeśa to Kajaṅgala. They did so also with a view to include their own motherland in the Madhyadeśa, which was highly respected from the ancient time.

The Chinese pilgrim Hsüan-Tsang[6] visited Kajaṅgala. He calls it Kie-chu-u-khi-lo or Kie-ching-kie-lo which is a

1. A.S.I. Vol. XVI, y. 19.
2. Vol. I, p. 197.
3. J. IV. 310.
4. P. 10.
5. *Milinda Pañho*, p. 10.
6. *On Yuan Chwang*, Vol. II. p. 183.

transliteration of *Kankjol.*[1] The pilgrim states that it was a district measuring about 2000 li or 300 miles in circuit. About the tenth or eleventh century A.D. it was a small independent state called Kayangala[2] Mandala, whose chief helped Rāmapāla[3] against his enemies. This place is known at present almost by the same name.

(B)

MĀHĀSALA

This was a nigama,[4] situated to the east of Kajaṅgala. It may have been on the border of Aṅga and Rāḍha. The place is not identifiable.

THE HAZARIBAGH DISTRICT

(A)

JAMBHIYAGĀMA

This place is often referred to in the Jain scriptures. Its Sanskrit name seems to be Jṛimbhikagrāma. Mahāvīra is said to have attained Kevalahood at this place which was on the bank of the Ṛijupālikā.[5] Munikalyāṇa Vijaya[6] understands that it was a flourishing "town stewn with tall ramparts and high buildings." He identifies it with Jambhigaon near the Damodara in the Hazaribagh district, but J.C. Jain[7] prefers to locate it somewhere in the region round modern Pāvā in the district of Patna. We find many references to Jain ascetics moving in the area round about the Pārasanātha hill and so it would be no wonder if Mahāvīra also went there to attain Kevalahood. The only objection to the identification of this place with Jambhigaon is that the place where Mahāvīra achieved enlightenment was on the bank of the river Ṛijupālikā which is identified[8] with the river Barakar. We cannot say how the village near the Dāmodara can be identified with

1. A.G.I. p. 548.
2. *Rāmacharita* II. 5 (Commentary)
3. *History of Bengal* Vol. I. p. 157.
4. *Vinaya* I. 197.
5. *Kalpasūtra*, p. 263.
6. S.B.M. pp. 357, 370.
7. *Life in Ancient India As Depicted in the Jain Canons.* p. 289
8. See above p. 81.

ancient Jambhiyagāma. It is possible that the Damodara may be flowing in that area through the old bed of the Barakar.

PĀVĀ

This place is often referred to in the Jain literature. It was the capital of the Bhaṅgī country which was one of the twenty five and half Aryan countries.[1] It should not be mistaken for modern Pāvā in the Patna district which is the Majjima Pāvā of the Jains. It is possible that Mahāvīra died in this village, which is in the locality of the Pārasanātha hill. As majority of the Jain Tīrthaṅkaras died on the Pārasanātha hill, it is no wonder if Mahāvīra also thought to do so, but expired in this village in the house of king Hastipāla, who may have been a local chief.

There is a village called Pawapur[2] in the Bagodar police area which may be the ancient Pāvā.

BHADDILAPURA

This was the capital of the Malaya kingdom, which is one of the twenty five and a half Aryan countries- of the Jain literature. The information of the Jain scripture is not corroborated by any other source and we cannot rely much upon them. However the place is identified with modern Bhadia[4] a village near the Kulha hills in the Hazaribagh district. It was the birth place of the tenth Tīrthaṅkara.

(B)

BHRAMARAŚĀLMALI, CHHIṄGATA, NABHŪTISAṆḌAKA

These three villages are recorded in the Dudhpani inscription[5] of probably the eighth century A.D. As its find-spot is in the Huntergunj police area of the Hazaribagh district, these villages should be somewhere in the same locality. But they are not identifiable.

1. *Brihat Kalpa sūtra* (with commentary) Part III, p. 913.
2. *Bengal Village Directory*, Vol. XLI. p. 105.
3. *Brihat Kalpa Bhāṣya Vritti* I, 32, 63 etc.
4. *Life in Ancient India As Depicted in the Jain Canons*. p. 272
5. E.I. Vol. II, pp. 344—45.

(C)

ITAKHORI

This place has mounds and ruins of a fort. The place lies on the way from Gayā to the southern districts. We do not know anything of its early history.

THE RANCHI DISTRICT

(A)

CHORĀYA

This place was visited by Mahāvīra. It has been identified with Chorey[1] in the Ranchi district, on the basis of similarity of name.

LOHĀGGALA

This place is referred to in the Jain scriptures.[2] On the basis of similarity of name, it may be identified with Lohardagga[3] the headquarters of a sub-division of the Ranchi district.

(B)

MADDANAGĀMA

This village is referred to in the Jain canon. Mahāvīra is said to have arrived here from Kuṇḍaka and left for Bahusalāga. It may have been somewhere in the Ranchi district or the Chhotanagpur region.

BAHUSALĀGA

It is stated that Mahāvīra travelled to this place from Maddana and left for Lohāggala. As Lohāggala is probably modern Lohardagga[1] this place also may be located in the Ranchi district. It is, however, not identifiable.

1. *Life in Ancient India As Depicted in the Jain Canons*, p. 277.
2. Ibid. p. 306.
3. Imperial Gazetteer, Vol. VIII, p. 475.

THE SARAN DISTRICT

(B)

THŪNĀ

This place is described as a *Sanniveśa* or settlement. The correct Sanskrit form of the name seems to be Sthūnā. The *Udāna*[1] places it in the country of the Mallas on the Gaṇḍaki which has since then changed its course. The place must therefore have been in modern Saran or Champaran district. It is not identifiable.

(C)

CHERAND

This is a big village in the district of Saran. There is a large number of ruins and mounds. Hoey[2] was inclind to identify the mounds of this place with Vaiśālī, but further research and excavations have proved his assumption wrong. We do not know the name by which it was known in the ancient time.

MANJHI

This is a village in the Saran district. It is full of ruins. W. Vast[3] identified it with the site of Vaiśālī, No historical account of the place can be given in absence of any archaeological excavation of the site.

THE DHANBAD DISTRICT

(A)

GOBHUMI

This place was often visited by Mahāvīra.[4] The *Mahābhārata*[5] mentions a locality called Paśubhūmi which we have identified[6] with the Chhotanagpur region. It is probable that the Gobhūmi and the Paśubhūmi may be identical. It is identified with Gomoh which is in the Dhanbad district.[7]

1. VII. 9.
2. J.R.A.S. (1901) p. 41.
3. Ibid. (1903) p. 583.
4. *Āvaśyaka Ṭikā*, p. 284a.
5. II. 27. 8.
6. See above p. 108.
7. *Life in Ancient India As Depicted in the Jain Canons*, p. 285.

THE SINGHBHUM DISTRICT

(A)

SUBHABHŪMI

The Jain literature often refers to this place. It may be modern Singhbhum[1] district which is still covered with wilderness.

DAḌHBHUMI

This was probably identical with Daṇḍabhūmi[2] and is said to have been inhabited by Mlechchhas. It is identified with Dhalbhum, a sub-division of the Singhbhum district.[3]

SOME OTHER PLACES

In Buddhist and Jain texts, we find some places about which we are not sure if they existed in Bihar or in the neighbouring states of Uttar Pradesh and west Bengal. Such places are considered in the following pages.

VĀCHĀLA

Mahāvīra came to this place[4] from Morāga. It was divided into two parts—north and south. The rivers Suvaṇṇakulā and Ruppakulā, about whose existence, we know nothing from any other source, flowed between them. The place may have been somewhere in north Bihar.

SURABHIPURA

Mahāvīra came to this place[5] after crossing the Gaṅgā. It seems to be in south Bihar.

PATTAKALAYA

From Kalaya, Mahāvīra reached this place. We cannot suggest any region for it.

1. Imperial Gazetteer, Vol. XII, p. 529.
2. S.B.M. II Part I, p. 473.
3. *Life in Ancient India As Depicted in the Jain Canons*, p. 278.
4. *Life in Ancient India As Depicted in the Jain Canons*,
5. Ibid.

HALDDUGA, NANGALA, AVATTAGAMA

Mahāvīra wandered through all these villages.[1] It seems that they may have been situated in the eastern part of Chhotanagpur from where he entered into the Lāḍha country.

Some places such as Jambusaṇḍa, Tambaya, Kuviya Sanniveśa seem to fall between Aṅga and Vaiśālī.

The places such as Ālabhiya, Kuṇḍāga, Unnāga may have been in south Bihar.

BHOGANAGARA

This seems to be an important place[2] which lay on the high road from Vaiśālī to Pāvā of the Mallas. The place may have been in Saran or Champaran district or in Deoria or Gorakhapur district of Uttar Pradesh.

CHHĀGALA

Tāranātha[3] refers to this place variously. He says that Vararuchi, the Pandit came from the land of *Chhāgala*, to the east of Magadha. But we know certainly that the territory of Aṅga was to the east of Magadha. It may have been a township of which we have no information in any other literature. The place is not identifiable.

1. Ibid.
2. *Āvaśyaka Chūrṇī*, II. 291.
3. XV, p. 74; XXIX, p. 210; XXXII. p. 233.

CHAPTER VII

COMMUNICATIONS

As long as men have existed, they have travelled from place to place. Long routes were discovered very easily in the course of the human migrations. With the discovery of land routes, rivers were also used for the same purpose. We generally find old routes running along the banks of rivers, probably because people wandered with their cattle in search of food and water along the rivers where they could easily procure these things. With the development of urban civilization, cities grew on river banks and they were linked together with other cities both by land and water.

The routes passing through mountainous areas have remained almost the same from time immemorial to our own day. In a hilly region it is very difficult to make or find out new routes, and as they have to run through certain passes, their number is always very few. But the roads running through the plains are apt to change, because people can move freely in such regions even without definite routes and such tracks after some time take the form of usual routes. In the plains, routes can be easily made to facilitate communications.

Bihar is not an exception to these generalizations. The land being plain, we find plenty of roads running from one part of the country to another. The *Rāmāyaṇa* and the *Mahābhārata* refer to such routes being traversed by the marching armies of the victorious kings. Chariots were driven on these routes and hence they were known as rathyās, meaning routes broad and firm enough for chariots.

The *Arthaśāstra*[1] refers to various types of roads, such as chariot roads, royal roads, and roads leading to *droṇamukhas*, country parts and pasture grounds, each of which is four *daṇdas* (24 ft.) in width. From the above statement we may arrive

1. *Arthaśāstra*, II. 4.

at the conclusion that there were various types of roads and that they varied in width according to the purpose they served.

In early days, when the whole country was divided into petty principalities, no big roads running throughout the length and breadth of the country could have been in existence However we find that routes connected state to state. With the development of the Mauryan empire, we find roads linking both ends of India. Kauṭilya[1] and Arrian[2] use the words 'royal roads' in their accounts. We really do not understand what the term 'royal road' signifies. It is not wholly clear whether it denoted a particular type of road used by royal personages and their troops and followers only, or main roads which crossed the country from one end to another. The latter interpretation seems to be more probable, and the term *rājamārga* may have had the same sense as the old English term "the king's high way", implying an important road maintained directly or indirectly by the state.

From the Greek accounts, it appears that special care was taken of roads during the Mauryas. Strabo[3] explicitly states that "they construct roads, and at every ten stadia set up a pillar to show the by-roads and distances." Such things could be expected only in a developed and highly civilized society and it is no wonder that so much attention was paid on roads during Mauryan times. But even then it is not to be expected that all roads in remote provinces could have been looked after so well.

Aśoka took special measures for the welfare of the state an even the roads could not escape his attention. In the second Rock Edict,[4] he states that wells were dug and trees were planted on roads for the use of men and animals. He emphasizes the same thing but more elaborately and explicitly in his 7th pillar Edict.[5] He says that he caused banyan trees to be planted on roads for giving shade to men and animals, and that wells were dug and rest houses built at a distance of eight *Kos*[6] and mango-gardens too were planted.

1. Ibid.
2. *Indika* (*Arrian*) II. 1.7.
3. XV. I. 50-52, pp. 707-709.
4. *Some Select Inscriptions*, p. 18.
5. *Some Select Inscriptions*, p. 66.
6. *Aṭhakosikya*—We support Hultzsch (C.I.I Vol. I, p. 135 n. 1).

These things are possible only when rulers are highly enlightened and peace and tranquility reign supreme in the country. In the disconnected and checquered history of ancient India, we do not know much about these roads.

Śukranīti[1], a later work, has some suggestions about the construction of roads. These show that in ancient India roads were never neglected and the attention of the rulers was drawn towards them from time to time by authors of great repute.

There must have been some dangers to these roads from infringement of their boundaries by cultivators and others as is clear from the *Arthaśāstra*,[2] which prescribes measures to be taken against this by the state.

We have no account of the nature of these roads whether they were metalled, brick-built or mud roads. The royal roads may have been brick built but the rest cannot be expected to have been so.

ROUTES TRACED IN THE RĀMĀYAṆA

The *Rāmāyaṇa*[3] traces a route through which Rāma had travelled in Bihar. The story tells us that Rāma and Lakshmaṇa led by Viśvāmitra came to the confluence of the Sarayu and the Gaṅgā. We do not know which route they took to reach the confluence, but the *Rāmāyaṇa* is explicit on this point that they crossed the Gaṅgā at the confluence and reached the forest, where they killed the demons. The hermitage of Viśvāmitra is traditionally located at the modern Buxar. It seems possible that Rāma followed some route which ran along the western bank of the Sarayu. However we do not find this route mentioned in any other work. After the completion of the sacrifice, they proceeded towards the north[4], but did not cross the Gaṅgā. They seem to have travelled to the east and come to the bank of the Śoṇa,[5] which may have flowed

against J. Bloch (*Les Inscriptions d' Asoka*, Paris, 1950, p. 170, n.1), who interprets the phrase as meaning half a *Koś*. Since Asoka also erected resting places at this distance apart, it is evident that he was thinking in terms of a day's journey.

1. Ch. I. pp. 34-35.
2. *Arthaśāstra*, II. 3.
3. Bāl. Chs. 23, 31, 35, 45, 47 etc.
4. Bāl. 31.16—Uttarām disi samuddisya prasthātumupachakrame.
5. Bāl. 31.20—Vāsam chakre munigaṇāgh Śoṇakūle samāhitāḥ.

in those days in the vicinity of modern Patna. Various routes leading to different directions[1] met on the western bank of the Śoṇa. One of them led to its junction with the Gaṅgā. The *Rāmāyaṇa* tells us here that they passed the whole night in crossing the river and in the morning landed on the other side, from where the palaces of Vaiśālī were visible. From this statement we can surmise that Rāma sailed from the western bank of the Śoṇa and landed on the eastern bank of the Gaṇḍakī, crossing the vast expanse of the Gaṅgā. Had he crossed the Gaṅgā directly it would have not taken the whole night, and thus it seems that he sailed diagonally across the main stream of the Gaṅgā. If the Gaṇḍakī flowed more to the west in those days, he may not have touched its banks.

Rāma probably landed on the northern bank of the Gaṅgā in the district of Muzaffarpur. Whatever may have been the course of the Gaṅgā in those days, it was never so northerly that the lofty palaces of Vaiśālī could be seen from the place where he landed. The poet either lacked the knowledge of geography of this region or he was using hyperbole to enhance the magnificence and splendour of ancient Vaiśālī. From Vaiśālī, they reached Mithilā via the hermitage of Gautama.[2] Rāma's journey to Mithilā from Vaiśālī probably indicates the route adopted by the Buddhists in the following ages.

If we analyse the whole journey of Rāma in Bihar, it will be apparent that there was a route from Ayodhyā or further west which touched the Saran district on its south-west. People crossed the Gaṅgā by boat at its confluence with the Sarayū and landed on its right bank near Buxar. A route ran from this place to the western bank of the Śoṇa, where other routes joined from various directions. Another route, which probably ran along the western bank of the Śoṇa, led to its junction with the Gaṅgā. People desirous of going to Vaiśālī or any place on the north of Gaṅgā, had to cross the river at this place. On the north of the Gaṅgā, the route led to Vaiśālī and the hermitage of Gautama, which is located

1. Bāl. 35. 4—Ayaṁ Śoṇaḥ śubhajalogāḍhaḥ pulinamanditaḥ Katarena pathā Brāhmaṇa saṁtarishyāmahe vayam.

2. Bāl. 48. 15.

at Ahiari[1] a village in the Darbhanga district, and then to Mithilā.

ROUTES INDICATED IN THE MAHĀBHĀRATA

The *Mahābhārata*[2] deals with the routes of ancient Bihar on two different occasions; once during the fight between Bhīma and Jarāsandha and again during Bhīma's conquest of the eastern quarter.

The Pāṇḍavas, headed by Kṛishṇa, left Kuru Pradeśa and took the route which ran on the north of the Gaṅgā. This was an old route and perhaps easier because we find many people travelling on this route in the Buddhist scriptures. They crossed the Sarayū somewhere in eastern Uttar Pradesh and reached Mithilā. The places along this route are not mentioned. They then followed the south-westerly route and crossed the Gaṅgā at its junction with the Śoṇa[3] The text says that they proceeded towards the east after crossing the river and reached Gorathagiri which is identified with modern Barabar hill. The Gorathagiri lay to the south east of the confluence of the Śoṇa and Gaṅgā. It seems that there was a route which went to the Gorathagiri from the eastern bank of the Śoṇa. This may be the route in continuation of another route which is traced in the *Rāmāyaṇa*[4] and along which Rāma had travelled. This route went to Rājagṛiha via Gorathagiri. At present there is no sign of any direct route from the Śoṇa to the Barabar hill. The Buddhist and Jain literature too are quiet about it. The Pāṇḍavas were travelling in disguise,[5] so they may have left the high road and travelled from one place to another along by -roads. The route from Gorathagiri to Rājagṛiha is still in use. The Pāṇḍavas had to follow this route because the area is hilly, and so naturally there are few routes.

Another route in the *Mahābhārata*[6] can be deduced from

1. Darbhanga District Gazetteer, p. 141.
2. II. 20. 30.
3. *Mahābhārata*, II. 20. 29. Atītyagaṅgāśoṇañcha trayste prañmukhāstadā kuśaschirachhadājagmuḥ Māgadham kshetramachyutāḥ
4. Bāl. 31. 16-20.
5. II. 20. 29.
6. II. 30.

Bhīma's conquest of the eastern territories. The kingdoms mentioned in this context have been put in such a haphazard way that no particular route seems to have been followed. From the list of the territories conquered one after another by Bhīma, it appears that the compiler of the epic had no knowledge of military strategy or geography. The conqueror sometimes goes far ahead leaving some territories unconquered.[1] This shows that the author had no knowledge of the geographical position of these states, nor of the high roads which are necessary for the movement of an army.

The road from Kuru Pradeśa to Rājagṛiha has been traced correctly, probably because that road had not lost importance even during the time when the *Mahābhārata* was being compiled or the author of that chapter may have been another man who knew these highways well.

ROUTES IN THE BUDDHIST AGE.

The Buddhist literature throws some light on the highways of its time which connected important cities of northern India. In those days it was definitely very difficult to cross the Gaṅgā except at important established ferry places. We therefore find that roads ran along the south and north banks of the Gaṅgā. These roads sometimes met at important places and again bifurcated.[2] This route system in the Indo-Gangetic valley has been followed throughout the ages and even in our own time railways run along those routes.

In ancient Bihar, important cities such as Rājagriha, Champā, Vaiśālī, Mithilā and later on Pāṭaliputra were linked together by highways, and were connected with other cities of the country, particularly of northern India.

To follow the line of these routes more clearly, we should start from a centrally situated city of Bihar and as such. Vaiśālī is perhaps the most important place, from which roads led to different quarters of the country.

A road started from Vaiśālī and connected it with remote cities of north-western India such as Taxila in one way or other. The *Suttanipāta*[3] refers to the important places lying

1. Ibid.
2. *Sārthavāha*, p. 17.
3. *Sutta Nipāta*, Verse 1013.

on this route; they are Bhoganagara, Pāvā, Kuśīnagara, Kapilavastu, Setaviyā, Śrāvastī and Sāketa, from which a further road led to Taxila and Purushapura. The *Dīgha-Nikāya Aṭṭhakathā*[1] goes into greater details about the places which lay between Vaiśālī and Bhoganagara : they are Bhaṇḍa-gāma, Hatthigāma, Ambagāma and Jambūgāma. This road continued to run to the south-west to Māhishmatī via Kośāmbī, Gonaddha and Ujjayinī. Bhoganagara, which lay on this route after Vaiśālī, was perhaps an important halting station. Buddha stayed there before he left for Pāvā. Although this place has not been identified, it can be assumed that it was somewhere on the north-western border of modern Champaran district. Thus it will be clear that from Vaiśālī, the road ran north-west to Pāvā and Kuśīnagara and beyond. The Buddha travelled along it several times.

From Vaiśālī , anotjaṅgala.te[2] led to Champā and further east to Kaṅkjol or Kalers em This road finally reached Tāmralipti, where travel The barked on ships for Ceylon and far eastern islands. Bhamost important place between Vaiśālī and Champā was Bhaddiyā which is identified with Monghyr by Rāhula Sānkṛityāyana,[3] while we think it was a village[4] near Bhagalpur. We cannot locate the exact spot where people crossed the Gaṅgā. At present the river is crossed at the Maniharighat, where it is not so broad. But in former days the Kośī may have joined the Gaṅgā a little west of the place where it falls now, and thus, avoiding the trouble of crossing the Kośī, travellers directly reached Champā after crossing the river Gaṅgā only. The road from Champā to Tāmralipti must have been very important, for the merchants. carried on sea-borne trade with eastern islands along this road.

A third route from Vaiśālī went to the south and reached Rājagiha. The places of importance on this road were Nādik, Koṭigāma, Pāṭaligāma, Nālandā, Ambalaṭṭhikā (which was probably a garden between Nālandā and Rājagṛiha where travellers used to take rest) and then Rājagṛiha.[5] Koṭigāma

1. D.A. Vol. II, p. 549.
2. *Sārthavāha*, p. 18.
3. Purātatva Nibandhāvalī (1939), pp. 33—35.
4. See above p. 178.
5. D. II. p. 72.ff.

seems to have been a ferry place opposite Pāṭaligāma. There was one more place, Ukkāchelā[1] between Koṭigāma and Vaiśālī, where the road coming from Vārāṇasī (Banaras) joined the southern route.

Motichandra[2] thinks that the road between Vaiśālī and Rājagṛiha ran via Pāṭaligāma, Uruvelā and Gorathagiri and then it reached Rājagṛiha. There may have been a route which ran along the eastern bank of the Śoṇa for some distance and then turned to the Gorathagiri and Rājagṛiha. This was the route on which the Pāṇḍavas travelled.[3] But Motichandra is definitely incorrect when he says that the route led to Uruvelā and then to the Gorathagiri. Uruvelā was farther south than the Gorathagiri and travellers would not have gone there and again come back to the Gorathagiri, covering a distance of almost 33 miles, for nothing. The land is quite level and there is no necessity of winding routes. There was another road from Uruvelā to Rājagṛiha along which Buddha journeyed to the sylvan grove of Uruvelā.

A road[4] seems to have run along the northern bank of the Gaṅgā from Vārāṇasī to Ukkāchelā which was somewhere to the south of Vaiśālī. This road joined the Vaiśālī Rājagṛiha road. Hsüan-Tsang[5] travelled on this road for some distance after crossing the Gaṅgā, somewhere near modern Arrah.

The city of Mithilā[6] was connected with Vaiśālī, where merchants flocked from different parts of the country. We have no clear evidence whether Mithilā was directly connected with Śrāvastī or whether the road passed through Vaiśālī. A road between Mithilā and Śrāvastī through Vaiśālī would be very long one, while we see no reason why these cities should not have been linked directly. It is possible that there was a road from Mithilā which joined the Pāvā-Vaiśālī route somewhere in the Champaran district. This city was linked with Champā[7] also. The road may have passed through Darbhanga

1. *Vinaya* II, 220.
2. *Sārthavāha*, p. 19.
3. See above p. 301.
4. *Vinaya* II. 220.
5. A.G.I. pp. 504—06.
6. See above p. 299.
7. IV. 32.

and Saharsa district and may have joined the Vaiśālī-Champā road somewhere to the north of the Gaṅgā before crossing the river.

As far as south Bihar is concerned, the central places whence routes led to different parts of the country were Rājagṛiha and Pāṭaliputra. There is a difference of time in the importance of these two places. In the early Buddhist period or even before, Rājagṛiha was the capital of Magadha and hence it was a flourishing centre of trade whose merchandise[1] was in demand in other territories also. Later on, with the transfer of the capital to Pāṭaliputra, Rājagṛiha began to decline, and the former became the centre of gravity. As it is said that all roads lead to Rome, similarly in a figurative sense all roads must have led to Pāṭaliputra in the Mauryan period. There were, however, certain roads which touched neither of the cities, but were equally important.

As has been said above, Rājagṛiha was connected with Vaiśālī via Pāṭaligāma. We find a few names of places on this ancient road, such as Nālandā and Ambalaṭṭhikā in the vicinity of Rājagṛiha,[2] which show that it was the same as that used in our own day. But we are not sure about the course of the route beyond Nālandā. Fa-hsien,[3] after covering a distance of nine *Yojanas* from Pāṭaliputra, came to a hill, which can be no other than that of Bihar Sharif. The road from Bihar-Sharif may have led to modern Fatuha via Hilsa and then, crossing the confluence of the Punpun with the Gaṅgā, may have directly led to Pāṭaliputra. Rājagṛiha may have been linked up with Champā by a highway, but we have no reference to any direct road either in the Buddhist or Jain literature. We can base our inference on the fact that there had been constant wars between Aṅga and Magadha and hence there must have been a movement of forces which required roads. Secondly both cities, Champā and Rājagṛiha, were prosperous trading centres, so they must have been linked up by a road.

From Rājagṛiha, one road led to Vārāṇasī[4] (Banaras)

1. *Rāmāyaṇa*, Ayo. 38.
2. *Vinaya*, III, 2.
3. *Record of the Buddhistic Kingdoms*, Ch. XXVIII. p. 66.
4. *Vinaya*, III. 2.

and further west to the cities of Prayāga, Kānyakubja, Mathurā and Taxila[1] through Gayā, along which the Buddha[2] himself journeyed to Ṛishipattana.

We do not know if any road connecting Rājagṛiha with an eastern port had been made at the time when Rājagṛiha was the capital of Magadha. Under the Mauryas, when Pāṭaliputra was the capital of the whole empire, a road ran from Tāmralipti, which was probably then on or very near the coast, to Purushapura in the north-west.[3] This road joined the two extremities of the Mauryan empire. Since then this highway has always occupied a unique place in the history of India and even now its importance cannot be denied. It passed through almost all the important cities of Āryāvarta and caravans could thus easily travel from one end of the country to another. In the west the foreign hordes easily penetrated into the plains of the Gangetic Valley along this highway. The *Mahāvaṁśa*[4] states that Aśoka travelled along this road to Tāmralipti in order to send off the sapling of the Bodhi tree to Ceylon. Tāmralipti could be easily reached by boat, but yet the emperor adopted a land route. To show his respect for the Bodhi tree he went to Tāmralipti with his force and retinue and so it was not possible for them all to travel by boat. Beglar[5] thinks that the Tāmralipti-Pāṭaliputra road passed through Ektesvara, Chatna, Raghunathapur, Telkupi, Jharia, Rajauli, Rajagriha and Patna. His assumption seems to be right, because the road at present runs along the southern side of the Vindhyā ridge. It probably entered Rājagṛiha through the southern gate. This highway must have touched Pāṭaliputra. Megasthenes[6] seems to have referred to this high road. At present we have no remains of this road beyond Pāṭaliputra. The modern Grand Trunk road, which was repaired from time to time, is probably the same ancient route. It runs via Dhanbad, Barhi, Gayā, Sahsram and Banaras. We cannot say when it ceased to

1. Ibid.
2. Ibid.
3. *Indika* (Arrian), II.1.7.
4. XIX. 6.
5. A.S.I. VIII. pp. 48—57.
6. *Indika* (Arrian). II. 1.7.

touch Rājagṛiha and Pāṭaliputra, but this may have been after the 10th or 11th century, when Pāṭaliputra was no longer an important town.

A road ran between Gayā and Pāṭaliputra. This road started from Gayā and running along the eastern bank of the Phalgu reached Tailāḍhaka via modern Islampur. Beglar[1] believes that there were two routes from Tailāḍhaka. One route, along which Hsüan-Tsang travelled, directly led to Pāṭaliputra, another passed via Hilsa and Fatuha. Beglar gives no clear reason, however, on which he bases his belief in the existence of the direct route. It does not seem logical that two different roads went to Pāṭaliputra from Tailāḍhaka, especially in those days when modern equipment was totally absent. Even at the present, there is no direct route between Teladha and Patna. A traveller will have to cross a large number of rivers on the way and so people generally prefer to go to Patna via Hilsa and Fatuha. There seems to have been one road only, which ran via Hilsa and Fatuha to Pāṭaliputra. The silence of the pilgrim about places between Pātaliputra and Tailāḍhaka may be due to the fact that these towns had not grown into prominence in those days, while Tailāḍhaka possessed a big *Saṁghārāma*.[2] Thus he travelled by the same old route which ran from Pāṭaliputra to Rājagṛiha via Fatuha and Hilsa while another starting from Hilsa led to Tailāḍhaka

Grierson[3] suggested that a road ran from Tāmralipti to Vārāṇasī via Ranchi and Palamau. The only purpose of this road seems to be for the speedy transport of merchandise to the eastern port. But this part of Bihar is even now full of jungles, and must have been even wilder in days of yore. A trading route generally takes a safe course, but here the case was quite the reverse. Grierson gives no clear evidence for his conjecture. We believe the trade between Vārāṇasī and Tāmralipti was carried on mainly by way of the Gaṅgā and along the route which passed through Gayā, Rājagṛiha and then to Tāmralipti. We find a record of three merchant brothers who had gone to Tāmralipti from Ayodhyā on business,

1. A.S.I. Vol. VIII, pp. 48—51.
2. *On Yuan Chwang*, Vol. II. p. 107.
3. *Notes on the District of Gayā*, p. 16.

at Dudhapani[1] in the Hazaribagh district. They probably travelled along this very route.

We are quite in the dark about the roads which passed through the interior of Jhārakhaṇḍa. We have no source available to show any of the routes passing from the north to the south and thus entering into modern Orissa. This problem becomes more difficult in the light of Samudragupta's invasion on Deccan. The Allahabad Pillar Inscription throws no light upon the route taken except to mention that Kosala[2] (which probably occupied the modern districts of Raipur-Sambhalpur and Bilaspur) was first to be vanquished. Dr. Davies,[3] tracing the route of Samudragupta's compaign, has drawn a line from Pāṭaliputra to the south via Bodh Gayā and modern Chhotanagpur across the Vindhyā. The Jhārakhaṇḍa area is even at present full of jungles and hence one would not expect that an army so big as to conquer the whole of the Eastern part of the Deccan Peninsula would pass through this tract. R. K. Mukherjee[4] states that "leaving the Jamna Valley, Samudragupta must have marched through the modern Rewa state and Jabalpore district and come up before his first object of attack, the kingdom of Kosala."

However, we would offer a third suggestion. It is not improbable that the whole force marched along the Pāṭaliputra-Tāmralipti road and from a place somewhere in modern west Bengal turned towards the west on a road which must have been in existence connecting the port of Tāmralipti with the fertile valley of the Mahānadī. This route may have passed through the region, through which the railways run between Calcutta and Nagpur in our own time. From modern Kharagpur one line goes to Orissa and another directly goes to Bilaspur and Raipur. Samudragupta may have followed the latter course. This Pāṭaliputra-Tāmralipti route may also have been followed by Aśoka when he attacked Kaliṅga. This is of course an assumption only and we cannot definitely reconstruct the route of Samudragupta's march to

1. E.I. Vol. II, pp. 343—47.
2. *Select Inscriptions* (note), p. 257.
3. See map facing a page 8, *Historical Atlas of the Indian Peninsula* (1949).
4. *The Gupta Empire*, p. 20.

the south. The routes hitherto suggested however, would have been exceedingly difficult for a large army.

The two Chinese pilgrims, Fa-hsien and Hsüan-Tsang, travelled widely in India and they have left accounts of their journeys which greatly help us in making an estimate of the routes in Bihar. We should not presume that they always travelled on high roads, though in an alien land a man would hardly like to travel off the road. But Hsüan-Tsang, in his journey in the region round Rājagriha, does not seem always to have followed a main road. He probably walked from one place to another and then, after completing his visit, he joined a road and went on to Champa. It seems probable that many of the smaller places he visited were merely linked by foot-paths, as at present.

Fa-hsien entered Bihar by the high road which led from Vaiśālī to Kuśīnagara and further west. He then crossed the Gaṅgā and followed the Pāṭaliputra-Rajagṛiha road. From Rājagṛiha he went to Gayā. He then went to Kukkuṭa-Pādagiri[1] which he wrongly located in the neighbourhood of Bodh-Gayā; but which we identify with the Gurupa hills. We do not know whether there was any direct route to Gurupa from Bodh-Gayā. He may have gone there along small paths. Fa-hsien then went to Pāṭaliputra whence he left for Kāśī and then he went to Champā. Then he followed the old Champā-Tāmralipti road and embarked for Ceylon.

The route followed by Hsüan-Tsang is not so easy to explain. He entered Bihar in the district of Shahabad after leaving the Chañchu country. He probably followed the old route along the southern bank of the Gaṅgā. He then crossed the Gaṅgā somewhere near modern Arrah and followed the road which led from Vārāṇasī to Vaiśālī along the northern bank of the Gaṅgā. From Vaiśālī he went to Mithilā along the highway mentioned above. He then entered the valley of Nepal. The pilgrim again came back to Vaiśāli and travelling along the Vaiśālī-Rājagṛiha road he reached Tailaḍhaka[3] (Ti-lo-shi-kia).

We have traced above the route between Pāṭaliputra

1. *Record of the Buddhistic kingdoms*, Ch. XXXIII. p. 83.
2. See above p. 196.
3. *On Yuan Chwang*, Vol. II. p. 107.

and Gayā along the eastern bank of the Phalgu, via modern Islampur. But the pilgrim probably left that route. After crossing a distance of 90 *li* (15 miles) he reached a hill which we identify with the Barabar hill. He then went north-west for 30 *li* (5 miles) and reached the Gunamati monastery which is located at the village of Dharawat.[1] He again turned and reached the Śīlabhadra monastery which was probably near the Kowadol hill.[3] The pilgrim says that after travelling for 49 or 60 li (7 or 10 miles), he reached Gayā after crossing the Phalgu. As the pilgrim seems to have travelled along the western bank of the Phalgu from Tailāḍhaka (Teladha) to Gayā, he did not need to cross the river. He probably could not correctly recollect the route he had travelled when writing his itinerary. From Tailāḍhaka, Hsüan-Tsang does not seem to have followed any highway, he covered the distance diagonally via Barabar and thus reached Gayā. Hsüan-Tsang then travelled 100 li (17 miles) and reached Kukkuṭapādagiri. We have suggested that Kukkuṭapādagiri or Gurupādagiri is identical with the Gurupa hills,[4] but the distance and places mentioned in its vicinity do not take us so far. The pilgrim may have forgotten the places which he visited in the vicinity of the Gurupa hills, though Cunningham[5] may be right in identifying the Kukkuṭapādagiri with the village of Kurkihar. Hsüan-Tsang then went along the route which Fa-hsien had already travelled. From the Kukkuṭapādagiri, he travelled to the north-west and visited places such as Buddhavana, Yashṭivana and Tapovana which are in the neighbourhood of Rājagṛiha. These are the places along the road from Gayā to Rājagṛiha. From the situation of these villages, it appears that either Hsüan-Tsang forgot to put them in the order in which he visited them or, as he was not well acquainted with these places, he made unnecessary journeys. From Tapovana, he went to Rājagṛiha through the Jethian-Rājagṛiha Pass. He then reached Nālandā along the highroad. From Nālandā he went to

1. *On Yuan Chwang*, Vol. II. p. 109.
2. A.S.I. Vol. VIII, p. 39.
3. Ibid. p. 37.
4. See above p. 48.
5. A.G.I. pp. 526—28.

Giriyek (Indraśailaguhā) and then proceeded through the hills of Shekhapura[1] to Rajauna[2] (Lo-pan-ni-lo), somewhere in the region round Kiul. He then went to Hiraṇya Parvat in the neighbourhood of Monghyr and from there Hsüan-Tsang reached Champā after travelling 300 li (50 miles). He then followed the Champā-Tāmralipti road and entered Bengal. The road from Nālandā to Champā seems to be old Rājagṛiha-Champā road.

The last route that we can trace in Bihar is that of Bakhtiyar Khilji's invasion (A.D. 1196-1203). Bakhtiyar had his fief[3] in the district of Mirzapur, near Bihar. He therefore must have known the main routes of this area. He easily captured this district and fell upon Maner.[4] In those days, the Śoṇa fell into the Gaṅgā at Maner.[5] So Maner must have then occupied an important position, being situated at the confluence of two big rivers. The invader crossed the Śoṇa at this place and proceeded to Bihar-Sharif. From there he took a route which led through the wild tract of Jhārakhaṇḍa.[6] This was probably the ancient Pāṭaliputra-Tāmralipti road, along which the invader travelled and penetrated into Bengal

Besides the land routes, there must have been some communication by water also. We get slight references to waterways in Bihar in ancient literature. The Gaṅgā is the biggest river, where vessels could be used throughout the year. The cities on the bank of this river soon became trading centres. Merchandise was taken from one place to another by the river. The trade of Champā with foreign countries was carried on mostly by the Gaṅgā and some sort of change in the course of the river of shallowness due to the silts deposited by other rivers, may be one of the causes of the decline of its city. Trade and communication by water was not limited to Champā only. Boats went further west via Pāṭaliputra, Vārāṇasī and Prayāga to Indraprastha.[7] The Khalimpur Inscription[8]

1. A.G.I. p. 544.
2. A.S.I. Vol. XV. pp. 13—15.
3. *History of Bengal*, Vol. II. p. 32.
4. Ibid.
5. See above p. 70.
6. *Foundation of Muslim rule in India*, p. 71.
7. J. VI. 447.
8. E.I. Vol. IV. p. 249.

of Dharmapāla gives a vivid description of boats in the Gaṅgā at Pāṭaliputra. This suggests that water communication was still flourishing in Bihar in the early 9th century.

Besides the Gaṅgā there is one more river in south Bihar where boats can be rowed throughout the year, the Śoṇa. The other rivers, being fed from the hills remain dry for the major part of the year. We do not find any reference to trade on the Śoṇa, but the location of Pāṭaliputra at its junction with the Gaṅgā, suggests not only the strong defence of the metropolis but also local trade by the water of the Śoṇa.

The rivers of north Bihar are mostly navigable and so local trade must have been carried on along them since time immemorial. But we have no definite evidence to support this. However the *Rāmāyaṇa*[1] furnishes one possible instance. The hermitage of Rishyaśriṅga was somewhere on the bank of the Kośī, which was probably in Aṅguttarāpa, whence the young sage was kidnapped to Champā in a boat, by the courtesans of Aṅga. They probably sailed through the Kośī and Gaṅgā to the capital of Aṅga.

The rivers of north Bihar were generally crossed by boats but we hardly find any reference to this effect in our ancient literature. The foreign pilgrims are also silent about any communication by water in Bihar.

1. Bāl. Ch. X.

BIBLIOGRAPHY

ORIGINAL SOURCES

PĀLI

Aṅguttara Nikāya	Pali Text Society
Aṅguttara Nikāya Aṭṭhakathā	—do—
Buddhavaṁśa	—do—
Dīgha Nikāya	—do—
Dīgha Nikāya Aṭṭhakathā	—do—
Jātakas	Edited by V. Fausboll, London 1877—1896.
Mahāvaṁśa	Pali Text Society.
Mahāvaṁśa Ṭīkā	—do—
Mahāvastu	Edited by Senart,
Majjhima Nikāya	Pali Text Society.
Majjhima Nikāya Aṭṭhakathā	—do—
Milinda Pañho	Edited by V. Treckner, London 1880.
Saṁyutta Nikāya	Pali Text Society.
Sārathappakāsinī	—do—
Sutta Nipāta	—do—
Sutta Nipāta Commentary	—do—
Theragāthā	—do—
Therīgāthā	—do—
Therīgāthā Commentary	—do—
Udāna	—do—
Udāna Commentary	—do—
Vimānavatthu Commentary	Pali Text Society.
Vinaya Piṭaka	Edited by H. Oldenberg, London and Edinburgh, 1879-1883.

SANSKṚIT AND PRĀKṚIT SOURCES.

Abhidhānachintāmaṇi	Bhavanagar, Veer Era 2451.
Abhidhānarājendra	Muni Vijaya, Rutlam, 1913-34.

Abhijñānaśākuntalaṁ	Kālidāsagranthāvalī, edited by Sitaram Chaturvedi, Banaras, 1950.
Arthaśāstra (Text)	Edited by Sham Sastri, Mysore 1909.
Arthaśāstra (translation)	Sham Sastri, Mysore, 1924.
Aṣṭādhyāyī of Pāṇini	Edited by S. C. Basu, Allahabad 1891.
Atharva Veda Saṁhitā	Sacred Book of the East. Vol. XLII.
Āvaśyaka Chūrṇī	Edited by Jinadasa Jain, Rutlam, 1928.
Āvaśyaka Niryukti	Edited by Jina Bhadra Jani Benares, 1915.
Āvaśyaka Ṭīkā	Edited by Haribhadra, Bombay, 1916.
Baudhāyana Dharmaśāstra	Edited by E.Hultzsch, Leipzig, 1884
Bhāgavata Purāṇa	Edited by Bhavani Charan Bandopadhyaya, Calcutta, 1830.
Bhagavatī Sūtra (Commentary)	Abhayadeva, Bombay, 1921.
Brahma Purāṇa	Edited by V. N. Mandalika, Poona,
Brihatkalpa Sūtra with commentary	Malayagiri and Kshemagiri, Bhavanagara, 1933-38.
Chaurapañcāsikā	Edited by S. N. Tadaparikar, Poona 1946.
Divyāvadāna	Edited by E. B. Cowel and R. A. Neil, Cambridge, 1886.
Gārgīsaṁhitā	J. B. O. R. S. (1928)
Garuḍa Purāṇa	Edited by M. N. Dutta, Calcutta, 1908.
Gauḍavāho of Vākpati	Edited by S. P. Pundit, Poona 1927.
Gopatha Brāhmaṇa	Edited by I. Vidyasagara, Calcutta, 1858.
Harshacharita	Edited by Kashinath Pandurang Parva, Bombay, 1925.
Harivaṁśa	Edited by Ramachandra Shastr Poona, 1936.

Kathāsaritsāgara of Somadeva (Translation)	C. H. Tawney, London, 1924-1927.
Kalpasūtra	Sacred Books of the East Vol. XXII.
Kāmasūtra of Vātsyāyana	Edited by K. Rangasvami Iyenger, Lahore, 1921.
Kāvyamimāṁsā	Edited by C. D. Dalal and R. Anantakrishana, Baroda, 1915.
Kumārasaṁbhava	*Kālidāsagranthāvalī*, edited by Sitaram Chaturvedi, Banaras, 1950.
Kurma Purāṇa	Edited by Nilamani Mukhopadhyaya, Calcutta, 1890.
Lalitavistara	Edited by R. L. Mitra, Calcutta, 1882.
Mahābhāraṭa	Edited by P. C. Roy, Calcutta 1887.
Mahābhāshya of Patañjali	Edited by Kielhorn, Bombay 1892-1909.
Mālavikāgnimitraṁ	*Kālidāsagranthāvalī*, edited by Sitaram Chaturvedi, Benares, 1950.
Manusaṁhitā	Edited by Gopala Sastri Nane, Banaras, 1935.
Mañjuśrīmūlakalpa	Edited by K. P. Jayswal and Sānkrityayan, Lahore, 1934.
Mārkaṇḍeya Purāṇa	Edited by F. E. Pargiter, Calcutta, 1888-1904.
Mudrārākshasa	Edited by R.S. Pandit, Bombay, 1944.
Nirukta of Yāska	Edited by F R. G. Bhandarkar, Bombay 1942.
Pañchaviṁśa Brāhmaṇa	Edited by Chinnaswami Shastri and Pattabhirama Shastri, Banaras, 1935-36.
Pariśishṭhaparva	Edited by H. Jacobi, Calcutta 1932.
Raghuvaṁśa	*Kālidāsagranthāvalī*, edited by Sitaram Chaturvedi, Banaras, 1950.

Rāmacharita of Sandhyākaranāndī — Edited by R. C. Majumdar and others, Calcutta, 1939.
Rāmāyaṇa of Vālmīki — Edited by Kasinatha Panduranga Parva, Bombay, 1888.
Ṛigveda Saṁhitā — Vedic Research Institute, Poona, 1933.
Śaktisaṁgama Tantra — Edited by D.C. Sircar, Indian Culture Vol. VIII.
Śatapatha Brāhmaṇa — Sacred Books of the East Vols. XII, XXVI.
Śukranīti (Translation) — B. K. Sarkar, Allahabad, 1914.
Svambhu Purāṇa
Vāyu Purāṇa — Edited by H. N. Apte, Poona, 1905.
Vārāha Purāṇa — Edited by Harikesa Sastri, Calcutta, 1893.

GREEK SOURCES

Ancient India As Described by Megasthenes and Arrian — Edited and translated by J.W. MacCrindle, Calcutta, 1926.
Ancient India As Described by Strabo and others — Edited and translated by J. W. MacCrindle, Calcutta.
Ancient India by Ptolemy — Edited and translated by MacCrindle, re-edited by S. N. Majumdar Sastri Calcutta, 1927.

CHINESE SOURCES

On Yuan Chwang — T. W. Watters, London, 1905.
The Record of the Western Kingdoms by Fa- hsien — Translated by H. Giles. London and Sanghai, 1897.

TIBETAN

Tāranātha's Geschichte des Buddhismus in Indian — Anton Schiefner. St. Petersberg, 1869.

PERSIAN SOURCES

Ain-i-Akbari of Abul Fazl — Translated by Col. H. S. Jarret, Calcutta, 1891-94.
Al-Beruni's India — Translated by Sachau, London, 1888.

Tabkāt-i-Nāsirī of Ibn Sira-jal-Din — Translated by H. G. Raverty, 2 Vols., Calcutta, 1881.

MISCELLANEOUS MODERN WORKS

Agrawal, V. S. — India As known to Pāṇini, Allahabad, 1953.

Allan, J. — Catalogue of the Coins of Ancient India, London, 1936.

Altekar, A.S. — State and Government in Ancient India, Banaras, 1949.

Barua, B. K. — Early Geography of Assam, Gauhati, 1952.

Barua, B. M. — Gayā and Buddha Gayā, Calcutta, 1931.

Barua, K.L. — Early History of Kamrupa, Shillong, 1933.

Basham, A. L. — The Ājīvikas, London, 1951.

Bhandarkar, D. R. — Charmichael Lectures, Calcutta, 1921.

Birt, Francies Bradley, — Chhotanagpur, London, 1903.

Chakldar, H. C. — Social Life in Ancient India. A study in Vātsyāyana's Kāma-sūtra, Calcutta, 1954.

Cunningham, Sir Alexander. — The Anciet Geography of India, edited by S. N. Majumdar Shastri, Calcutta, 1924.

—do— — Mahābodhī, London, 1892.

Darby, H. C. — An Historical Geography of England before A.D. 1800. Cambridge, 1951.

Davis C. C. — Historical Atlas of the Indian Peninsula, Oxford, 1949.

Dey, N. L. — Geographical Dictionary of Ancient and Medieval India, London, 1927.

Dikshitar, V. R. — Purāṇa Index, 3 vols. Madras, 1955.

East, N. G. — Geography Behind History, London, 1958.

Eggermont, Dr.P.H.L. — The Chronology of Asoka Moriya Leiden, 1956.

Eliot, Charles — Hinduism and Buddhism, London 1921.

Fergusson, J. — A History of Indian and Eastern Architecture, London, 1876.

Fleet, J. S. — Corpus Inscriptionum Indicarum, Vol. III, Calcutta, 1888.

Franklin, N. — Inquiry Concerning the Site of Ancient Pātaliputra.

Grieson, Sir G. A. — Notes on the District of Gayā, Calcutta, 1893.

—do— Linguistic Survey of India, Calcutta, 1911.

Habibullah, A.B.M. — Foundation of the Muslim Rule in India, Lahore, 1945.

Hardy, R.S. — Mannual of Buddhism, London 1853.

Hultzsch, — Corpus Insprictions Indicarums Vol. I, Oxford, 1925.

Jain, J.C. — Life in Ancient India as Depicted in the Jain Canons, Bombay, 1947.

Kane, P. V. — History of the Dharmaśāstras

Konow, S. — Corpus Inscriptions Indicarums Vol. II, Calcutta, 1929.

Law, B. C. — Historical Geography of Ancient India, Paris, 1954.

—do— Kshatriya Tribes in Ancient India, Calcutta and Simla, 1923.

—do— Ancient Mid-Indian Kshatriya Tribes, Calcutta and Simla, 1924.

—do— Tribes in Ancient India, Poona, 1943.

—do— Bhārater Puṇya Tīrtha, Calcutta, 1944.

—do— Geographical Aspect of Kālidāsa's works, Calcutta 1954.

—do— Geographical Essays, London, 1937.

—do— Geography of Early Buddhism London, 1930.

—do— Mountains of India, Calcutta 1944.

—do— Rivers of India, Calcutta 1944.

MacCrindle Invasion of Alexander

Macdonell and Kieth Vedic Index, 2 Vols. London, 1912.

Majumdar, R. C. History of Bengal, Vol. I, Dacca, 1943.

Majumdar, R. C. Ancient India, Banaras, 1952.

Martin, R. M. The Eastern India, London, 1838.

Malalasekara, G. P. Dictionary of Pali Proper Names London, 1937.

Mitra, G. Birabhumer Itihasa, Calcutta, 1925.

Mitra, R. L. Budha Gayā, Calcutta, 1878.

—do— Sanskrit Budhist Literature of Nepal, Calcutta, 1882.

Morgan, K. The Religion of the Hindus, New York, 1953.

Motichandra Sārthavāha, Patna, 1953.

—do— Geographical and Economic Studies in the Mahābhārata, Lucknow, 1945.

Mukharjee, R. K. Ancient Indian Education, London, 1947.

—do— The Gupta Empire, Bombay, 1947.

Narain, A. K. The Indo-Greeks, Oxford, 1957.

Oldenberg, H. Budha, Edinburgh, 1882.

Pandey, Rajbali Gorakhpur Janpad Aur Uski Kashatriya Jatiyon Ka Itihasa Gorakhpur, 1946.

Ray, H. C. The Dynastic History of Northern India, Calcutta, 1931-36.

Raychaudhuri, H. C. The Polital Histrory of Ancient India, Calcutta, 1953.

Raychaudhuri, H. C. Studies in Ancient Indian Antiquities, Calcutta, 1931.

Rennell, Memoir of Maps of Hindoostan London, 1887.

Sānkṛityāyana, Rāhula — Buddhacharyya, Banaras, 1931
—do— — Vinaya Pitāka (trans.), Saranath 1935.
Sen, B. C. — Political Aspects of Inscriptions of Bengal, Calcutta, 1942.
—do— — Studies in the Jātakas, Calcutta, 1930.
Sankalia, H. D. — Studies in the Historical and Cultural Geography and Ethnography of Gujarata, Poona, 1949.
Singh, S. N. — History of Tirhut, Calcutta, 1922.
Sinha, B. P. — The Decline of the Kingdom of Magadha, Patna, 1954.
Sircar, D. C. — Select Inscriptions, Calcutta, 1942.
Sorenson, Soren. — Index to the Mahābhārata, London, 1904.
Spate, O. H. K. — India and Pakistan, London etc., 1954.
Suri, Vijayendra, — Vira-vihara Mimanasa, Delhi, 1946.
Thomas, E. G. — The Life of Buddha as Legend and History, London, 1931.
Vidyalankara, Jayachandra. — Bhāratabhūmi Aur Uske Nivāsī, Agara, 1931
—do— Satyaketu — Pāṭaliputra Ki Kathā
Vijaya, Muni Kalyāṇa — Abhidhāna Rājendra, Allahabad, 1949. Rutlam, 1913-34.
Vijaya, Muni Ratnaprabha — Śramaṇa Bhagavān Mahāvīra, Ahmadabad, 1948.
Warmington, E. H. — The Commerce between the Roman Empire and India, Cambridge, 1928.
Wilson, H. H. — Essays and Lectures Chiefly on the Religions of Hindus, London, London, 1862-77.

District Gazetteers of Bihar.

Bengal Village Directory, Calcutta 1888.

ARTICLES

Abbot, J. E.	The topographical list of the Bhāgavata Purāṇa, I.A. (1899) pp. 1—6.
Acharya, Paramananda.	A note on the Bhum Countries of Eastern India, I.C. Vol. XII. pp. 37-46.
Agrawal, V. S.	Geographical data in Pāṇini, I.H.Q. (1953), pp. 1-34.
Ball, V.	Stone Monuments in the district of Singhbhum in Chhotanagpur, I.A. Vol. I, pp. 291-92.
Banerjee, Adris.	The Antiquities of Bihar-Sharif, I.H.Q. (1951) pp. 151-60.
Banerjee, Mahagovind.	Name 'Chhotanagpur', J.B.O.R. S. Vol. XXVI, pp. 188-223.
Banerjee Sastri, A.	India beyond the Ganges, J. B. O. R. S. Vol. XXVIII, pp. 297-362.
—do—	Keur, A probable site of Vikramasila, J.B.O.R.S. Vol. XV, pp. pp. 263-76.
—do—	Vishvāmitra in Bihar, J.O.C. VI. pp. 185-88.
Bloch, T.	The Modern Name of Nālandā, J.R.A.S. pp. 440-43.
—do—	Excavation at Basarh, A.S.I.A.R. (1903-04) pp. 81-122.
Bose, Atindranath	Oldest Indo-Aryan Cities, J.I.H. (1942) pp. 60-82.
Bose, K. K.	Some old Accounts of Bhagalpur, J.B.O.R.S. Vol. XXI, pp. 139-19.
Broadley, A. M.	The Buddhistic Remains of Bihar, I.A.S.H. (1872) 207-312.
Chakaldar, H.	Contribution of Bihar to Vedic Culture, J. O. C. Vol. IV, pp. 507-15.
Chaudhari, P. C.	Ajapur of Skandagupta and area round Bihar J.B.O.R.S., Vol. XIX, pp. 337-44.

Chaudhari, S.B. — The Malavas, I.H.Q. (1948), pp. 171-79.

—do— — Aryavarta, I.H.Q. (1949) pp. 111-22.

Cunningham, Sir, A. — A.S.I. Vols. I, III, VIII, XI, XII, XV, XVI, XXIII.

Dalton, Col. E.T. — Rude Stone Monuments in Chhotanagpur and other places, J.A.S.B. (1873) pp. 112-19.

Dayal, P. — The Umga Hill Inscription in the Gayā district, J.A.S.B. (1906) pp. 23-30.

Dey, N. L. — The e Early Course of the Ganges, I.A. (1921) pp. 8,33,65.

—do— — Notes on Chirand in the district of Saran, J.A.S.B. (1903) pp. 87-90.

Fleet, J. F. — Dimensions of Indian cities and countries, J.R.A.S. (1907) pp. 641-56.

Ganguly, D.C. — Vaṅgāla deśa, I.H.Q. (1943), pp. 297-317.

—do— — Yādavaprakāśa on the ancient geography of India, I.H.Q. (1943) pp. 214-24.

Ghosh, A. — Rājagṛiha, A.I.(1950) pp.66-78.

Ghosh, J. C. — Antiquity of Gayā, J.B.O.R.S. Vol. XXIV, pp. 89-111.

Ghoshal, U. N. — Studies in Early Buddhist Histiriography, I.H.Q. (1941), pp. 149-61.

Grierson, Sir, G. A. — The Māgadhapura of the Mahābhārata, J.B.O.R.S. Vol. II, pp. 95-96.

Hodgon, B. H. — A memorandum relative to the seven Kośīs of Nepal J.A.S.B. Vol. XVII, pp. 646-49.

Hoey, W. — On the identification of Kuśīnārā, Vaiśālī and other places, J.A.S.B. (1900), pp. 74-88.

—do—	The five Rivers of the Buddhists, J.R.A.S. (1907) pp. 41-46.
Jackson, V. H.	Journal of Francies Buchanan (Patna and Gaya) J.B.O.R.S., Vol. VII, pp. 145-366.
—do—	The Shahabad Journal of Dr. Francis Buchanan, J.B.O.R.S. Vol. XI, pp. 201-387.
—do—	Hieüntsang's route in South Bihar, J.B.O.R.S. Vol. V, pp. 293-316.
—do—	The New Inscription from the Barabar Hills and an identification of Gorathagiri, J.B.O.R.S. Vol. II, pp. 159-71.
Jayswal, K. P.	A note on certain Sanskṛit Geographical and Ethnic terms, J.B.O.R.S. Vol. XVIII, pp. 97-98.
Johnston, E. H.	Two Notes on Ptolemy's Geography of India, J.R.A.S. (1941) pp. 208-22.
Joseph, T. K.	The India of Greeks and Romans of B.C. 326 to 641, J.B.O.R.S., Vol. XXXII, pp. 33-34.
Kale, Y. M.	Geographical position of certain places in India, I.A. (1923), pp. 262-63.
Keny, L. B.	Nāgas in Magadh, J.B.O.R.S. Vol. XXVIII, pp. 152-75.
Kittoe, Major, M.	Notes on the caves of Barabar, J.A.S.B., Vol. XVI, pp. 401-16.
—do—	Notes on the Vihāras and Chaityas of Bihar, J.A.S.B. Vol. XVI, pp. 272-79.
—do—	Notes on the Places of Bihar, J.A.S.B. Vol. XVI, pp. 953-70.
Kunhar, C.	The Malaya mountain, I.H.Q. (1947), p. 69.
Law, B. C.	Geographical data from the

	Mahāvaṁśa and its commentary, I.C. Vol. II, pp. 814-21.
—do—	Aṅga and Champā in Pali literature, J.A.S.B., (1925), pp. 137-42.
—do—	Rājagṛiha in Ancient Indian Literature, M.A.S.I. No. 58.
Long, Rev. J.	Notice of a ruin in Singhbhum, J.A.S.B. Vol. XX, pp. 283-84.
Mackenzi, Col.	Extract from the Journal of Col. Mackenzi's Pundit of His Route from Calcutta to Gaya, I.A. Vol. XXXI, pp. 65-75.
Majumdar, S.S.	Pīṭhī and Pīṭhīpati, I.C. Vol. V, pp. 379-85.
Majumdar, R. C.	Identification of some old sites in Rājagriha, J.A.S.B. (1949) pp. 65-80.
Martin, J.W.B.	On the Archaeological Remains of Bharatapur in the district of Bhagalpur, J.A.S.B. (1875) p. 128.
Marshall, J. H.	Rājagṛiha and its Remains, A.S. I.A.R. (1905-06) pp. 86-106.
Maulavi, A. W.	The Etymology of Ranchi, J.A. S.B. (1908) pp. 599-601.
Misra, Y.	Bihar in Agnipurāṇa, J.B.R.S., Vol. XL, pp. 1-7.
Mitra, Panchanan.	Pre-historic Trade Routes and commerce, I.C. Vol. II. pp. 77-92
Modi, J. J.	Ancientt Pāṭaliputra, J.B.R.A.S (1916-17) pp. 457-532.
Nahar, P. C.	The Jain Tradition on the Origin of Pātaliputra, J.O.C., Vol. VI, pp. 169-71.
Nigvi, B. K.	Legendary Origin of Patna, I.A. Vol. III, pp. 149-50.
Pandey H.	Notes on the Vajji country and the Mallas, J.B.O.R.S., Vol .VI, pp. 259-65.

Pandey, H. The Janibigha Inscription J.B.O.R.S. Vol. IV.

Pargiter, F. E. Ancient countries in Eastern India, J.A.S.B. (1897), pp. 85-112.

Peppe, W. Rough Notes on some of the Antiquities of the Gaya district, J.A.S.B. Vol.XXXV., pp.49-59.

Ray, U. N. Fortification of cities in Ancient India, I.H.Q. (1954), pp. 237-44.

Renny, T. Notes on the Locality of Rājagṛiha of the town of that name in Bihar, J.A.S.B. Vol. III, p. 366.

Rhysdavids, T. W. The Middle Country of Ancient India, pp. 83-93.

Roy, B. C. Distribution and Nature of Asur Sites in Chhotanagpur, J.B.O.R.S. Vol. VI, pp. 393-423.

Sarkar, S.C. Ancient Indian Geography, I.C. Vol. VII, pp. 137-89.

Sastri, H. P. Two eternal cities in the province of Bihar and Orissa, J.B.O.R.S., Vol. VI, pp. 23-33.

Sastri, H. Nalanda and Its Epigraphic Material, M.A.S.I.No. 66.

Sen, D. N. Sites in Rajagir, J.B.O.R.S. Vol. IV., pp. 113-35.

—do— Rājagṛiha in the Buddhist Scripture, J.O.C. Vol. II, pp. 613-24.

Sheawill, W. S. Notes on a tour through the Rajamahal hills, J.A.S.B., Vol. XX, pp. 544-606.

Shillingford, F. A. Changes in the course of the Kośī river, J.A.S.B. (1895), pp. 1-24.

Sinha, A. N. Notes on Kharakpur, J.B.R.S., Vol. XXVIII, pp.

Sinha, P. N. The word Kīkaṭa in the Ṛigveda in reference to South Bihar, J.B.O.R.S., Vol. IV, pp. 487-91.

Shende, S. R. — Routes between Āryāvarta and Dakshināpatha, B.C. Law Memorial, Vol. I, pp. 519-26.

Sircar, D. C. — An account of fifty-six countries in and on the border of India, I.C., Vol. VII, pp. 33-64.

—do— Origin of the name of Bengal I.H.Q. (1947) pp. 62-65.

—do— Kuntala and Aśmaka, I.H.Q., (1947) pp. 65-69.

—do— An Inscription from the Patna district, I.H.Q.(1953), pp.395-99.

—do— Text of the Puranic list of the peoples, I.H.Q., (1945) pp.

—do— Gayā Tīrtha, J.I.H. (1594) pp

Sikkadar, J. N. andThakur,A. — Panchobh Copper Plate of Sangrāmagupta, J.B.O.R.S. Vol V, pp. 582-96.

Smith, V. A. — Nepal, Tirhut and Tibet, J.B.O. R.S., Vol. III, pp. 555-56.

—do— Vaiśālī, J.R.A.S. (1902), pp. 267-88.

—do— Kuśīnārā or Kuśīnagara and other Buddhist places, J.R. A.S. (1902) pp. 139-63.

Sohoni, S. V. — The location of Seigerdis J.B.R.S. Vol. XVVV, pp. 35-36.

—do— Khandika and Kalinga, J.B.R.S. Vol. XXXV, pp. 91-92.

Stephen, J. — Excursions to the ruins and site of an ancient city at Bakhra, 13 Cos north of Patna and 6 Cos north from Singhea, J.A.S.B., Vol. IV. pp. 544-606.

Trivedi, Harihar V. — The Geography of Kauṭilya, Vol. I pp. 247-61.

Venkataramayya, M, — The Ancient Mālavas, I.H.Q (1953), pp. 80-93.

Vost, W. — Rāmanagara to Kuśīnārā, J.R. A.S. (1903), pp. 367-68.

—do— Kauśāmbī, Kasapura and Vaiśālī, J.R.A.S. (1903), p. 583.

Waddel, L. A. Discovery of Bud dhist remains at Mt. Uren in the Monghyr district, J.A.S.B. (1892), pp. 1-23.

Wilford, Col. F. An essay on the comparative Geography of Ancient India, J.A.S.B. Vol. XX, pp. 227-72 470-80.

—do— On the ancient Geography of India, Asiatic Researches, pp 373-470.

INDEX TO IMPORTANT PLACE-NAMES

(Ancient Indian names in Roman foreign forms Italicised, modern names in small type)

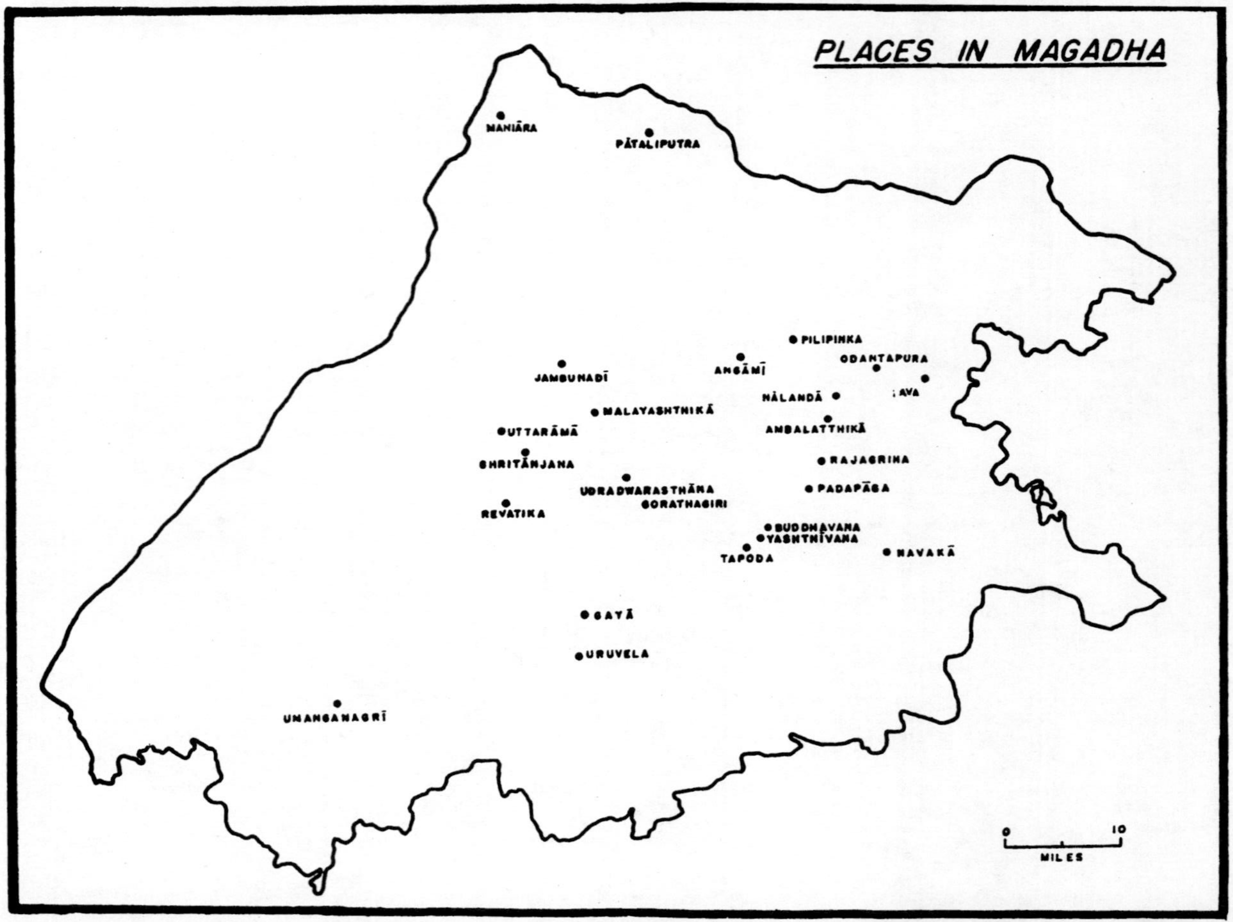
PLACES IN MAGADHA
MANIĀRA
PĀTALIPUTRA
PILIPINKA
ODANTAPURA
ANGĀMĪ
JAMBUNADĪ
NĀLANDĀ
AVA
MALAYASHTHIKĀ
UTTARĀMĀ
AMBALATTHIKĀ
SHRITĀNJANA
RAJAGRIHA
UDRADWARASTHĀNA
GORATHAGIRI
PADAPĀSA
REVATIKA
BUDDHAVANA
YASHTHĪVANA
TAPODA
NAVAKĀ
GAYĀ
URUVELA
UNANGANAGRĪ
0
10
MILES

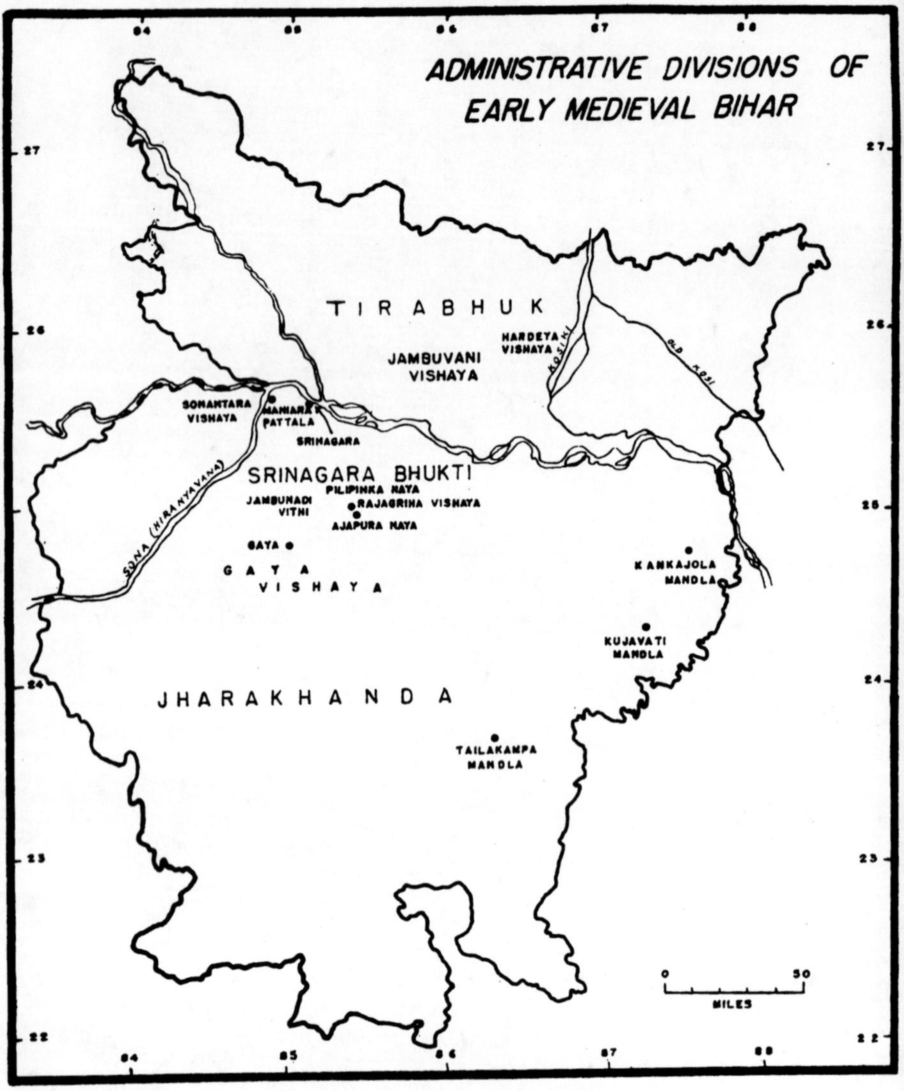
ADMINISTRATIVE DIVISIONS OF EARLY MEDIEVAL BIHAR
TIRABHUK
JAMBUVANI VISHAYA
HARDEYA VISHAYA
KOSIKI
OLD KOSI
SONANTARA VISHAYA
MANIARA PATTALA
SRINAGARA
SRINAGARA BHUKTI
PILIPINKA NAYA
JAMBUNADI VITHI
RAJAGRIHA VISHAYA
AJAPURA NAYA
GAYA
SONA (HIRANYAVANA)
G A Y A V I S H A Y A
KANKAJOLA MANDLA
KUJAVATI MANDLA
J H A R A K H A N D A
TAILAKAMPA MANDLA
0 50
MILES
84
85
86
87
88
27
26
25
24
23
22

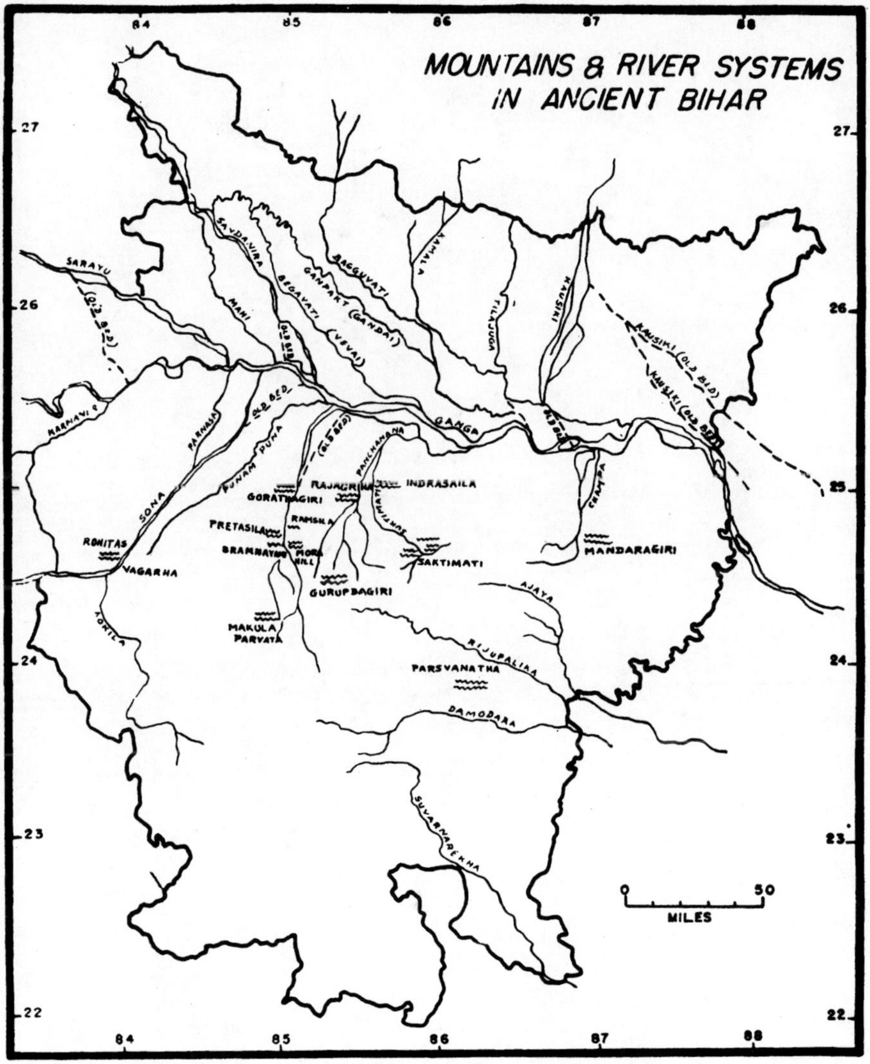
MOUNTAINS & RIVER SYSTEMS IN ANCIENT BIHAR
SARAYU
SAVDANIRA
MAHI
BAGGUVATI
GANPAKT (GANDAI)
BEGAVATI
(VEVAI)
KAMALA
TILAJUGA
KAUSIKI
KAUSIKI (OLD BED)
GANGA
SONA
PUNAM PUNA
OLD BED
RAJAGRIHA
INDRASAILA
GORATHAGIRI
PANCHANANA
PRETASILA
RAMSILA
ROHITAS
VAGARHA
SAKTIMATI
CHAMPA
MANDARAGIRI
GURUPDAGIRI
AJAYA
KOKILA
MAKULA PARVATA
PARSVANATHA
DAMODARA
SUVARNAREKHA
0
50
MILES
84
85
86
87
88
27
26
25
24
23
22

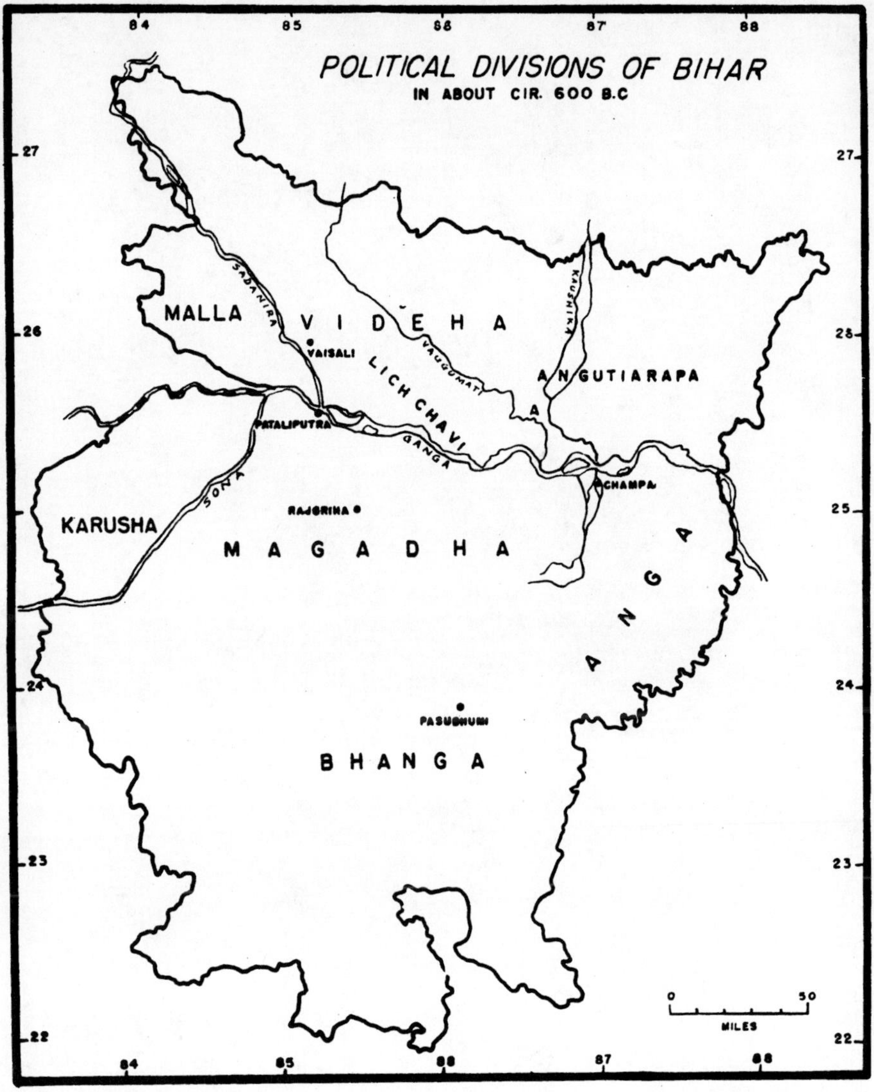

POLITICAL DIVISIONS OF BIHAR
IN ABOUT CIR. 600 B.C
MALLA
VIDEHA
VAISALI
LICHCHAVI
ANGUTIARAPA
SADANIRA
VAGUMATI
KAUSHIKA
PATALIPUTRA
GANGA
SONA
CHAMPA
RAJGRIHA
KARUSHA
MAGADHA
ANGA
PASUBHUMI
BHANGA
MILES

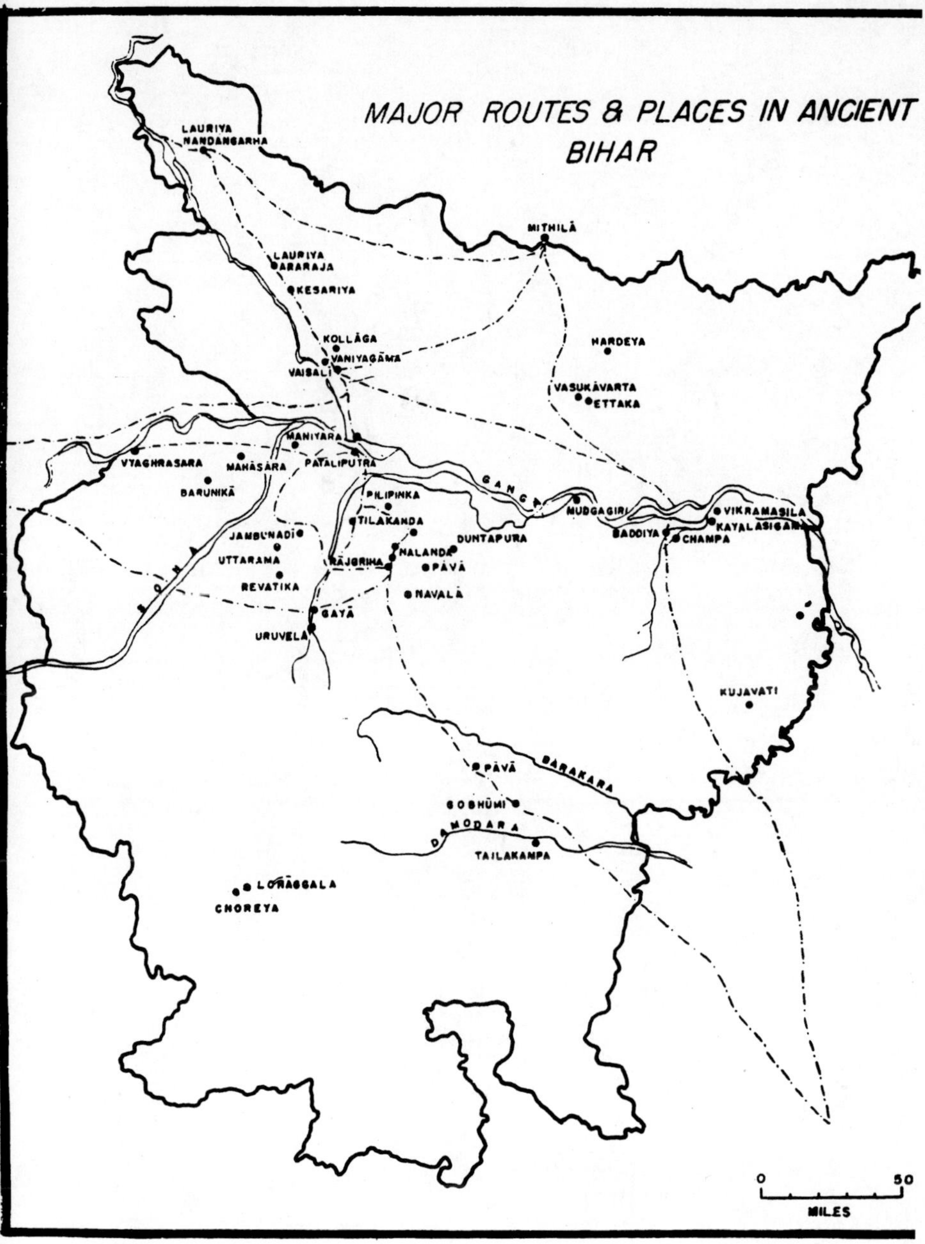
MAJOR ROUTES & PLACES IN ANCIENT BIHAR
LAURIYA NANDANGARHA
MITHILĀ
LAURIYA ARARAJA
KESARIYA
KOLLĀGA
VANIYAGĀMA
VAISALĪ
HARDEYA
VASUKĀVARTA
ETTAKA
MANIYARA
PATALIPUTRA
VYAGHRASARA
MAHĀSĀRA
BARUNIKĀ
GANGA
MUDGAGIRI
VIKRAMASILA
KAYALASIGAMA
BADDIYA
CHAMPA
PILIPINKA
TILAKANDA
JAMBUNADI
UTTARAMA
REVATIKA
NALANDA
DUNTAPURA
RĀJGRIHA
PĀVĀ
NAVALĀ
SONA
GAYĀ
URUVELĀ
KUJAVATI
PĀVĀ
BARAKARA
GOBHŪMI
DAMODARA
TAILAKAMPA
LORĀGGALA
CHOREYA
0
50
MILES

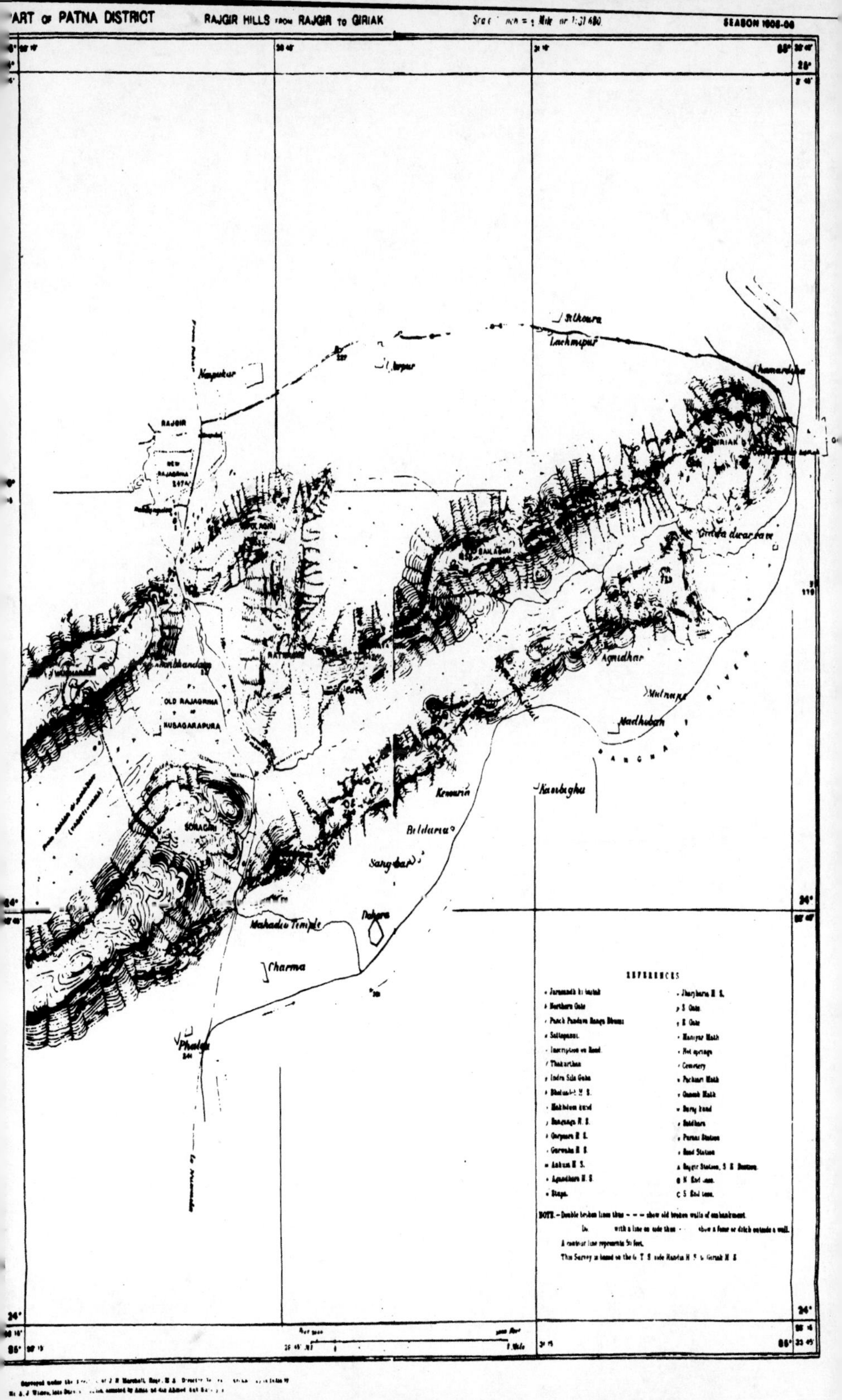
PART OF PATNA DISTRICT
RAJGIR HILLS FROM RAJGIR TO GIRIAK
SEASON 1905-06
RAJGIR
NEW RAJAGRIHA
Lachmipur
Chamardiha
GIRIAK
SAILAGIRI
RATNAGIRI
OLD RAJAGRIHA or KUSAGARAPURA
SONAGIRI
Agnidhar
Madhuban
Kasbigha
Belduria
Dabora
Mahadeo Temple
Charma
REFERENCES
Panch Pandava Ranga Bhumi
Inscription on Road
Thakurthan
Indra Sila Guha
Cemetery
Hot springs
Stupa
A contour line represents 50 feet.